EVERY BUSH AFLAME

EVERY BUSH AFLAME

SCIENCE, GOD AND THE NATURAL WORLD

JOHN FEEHAN

VERITAS

Published 2021 by
Veritas Publications
7–8 Lower Abbey Street
Dublin 1
Ireland
publications@veritas.ie
www.veritas.ie

ISBN: 978 1 84730 948 8

10 9 8 7 6 5 4 3 2 1

A catalogue record for this book is available from the British Library.

Designed by Clare Meredith, Veritas Publications
Typeset by Padraig McCormack, Veritas Publications
Cover design by Jeannie Swan, Veritas Publications
Printed in the Republic of Ireland by SPRINT-print Ltd, Dublin

Veritas books are printed on paper made from the wood pulp of managed forests. For every tree felled, at least one tree is planted, thereby renewing natural resources.

CONTENTS

Pour Malo, Lua et Briac

Quelle drôle de planète! pensa-t-il alors. Elle est toute séche, et toute pointue et toute salée. Et les hommes manquent d'imagination. Ils répètent ce qu'on leur dit... Chez moi j'avais une fleur: elle parlait toujours la premiére ...

Le Petit Prince, Chapitre XIX

FOREWORD

I first met John Feehan in September 1972, the same autumn he wrote, 'I am filled with trust/at all that is, charged with trust/for all that is, unto dust,/dust of the desert's rock, dust of the way,/dust of my own decay' ('October Poem 1972'). Back then in Salesian College, Heywood, I was enthralled to meet someone so enthused with a sense of place, breathless almost in his desire to share with his students what wonders lay beyond the classroom door.

'Encounter' as word and doorway is key for him. It is there in our first intake of breath and in any transfigured moment we attend to; something impossible to express though best approached in poetry – his 'no words to utter but my wordlessness/before ripples on rocks and autumn's mystery/striking my soul from his horse' ('October Poem 1972'). Only this direct encounter with the natural world, he maintains, can satisfy our deepest need for the company of other creatures, the chatter of mountain streams, for woodland, a starry sky, wildness and wet.

This present book I see as a companion volume to *The Singing Heart of the World: Creation, Evolution and Faith* and, like it, a continuation of John's ongoing reflection on what it means to be a fully human participant in the unfolding of creation. His range of reference is wide; from the physical sciences to philosophy, theology and to the history of ideas and culture and so he is able to welcome guests from many backgrounds to his table.

If encounter with the natural world is an underlying theme then a commitment to the best use of our reason is another. John makes the point regularly that it is within the world of science that we are provided with the surest way to proceed towards understanding and it is science, in its truest sense, which leads us to a place of depth, to what, for the person of faith, is the apprehension of creation as ultimate Mystery revealing itself.

In this awareness, to walk out each morning to greet the day is to do a graceful thing, just as it is to bend over a microscope, to tend flowers, gardens, animals, to raise children, study, acclaim, love; by such we become human and learn to know our place in a larger community of life.

As we follow the different tracks through *Every Bush Aflame: Science, God and the Natural World* – some of them challenging but all enlightening – a sense of our own responsibility increases. What are the virtues we must practise to help us thrive if not those we have always known – discipline, justice, wisdom, courage, Eucharist in all its forms, simplicity of life – thereby making space for brothers and sisters including those other kin whose unique embodiments of divine presence draw us into communion?

It has been a pleasure to read through this new work in which the author returns to matters close to his heart and takes up lines of enquiry he has not found opportunity to comprehensively pursue until now. His grasp of large and complex issues is as impressive as ever as he clears a path for his reader; his findings always ample as he inspects the boundaries, checks new landmarks against older maps, reaches for a language capable of recognising where the line runs out and unknowing deepens. To quote a line from his early poem 'Song for the Chaplains', 'my answers, none; I only think of Francis'; the Francis in question is the divinely mad man of Assisi who would ring the church bells to rouse his neighbours to witness a full moon.

This book rings quieter bells but no less insistent. It calls us to the new kind of consciousness that is required if we are not to destroy our planetary home and in the process a future for children and grandchildren and the ailing child within each of us.

In the preface to his poetry collection, *Eireaball Spideoige*, Seán Ó Ríordáin creates this scene. A horse is going down the street. A child and his father listen. The father looks out and states 'that's Mary's horse' but the horse does not enrich his life. For the child it's different. The clopping of the horse's hooves fills his whole being: 'he feels the sound of the horse in his bones. He licks his lips with the sound of the horse'. He is one with the animal. *Every Bush Aflame* directs the reader towards that ecstatic response to the living world. More than simply a book to read, it invites us to approach it imaginatively as a field trip with ditches to clamber over, muddy laneways, uphill hikes and sudden vistas. Time to lace up our boots!

It is fitting that a last word should go to John's great and early mentor, Pierre Teilhard de Chardin, for in the following passage something of their shared life's commitment is to be found: 'As for me, dominated as I am by a vocation which springs from the inmost fibres of my being, I have no desire, I have no ability, to proclaim anything except the innumerable prolongations of your incarnate Being in the world of matter' (*Hymn of the Universe*).

HUGH O'DONNELL

PREFACE AND ACKNOWLEDGEMENTS

This book had its beginnings in the Masters Programme at Dalgan Park, and its progress over the last ten years has been catalysed by discussion with the participants on that programme at Dalgan and All Hallows, and on the sabbatical programme at the Dominican Ecology Centre (An Tairseach) in Wicklow. It would in all probability, however, have remained as a *cnuasach* of scattered and disconnected reflections and responses without the stimulus provided by Sean McDonagh's encouragement to prepare it for publication: and it has been a priviledge to do so, and an acknowledgement of my own debt to Sean and to Dalgan. Hugh O'Donnell has read the text in draft form several times, his critical comments greatly helping to give more coherence to a text in which words struggle time and again to hold onto meaning. I am also grateful to Peter Cowan, Daniel Kelly, Sean McNulty and John J. Ryan for critical comment and suggestions.

I explore several themes in the book. First of all the notion that creation is an evolutionary process in two senses: in and of itself, as the progressive unfolding of possibility implicate in material reality from the very beginning; but also in the way our human ability to understand what is going on also evolves, becomes more insightful, and in that enlargement becomes ever more aware of its own infinite distance from Ultimate Understanding. This places on the religious response the demand to keep pace with the forward advance of reason's enquiry, and, in this, religion lags far behind (theologically, socio-politically, economically, and in terms of meaningful ritual).

Second, I discuss and attempt to critically evaluate the human response to all of this, and explore some of the implications for everyday living and interreligious dialogue. This last requires a digression in order to make the argument that far from religion being divorced from reason, some sort of 'religious' response is what *unrestricted reason* demands (however challenged by reason all our attempts prove to be as they grope their way to less inadequate articulation of what they intuit). Third, I explore the question of what it is that we respond to in our encounter with the creation before us; and the attention that is required of us if we are to hear what is being said.

At a time when exposition of the great truths of human life is grounded in theological concepts too outdated to metamorphose at a rate sufficient to the need of the times we live in, we may need to lay aside for the moment our attempts to direct the course of human affairs under the direction of scriptural modes of revelation, and teach our lessons from the other, primary book of revelation that is created reality itself. I suppose this book could be considered an extended reflection on Pope Francis' references to this other, greater book in *Laudato Si'*, the latest statement of an oft- (if faintly) repeated echo in earlier Christian tradition, and indeed in the tradition of all religions.

Early impressions to the contrary, there can be no essential contradiction between these two revelations, however opposite they may appear on first acquaintance. Cardinal Newman (in his careful way) states as much in his *Idea of a University*:

> He who believes Revelation with that absolute faith which is the prerogative of a Catholic … is sure, and nothing shall make him doubt, that, if anything seems to be proved by astronomer, or geologist, or chronologist, or antiquarian, or ethnologist, in contradiction to the dogmas of faith, that point will eventually turn out, first, *not* to be proved, or, secondly, not *contradictory*, or thirdly, not contradictory to any thing really *revealed*, but to something which has been confused with revelation.[1]

The book opens in chapter one with an exploration of the central role of attention and openness in our encounter with the natural world, and the fundamental nature of sensory experience in that encounter: in quest of that which human intuition wordlessly touches, and for which scientific method is an indispensable tool. A theme that echoes throughout these pages is an insistence that the way of knowing we call 'science' reveals progressively the presence of God: but a God infinitely beyond the small god our embryonic reasoning grew up with: and realise that we are called to a spiritual response that is proportionately mature: in our understanding and in our living, so that far from being outmoded, our spiritual response is seen as the *unum necessarium*: what takes over our lives, what gives life true meaning.

Chapter two then explores the evolutionary nature of the world of the encounter: not only is creation an unfolding reality in and of itself, but so

---

1   Newman (1852), 'Christianity and Scientific Investigation', in *The Idea of a University*.

too is our human understanding of it and of what lies behind and beyond it. It includes a brief historical overview of the evolution of evolutionary thinking, and of our ability to see and better understand the world and in particular other creatures. Chapter three focuses on the dignity of individual other-than-human lives, and chapter four looks at the revelatory nature of our human encounter with the rest of the living world and explores the new meaning of incarnation demanded of us by a deeper appreciation of what all of this signifies. A constant refrain in the text is an insistence that we access this deepest something at the heart of every creature's existence through *encounter*: physical and emotional contact that may be further enhanced and deepened by intellectual understanding and prayerful contemplation. Chapter five explores this concept further, particularly in relation to the treatment of biodiversity in *Laudato Si'*. This central chapter is really an attempt to explore the deeper roots of a wonderful passage in Pope Francis' encyclical: 'Each of the various creatures, willed in its own being, reflects in its own way a ray of God's infinite wisdom and goodness. Man must therefore respect the particular goodness of every creature, to avoid any disordered use of things' (*Laudato Si'*, 69).

Chapter six explores the key question of purpose and design in evolution, consideration of which is the first step in the development of the rational underpinning of 'faith'. Here I ask for myself that perennial question all people of faith must face: what kind of God is it that calls into being a world in which evil, pain and suffering are such all-pervasive constituents; and I have tried to see whether the question looks any different from the perspective of our age.

In chapter seven, I step over the threshold of my philosophical door to explore the ways in which some aspects of our everyday living are influenced by these earlier reflections. Chapter eight, reflecting further on this, is a more extended treatment of the theme of evolution introduced in chapter two. Chapter nine is a reflection on what it all means for the deeper ecumenism we are so urgently called to embrace and develop in our time.

Syngefield, Birr
Easter 2020

Now Moses kept the flock of Jethro his father-in-law, the priest of Midian; and he led the flock to the backside of the desert, and came to the mountain of God, even to Horeb. And the angel of the Lord appeared unto him in a flame of fire out of the midst of a bush; and he looked, and, behold, the bush burned with fire, and the bush was not consumed. And Moses said, I will now turn aside, and see this great sight, why the bush is not burnt. And when the Lord saw that he turned aside to see, God called unto him out of the midst of the bush, and said, Moses, Moses. And he said, Here am I. And he said, Draw not nigh hither: put off thy shoes from off thy feet, for the place whereon thou standest is holy ground. Moreover he said, I am the God of thy father, the God of Abraham, the God of Isaac, and the God of Jacob. And Moses hid his face; for he was afraid to look upon God.

Exodus 3, 1-6

Earth's crammed with heaven,
And every common bush afire with God;
But only he who sees, takes off his shoes,
The rest sit round it and pluck blackberries.

Elizabeth Barrett Browning, *Aurora Leigh*, Book VII

The universe unfolds in God, who fills it completely. Hence, there is a mystical meaning to be found in a leaf, in a mountain trail, in a dewdrop, in a poor person's face. The ideal is not only to pass from the exterior to the interior to discover the action of God in the soul, but also to discover God in all things. Saint Bonaventure teaches us that 'contemplation deepens the more we feel the working of God's grace within our hearts, and the better we learn to encounter God in creatures outside ourselves.'

Laudato Si', 233

Nor is the light of faith, joined to the truth of love, extraneous to the material world, for love is always lived out in body and spirit; the light of faith is an incarnate light radiating from the luminous life of Jesus. It also illuminates the material world, trusts its inherent order, and knows that it calls us to an ever widening path of harmony and understanding. The gaze of science thus benefits from faith: faith encourages the scientist to remain constantly open to reality in all its inexhaustible richness. Faith awakens the critical sense by preventing research from being satisfied with its own formulae and helps it to realise that nature is always greater. By stimulating wonder before the profound mystery of creation, faith broadens the horizons of reason to shed greater light on the world which discloses itself to scientific investigation.

Lumen Fidei, 34: AAS 105 (2013), 1107

CHAPTER 1

ATTENDING TO CREATION

Reaffiliating with the biosphere is an empathic experience that has to be felt as well as intellectualised to be meaningful. It also has to be practised.

JEREMY RIFKIN, *THE EMPATHIC CIVILIZATION*, P. 611

How do we hear what is being said to us through our encounter with reality: with creation? Not by listening with our sense of hearing alone, nor indeed if we use the word metaphorically and extend our 'hearing' to all the senses. A deeper mode of attention is required of us.

Our responsiveness to the natural world, the measure of our attunement, of our ability to pick up on what is being said to us by its being, our degree of intuition to the presence at its very heart, is born of the attention we pay to it: to stones and weather and stars, and to all that is alive. There is a discipline to the practice of attention, and this is something to be learned; but it is in part also genetic, some of us are born with a greater capacity than others, as is the case with other character traits. Nor do I need to feel unfulfilled because I am not born with this heightened capacity, any more than I would feel unfulfilled intellectually because I am not a genius.

We have to respond first of all on a sensory level, as does all creation, each creature differently in accordance with its particular sensory and emotional capacity. What we respond to on this level is the *thatness* of creatures: their sheer, given reality. But human appreciation is heightened through our ability to understand in some measure how this being is achieved, and this understanding is something that grows in human awareness over time; first of all, over the course of the individual life of each one of us; and secondly in humanity as a whole, over the collective time of history.

It is this process of *epistemic unfolding* that we will explore first of all, before we move on in the next chapter to look at that other process of *evolutionary unfolding* by which the being of creatures has been achieved.

Experience of creation comes first

As we try to reach a deeper understanding of What It is All About, we have to think things through; each generation does this anew in the light of increasingly informed understanding of reality. This can be a delicate exercise, because it is not the *explanation* that counts most of all in the first place. It is our experience of that *of which* it is an explanation – the latest, but ever partial, tentative, limited attempt at explanation. We need always to return and plunge ourselves into our human experience, our encounter with creation. This is the truly essential dialectic.

The response our existence calls for from us is rooted in the direct experience of personal encounter: with sun, wind and rain; flower and forest; love and evil; ecstasy and pain. We need to return constantly to this recurring dialectical confrontation with reality in the way of our knowing, and as it advances and develops, any conceptual superstructure we built on it needs to be advanced and developed in proportion. This we have tended not to do in theology. Instead, we seek to re-model the upper stories of the building, content to change the furniture from time to time.

Our experience of reality – the encounter through which creation reveals itself to us – is a sensory experience, and we can only *describe* it in sensory terms. The more we *attend* – with all our senses first of all, and then with the more penetrating attention that is scientific enquiry – the more wonderful becomes our awareness of what it is that we apprehend through sense and intellect. For most of the time our attention is minimal. We live lives endlessly distracted from what is being said by the creation around us, *so that we no longer live in the real world.* 'To think of a thing,' wrote Coleridge, 'is [as] different from to perceive it as "to walk" is from "to feel the ground under you".'[1]

But behind all that we can sense (or rather, not behind, but at the heart of), *something* is reaching to us from the depths of that attentive experience: something we rather intuit, and it is this sense of an Ultimate Something that religion tries to capture so that we humans may live our lives in harmony with what It or He/She or They intends. But unlike our discourse about 'things', we cannot talk about this Ultimate Something. And when we try, we lose the 'sense' of it.

And it is the *search* that matters, not the explanation we give of what we think we are doing in the sense of 'why' am I doing it. It is worth emphasising again that the spark that inflames the tinder of our human thirst for God is our physical, emotional and intellectual *encounter* with creation in the first instance. The leap of recognition that finds expression in our joy at what we find there is the same for the spirit of a Stone Age me gazing at the sunset or at shoals of salmon swimming upstream to spawn, as it is for modern me thrilling to the beauty of the Krebs Cycle or the equations to which electrons dance, or the newly discovered intricacies of the lives of orchids or bats.

There is no substitute for this encounter. It might be thought that – with the advance in technology, the stupendous increase in the sophistication and resolution of computers and imaging systems, and the advent of virtual reality – it can be substituted by forms of mediated experience. But such experience is entirely dependent on the natural world itself. Late in the nineteenth century, the great Belgian scientist and explorer Jean-Charles Houzeau perceptively remarked that we encounter true novelty only in nature itself: 'our imagination, as powerful as it seems at first, is only rich in combination of things that are already known'.

> The invention of the microscope and the telescope has therefore not just contributed in opening up a new world for us, so vast that we cannot yet appreciate its whole extent; it has also shown us the contrast between the reach of our mental faculties and the actual richness of nature. We have there a palpable proof that imagination, as powerful as it seems at first, is only rich in combination of things that are already known. It forms assemblages of great variety, often odd and monstrous; it knows how to amplify or to diminish its pictures in all proportions. But, from its own depths, it does not draw anything that is really new; and as inventive as it thinks itself it would find nothing if nature did not furnish the models.[2]

The kernel we uncover when we strip away these layers is the centrality of direct sensory encounter with the natural world. In and through this, and only this, its outlines dimly reproduced in atoms and molecules and patterns of energy flow in a way that we can see we come in touch with that Deepest Something reaching out to us, beyond the capacity of words to express; it pops like soap bubbles when we touch it with the finger of words. In itself it is independent of matter. Plato's (c.428–c.348 BC) primary focus is on what it is that is reflected; what, for want of a better word, he calls the *ideas*. Aristotle (384-322 BC) alters the focus. His primary focus is the reflections themselves, because it is only in and through these that we come to know the Ideas and what generates them, as far as human capacity is capable of this.

The great philosopher A.N. Whitehead once remarked that all of western philosophy consists of little more than notes to Plato. And indeed it may be: but each new generation, re-reading Plato in the light of its own new insights, augmented in each generation by the progress of human understanding over time, sets out to express it anew, in a way that is enriched by its wider view, able to survey the terrain below and behind from this new viewpoint higher up that mount of ascent. However, but in doing so it is adding another layer; and so we find ourselves having to peel away layer after layer, remembering as we must that the author of each layer believes his exposition to be definitive: and there is the danger that the original platonic core will have been smothered under the weight of all that suffocating verbiage. In working our way back through the various corrective lenses, distracted by their fascinating optics, we may fail to focus sharply enough on what was so central for Plato.

After all our high flying in cosmic physics, juggling with the alternative hypotheses of inflation from a singularity, the collision of interacting four-dimensional 'branes' generating a big bang, the meshing of possible quantum histories to weave a real universe, or a universe that is a holographic projection from the edge of reality, we are returned to the fragments and riddles of life out of which we have to make a whole.

As if working out the 'grand unified theory' was the real question: rather than the sheer *thatness* of it: 'the achieve of the thing' in Hopkins' poem. And the 'achieve' is only *appreciated* through experiential encounter. The measurable defines no more than the dimensions the thing occupies. Our mind, though again through the senses, takes hold of the existent that is realised within these unique spatial parameters (and these range from nanoscopic to cosmic). Our approach to reality needs to be participatory (i.e. empathic) as well as detached. We must strive to enter into *all* that it is.

William Paley gave a sermon at an Ordination Service in July of 1781 in which he laid before the young Anglican ordinands a very short set of the 'rules of life and behaviour' that should characterise the life of the young vicar. The habit he thought 'the foundation of almost all other good ones' was what he called 'retirement'. 'Were I required to condense my advice to young clergymen in one sentence, it should be in this, Learn to live alone.'³ It is very much a sermon of its time, written and delivered out of the conservative Anglican Christianity of his day. But one striking feature of it is his advice on how to use all the time that would be freed up by this solitary existence: 'take in hand any branch of useful science, especially of those parts of it which are subsidiary to the knowledge of religion.' In other words, retain through the days and years of your dedicated life the space to cultivate attention to *the reality that enfolds us* and that you have elected to bear witness to or find yourself elected to witness: and which is drowned out in the noise and distraction of the 'world'. I think this helps to explain why it was that so many clerics of the age became ardent naturalists, 'feeling the ground' on which they walked; not just seeing the narrow path that channels the course of our human life, but leaving ourselves open to everything in the forest of experience through which it passes.

Illumination through attention

In the lives of some of those who pursue a conscious search for God, there are explosive moments of enlightenment, when everything springs into focus in a way that has nothing to do with intellect. It is not as if suddenly the *solution* to the problem presents itself. Such moments can be precipitated by the most trivial of things: Hildegard of Bingen's migraine; a bang on the head, whether (as in Paul of Tarsus' case) from falling or (in the case of Thomas Aquinas) banging it on an overhanging branch. It happened in the life of Thomas Merton when he found himself in the presence of the great stone Buddhas at Polonnaruwa in Sri Lanka (not during his years of meditation or prayer in his monastery at Gethsemane).⁴

But – important as they are – there is nothing essential to human fulfilment in such moments. What is essential is the readiness for such a moment – should it come – that *attentiveness* to the world *about* us presents us with: the sort of attention that allows our human mind to penetrate to the depth of things as far as the limits of our human mind allow us to penetrate, as far as our individual mind is able to go. This is best cultivated and learned in a place to which we become intimate: and the cultivation of intimacy is at the very heart of our quest.

We are not just waiting. Like the Five Wise Virgins of the parable we *attend* with all our senses to the detail of each element of our surroundings – in the ecosystem community of which we are a part – and to the inter-relationships of these elements. While *thinking* is what enables us to, as one presumptuous scientist put it, 'know the mind of God', it also short circuits the intensity of the sensuous encounter we have in direct experience. In creation spirituality, contemplation differs from meditation in disengaging the wire of thought: it stops thinking about in order just *to be in the presence of.*

Cultivating attentiveness in the present – a present that gathers to itself all the past and the future – is the only way to appreciation: to seeing as fully as we may every detail that is around us, and through it what lies within/ beneath/beyond …

In the spiritual practice of the early medieval period meditation was conceived as the practice of intensive concentration on a text – which was read aloud – and pondering the *depth* of its meaning: with the whole person, not just mental processes of attention, memory and intellect, but also engaging all the faculties of body, mind and spirit. This is the kernel of the sort of concentrated attention we are talking about here, but using a particular experienced reality *as text*: the attention that enables its being to unfold before us: attention for the Mystery its being embodies, attention of the senses first of all, followed by attention of the enquiring mind.

We find something resembling this three-stage progression in appreciation of creation in the reflections of some of the earliest writers on Christian mysticism (and they were building on earlier eastern practice and reflection). Hugh of St Victor (1078-1141) and his pupil Richard of St Victor (1123-1173) wrote of the three sets of eyes with which we look on creation: first the bodily eyes with which we take unto ourselves the evidence: that which is sensually presented to us. Second, and building on this, there is the eye of reason, with which we think about what we see and hear; and thirdly there are the eyes of true understanding that enable us, through contemplation, to penetrate deeper, to what breathes fire into the reality we behold.

Interlude

When I go for a walk in the woods, I am surrounded by trees and all the life that goes with them, green and otherwise, which I encounter through the experience of all my senses. On this level my experience is less intense than that of the badger or wood mouse or jay – or beetle – that lives here, because their lives depend on it. In earlier times the human experience was sharper in this sensory way also because to an extent *their* lives depended on it. Where our human encounter differs from the animal's is that it rises above the experience to question in wonder. In us there is something new, something never before seen in any of the endless forms life has taken in its four-billion year journey: the *question*. What is going on?

The leaves are green. What is green? Why are leaves green? And the question, pursued relentlessly by reason over the centuries, is the essence of scientific enquiry. But these questions are not just 'science' questions, 'what is it?', 'how is it?' questions. They are 'why?' questions: 'what is going on?' questions, ultimately 'what is God about?' questions. Science questions are theology questions.

I marvel at the wonder of it all, and our collective mind pursues that wonder through my life and down the ages. I inherit the progressively-advancing insight of the generations before me, and in this incremental way, albeit ever so slowly, I am allowed a closer approach to what is really going on. The cumulative growth in human understanding is a communal affair that grows through time and across space – as is science as a whole. Paying attention therefore has two dimensions to it. There is my *individual* attention first of all. But not only is the enrichment this progress in attention brings to me something that takes place in my individual life. There is also a *collective* attention that grows over time, over years and across centuries and millennia, and my attention must also be directed towards this, because it lifts the meaning of what I apprehend with my own senses and intellect.

The first step in developing the *appreciation* that makes possible the *contemplation* of creation of which Pope Francis speaks in the encyclical is *attentiveness* – paying attention. This is the neglected other side of *mindfulness*.

When we attend to the world about us in this prayerful way, it begins to come into focus. The tall woody plants that dominate the vegetation are no longer just trees and shrubs. They have names, knowing which is the first step in an acquaintance that can, if we will, become deeper and deeper until we reach a stage where we are intimate with them, inasmuch as this is possible to us. The same is true of the flowering herbaceous plants, whose achievement we first acknowledge by getting to know them by name before attempting to reach a glimmer of understanding of how God knows them. But how much remains hidden, how much requires our attention and the extension of our eyes the microscope provides us with, before we can share in the depth of their beauty and the wonder of their being?

Even the mere circumstance of knowing the scientific name of an object may prove of the first service in leading us to a knowledge of all that is known respecting it.[5]

When I walk in the woods I now see the variation in the form and arrangement of leaf in different flowering species; with my new attention I can follow their progress through the year – at least as far as what I see above ground allows me. Much else is going on below ground, and we have to dig deeper in every sense to see that, and in any case we are still discovering with amazement how much is going on among the roots. Careful investigation in recent decades has shown that a web of fungal threads unites the roots of trees, often of different species, into a single mycorrhizal network. Research suggests that plants can transmit alarm calls to each other across this mycorrhizal internet: they are genuine social networks.

But underneath the canopy of leaves there is another carpet of green, to see which we must take our focus to a higher level. What is it? It is moss of course, but now that my attention is drawn to it I begin to see a pattern. The moss plants are not all the same. Now that I look more closely I begin to see that there are different kinds, and although they lack colourful flowers to make differences between them more obvious to human eyes, they are as different from each other as flowering plants are. In any corner of the wood there are likely to be several dozen species of mosses – more perhaps then there are flowering plant species.

Here is one that is more abundant and conspicuous than the others, clearly one of the dominant species in this habitat. With a hand lens and in good light I can see its beauty. It has the form of a miniature tree, 5-20 cm tall, with downcurved branches of varying length held out from the main stem more or less at right angles. All the stems are red in colour, and closely invested with pale green and rather chaffy-looking leaves that stick out in all directions and are arranged in a somewhat raggedy fashion. The tip of the leading shoot always takes a characteristic turn to one side; and the leaves are so densely clustered at the tips of the shoots that the stem is hidden (the tips of the uppermost branches are somewhat similar). It grows in dense tufts that sometimes form a continuous carpet on the woodland floor. This is *Rhytidiadelphus triquetrus*, for which the uninspiring English name 'Big Shaggy-moss' has recently been coined.

The dominant moss on my lawn, living unobtrusively between the grass plants and safely below the level of the lawnmower blades, is a close relative of my woodland moss. Is does not have the same stature (2-15 cm tall), but it too forms miniature forests among the grass. The leaves are arranged all the way round the stems, but the free end part turns back at right angles, giving the tips of the shoots a star-like appearance. The broad leaf base clasps the stem so that it is visible only through the leaves. This is *Rhytidiadelphus squarrosus* ('Springy Turf-moss'). Beside the track through the conifer forest where I walk sometimes is another close relative, *Rhytidiadelphus loreus* ('Little Shaggy-moss'). It has something of the stature of *Rhytidiadelphus triquetrus* but here the upper part of the leaf is narrower, tapering to a distinctive long, tapering tip. The leaves all curl in the same direction, which immediately distinguishes the species from its more robust relative.

Rhytidiadelphus is just one genus of mosses among hundreds. It is a small genus, with only a handful of species, but many genera have dozens of species; some have hundreds. Altogether we know of something in the order of twelve thousand species of mosses in our world at this moment of geological time – not counting those that have never been described: and perhaps never will be.

But even the wonderful identification handbooks available these days for the more favoured parts of the world tell us little about their scarcely understood relationships to wood and light and levels of moisture, or the mites and tardigrades, nematodes and spiders that live in their canopies. And the green kaleidoscope of moss is but one stroke of colour in the living portrait of landscape, the lives of mosses one green note in the symphony of one ecosystem, which meshes with every other ecosystem to weave the unfolding tapestry that is the living world.

Reduced opportunity for encounter

In the short space of one lifetime there have been two profoundly significant developments that relate to the opportunity for personal encounter with the natural world. The first is the extent of its *loss*: the dimming of the rainbow of living diversity and of the natural habitats that sustain it. 'Loss is everywhere, and the defining characteristic of the natural world in the twenty-first century is no longer beauty, nor riches, nor abundance, nor, if you like, life force, but has become vulnerability.'[6] More than half the Earth's rainforests have gone; one-fifth of all vertebrates are threatened with extinction; more than half of the wildlife of Great Britain has gone since the end of World War Two. And with this reduction in the diversity and abundance comes the lessening of opportunity to encounter it.

Second, our senses and our capacities have become increasingly divorced from direct and real encounter with the Earth. We have become progressively distanced from nature's touch over this last century: first by radio, then television and now in recent years by the cybernetic revolution. I still find it hard to get used to people walking through a world of birdsong while voluntarily trapped inside the sound bubble of their earbuds, staring at the screens on their smartphones, never alone with themselves, and whose substitute for community is the disembodied contact of Facebook and YouTube. Richard Louv, who refers to this as Nature-Deficit Disorder, describes how in the space of a century our experience of nature has gone 'from direct utilitarianism to romantic attachment to electronic detachment.'[7]

On the other hand, the digital revolution of our time has made the personal acquisition of the information about the natural world possible for everybody with an ease and facility undreamt of even a generation ago, and it has also made access to sophisticated tools such as the microscope and camera much easier, at the same time as these tools become ever easier to use and better at what they do.

The other defining element of wild places – apart from biological diversity and the predominance of natural ecological processes – is silence. Silence is not the absence of sound: it is the absence of distraction.[8] Indeed, sound (if our definition of sound is confined to auditory sensation) is an integral part of this true silence: the sounds that are an integral part of the community of life-at-home here. So too all the other sensory outputs that we are capable of tuning in to are integral to it (smell, texture, colour etc.). And distraction is brought about not only by the intrusion of the noise of machines, or the conversation of others in our company, but by our own thought processes. Important – essential – though the reflective mind is to our appreciation of the world, it can only do so fully and properly by weaving itself into the fullest sensory engagement with each expression of life (species) we are capable of.[9]

This is difficult and demanding of personal discipline at the best of times. Each of us is different in our capacity to respond – as different in this as we differ in all other ways: physically, emotionally, intellectually. And the potential and limits conferred and imposed by our capacities in these ways are paralleled by the limits (and opportunities) imposed or presented by our place in the flow of human history and geography: essentially different in this regard between (for example) somebody living in aboriginal Australia or medieval Europe, and somebody in our postmodernist world.

This sea change, which has happened in our lifetime, seems to have slipped past our attention almost unnoticed. In the Developed World, as we call it, the generation now growing up is effectively cut off from the world outside, from the world of real things, never alone, never quiet, attention siphoned off by iPod, iPad, Facebook, their capacity to respond anaesthetised, leading to what a recent heartbreaking book on loss of the experience of natural diversity describes as 'the blank-faced indifference which is a major response to nature today, especially amongst young people seduced by screens and living electronic lives.'[10] A hundred years ago we might have expressed reservations about the distracting influence of radio. Fifty years ago, we might have voiced our anxieties about the extension of that auditory distraction to the visual distraction of television, but this is distraction of a different order. At the same time, it is important to emphasise that such reservation is in no sense a condemnation of these extraordinary augmentations of the human capacity for communication, but rather of their unconsidered, inadequately evaluated application to human life.

CHAPTER 2

THE EVOLUTION OF HUMAN UNDERSTANDING

In this chapter we will highlight the fact that creation is an unfolding process: in itself across cosmic and geological time and at every level from sub-atomic particles to persons; and in the way our knowledge of it grows over historical time and the span of individual lives. We see the same spectrum of intellectual capacity today as there was at any earlier stage of human history. Ever since our species appeared on Earth human beings have been endowed with the same intellect. There were people with the intelligence of Einstein or Thomas Aquinas or Dante in the Stone Age and in every culture, but all they were capable of was the making of stone tools by chipping flakes from a core of flint held in one hand with a hammer-stone of flint held in the other. They could not *divine* at some deeper level the equivalence of matter and energy, or string words together that would be capable of holding in the mesh of their meanings the otherwise inexplicable depth of human feeling and longing. They encountered the world with the same spectrum of senses as ours, and because of that unique human capacity to *reason*, they were able gradually and incrementally to understand what is really going on, but they needed *tools* to extend the reach of the human senses in order to do this.

Each of us is born into a particular culture at a particular time in its history, and we are shaped and influenced on every level by this endowment. Our deepest convictions, that which is most essentially me and mine, are coloured by that endowment to an extent greater than any of us can appreciate even after decades of reflection and introspection. Indeed, the explanation and action through which these convictions become *real* in the world must of necessity be refracted through that prism if they are to become visible and active.

There is always the danger of seeing the cultural framework as actually *defining* the unique personal identity these convictions kindle. And we are always in danger, to a greater or lesser extent, of seeing our physical and mental endowment, or the level of intellectual apprehension of our particular stage in history, as defining it. Such may be the level of 'certainty' here that these false convictions take over our lives.

Some years ago, I found myself in Prague, en route to a meeting in Hungary. I knew nothing about the place except one thing, and hadn't done any homework about what sights a visitor might to take in. The one thing I knew about Prague was that in the Church of the Discalced Carmelites in Malá Strana I would find the Child of Prague: and so I set out to pay him a visit.

The Infant of Prague is a statue of Jesus as a child believed to have belonged originally to Teresa of Ávila, and which was gifted in the late sixteenth century to the Carmelites here in the Bohemian capital. All you can see is the face, because it's swaddled in several layers of regal vestments of the most elaborate sartorial elegance you can imagine. Anyway, I found the Church of Our Lady Victorious where the Infant of Prague resides, and I saw the Infant – just about, because it is the centrepiece of the most elaborate golden Baroque altar you ever saw – but what astonished me was not so much the little child in the robes so familiar to properly pious post-war Irish Catholics, but the museum upstairs, which is lined with glass cases filled with dozens and dozens of ersatz children of Prague, all dressed in the different costumes which the Real Child had worn down the centuries, changing as fashion changed: it was like a bizarre collection of Byzantine Barbies. It is one of those memories that remain with you through life ever afterwards – whether you want them to or not.

But the Infant of Prague is really just a little wax doll, 48 cm high. And all this ornate eye-catching sartorial panoply – by which we instantly recognise it – is just the package in which it is carried. Not the best metaphor perhaps, but it served to remind me how easy it is to miss the point: to see the 'container', the 'costume' as the important thing, and miss what lies at the heart of it. And if we have this problem of isolating the essential kernel, then for the majority of people, who simply don't bother to think about this sort of stuff at all, the whole thing is nonsense and irrelevant, belonging to the childhood of modern man, and another reason to put religion behind us.

In the early twelfth century, the great scholar Adelard of Bath put pen to paper to make a list of what he considered the great unsolved problems of natural enquiry, the *Perdifficiles Questiones Naturales* as he called them: the *really difficult questions* about the natural world to which we didn't have answers at that time. Here is a selection chosen more or less at random from his list of seventy-six:

> Why plants are produced without the sowing of seed.
> Why certain beasts chew the cud, and certain others not at all.
> Why the fingers were made unequal.
> How or why the globe of the Earth is held up in the middle of the air.
> How the Earth moves.
> Why the waters of the sea are salty.
> Whence the ebb and flow of the tides come.
> What food the stars eat, if they are animals.[1]

How far removed from this are the *Perdifficiles Questiones Naturales* of today! How thrilling to be alive at this time, when we understand in such depth and detail the workings of the universe as the result of an intellectual quest that began as soon as the capacity to ask such questions arose in our first human parents. Our concept of who or what God is is founded on the answers we frame to these questions, and so must evolve as the answers themselves mature and become less inadequate. But our theological concepts are still restrained by clinging conceptual cobwebs that originated out of outmoded or false attempts at explaining how things actually work. In this chapter we will review the way in which the human grasp of the nature and meaning of reality has advanced through the development of scientific understanding.

Advance in the practical sciences associated with metallurgy (much of it in the early years by alchemists) was necessary in order to fabricate the metal components of the microscope. If you look carefully at Robert Hooke's famous microscope you will see another area where advance in scientific understanding would, in time, transform our ability to see more clearly – and that is in *illumination*. The object under observation needs to be lit before it can be studied. Out of doors the sun is the ideal source, but indoors the only source is a candle, whose light is transmitted by the globe of oil you see in the illustration. There is no electricity.

By the time of the Romans, glass-making technology had advanced sufficiently for artisans to craft bean-shaped globules of clear glass that would focus rays of light and thereby magnify objects viewed through them. Because of their shape these 'burning glasses' were called lenses (because they were shaped like lentils). By the end of the thirteenth century craftsmen were making pairs of lenses that could be worn as glasses, and naturalists were beginning to use simple magnifiers in the late 1550s. The first microscopes, in which two lenses are arranged one above the other, thereby multiplying the magnifying effect of a single lens, appeared in Holland in the 1590s, but the first really effective microscopes are credited to Antonie van Leeuwenhoek (1632-1723) in the 1600s. Leeuwenhoek was incredibly skilled at grinding and polishing the lenses he used. His microscopes were difficult to use effectively: but with these tiny instruments – each made for a specific investigation – he made countless observations, including things such as red blood cells and spermatozoa, protozoa in water everywhere, even bacteria.[2]

The familiar compound microscope we use today was devised by Robert Hooke, and his book on what it revealed (*Micrographia*, 1665) had an enormous impact. Hooke was Robert Boyle's assistant early on in life, before he went on to became the first Curator of Experiments for the newly formed Royal Society of London and a university professor. His microscope was only one of an extraordinary range of important contributions to a wide spectrum of scientific enquiry.[3] The microscope made it possible for the human eye *to see for the first time* the detailed structure of small creatures: what (in the words of Linnaeus) 'has been for all the ages closed': and what they saw astonished and mesmerised the early microscopists.

In the chapter in his book where he provides the first detailed description of the flea he has viewed through his early, simple microscope in 1665 his description is noteworthy for two things in particular: first of all there is the refreshing simplicity of the language; there are no words as yet, no technical vocabulary, for the parts of an insect; and second his observation that, its relationship with us apart, its *beauty* ('The strength and beauty of this small creature, had it no other relation at all to man, would merit a description.'[4]). And of course, that is only the start. The most powerful of today's microscopes allow us to see down to a resolution of thirty-five trillionths of a metre, enabling us to see even the smallest creatures as they really are, in the most minute detail.[5]

Robert Hooke remarks that even if this creature were of no practical interest to us it would deserve our admiration on account of 'its strength and beauty'. The devout literature of the next two and a half centuries is replete with expressions of admiration at the marvels of creation, increasingly so as the advance of microscopy, and a vast increase in the number of people using microscopes, revealed it in ever-greater scope and detail. Much of this was gathered together at the end of the eighteenth century in one of the great classical works of natural theology by William Paley: a book remembered nowadays only to jeer at the famous metaphor of creation as the watch on the heath, but at the same time this was one of the carefully chosen volumes brought on board the *Beagle* by Charles Darwin when he left England on his famous voyage round the world in 1831.

It is possible to magnify objects up to two thousand times with skilled use of the microscope. This limit is set by the *wavelength* of light, a limitation that is overcome by using an accelerated beam of *electrons* rather than a beam of light. Because the wavelength of an electron can be one hundred thousand times shorter than that of a photon of visible light, electron microscopes have higher resolving power (50 picometres as against 200 nanometres for a light microscope), resulting in magnifications of up to ten million and beyond compared to two thousand for a light microscope.[6]

One big disadvantage with the more powerful electron microscopes is that they cost a small fortune. Another is that they require extremely thin slices of the object being viewed, and it is technically very challenging to achieve this. Of particular importance in terms of our discussion here is the scanning electron microscope (SEM), which produces images by scanning the surface with the electron beam and translating the information into images. It has a great depth of field, so it enables us to see the surface of the object in exceptional detail and in three dimensions.

Technical advance in the science of the microscope has continued at an exponential rate. We now have microscopes that can magnify millions of times, revealing the complexity of living things in ever greater detail: not just morphological complexity – the form and shape – but complexity on every level: chemical, physiological, genetic, behavioural. Linnaeus could exclaim, *Natura in minimis maxime miranda!* ('Nature is at its most-to-be-marvelled-at in the smallest creatures!') Words fail us today.

Allied to this is the equally spectacular advance in our capacity to *image* what is revealed by the microscope. Early microscopists such as Robert Hooke and Antonie van Leeuwenhoek could only sketch what they saw through their primitive microscopes. The invention of the camera elevated our imaging capacity to a new level, and in our own day the development of digital technology has utterly transformed our ability to share what life is *really* like. The capacity to *magnify* and *image* has advanced in parallel with an incredibly complex range of other investigative techniques, enabling us to see and understand living creatures for what they really are. It altogether extends our sense of the true depths of beauty and the scale of living diversity.

How our understanding of life has evolved

In a way that is directly comparable to that by which our understanding and appreciation of the universe at large have been extended – to a degree utterly beyond anything that could have been envisaged even a century ago – by the invention and progressive development of the telescope, our understanding and appreciation of life has been extended – again to a degree utterly beyond anything that could have been envisaged in earlier centuries – by the invention and progressive development of the microscope. The earliest microscopes could magnify only a few tens of times; today's instruments can magnify hundreds of thousands of times, enabling us to see the structure and workings of the smallest creatures in the most minute detail, right down to its very molecular structure.[7]

The same progress is true of telescopic vision. The mirror on Newton's first reflecting telescope had a diameter of 10 centimetres. Europe's Extremely Large Telescope (E-ELT) will be 39 metres: a mosaic of small mirrors with a total collecting area more than a hundred thousand times larger. And Martin Rees imagines a possible future when we reach the centenary of the Apollo 8 'Earthrise' image in 2068, when there might be 'an array of vast space telescopes, each with gossamer-thin kilometre-scale mirrors, being assembled in deep space by robotic fabricators,' and capable of seeing other earths orbiting distant stars.[8] But will human wisdom take us that far? ('The outcomes of future technological evolution could surpass humans by as much as we [intellectually] surpass slime mould.'[9])

The ground of our admiration itself undergoes an unfolding as we come to understand more: on every level of reality – stars, clouds, rocks, plants, animals: every individual species. It is in its way the exposition of the mystery 'of things hidden since the foundation of the world …': on every level on which the real is manifested, physical or chemical, biological or psychological.

Our admiration is directed in the first instance at the thing in itself, the individual species we encounter, and what we can see and understand of that. This is the first level of wonder: first of all, in our individual life and second in our experience as a species. And on this level of encounter no number of lives could exhaust the experience. But as we come to understand more and more, our apprehension of *how the Thing is achieved* grows apace, and that takes us into the succession of levels explored by the individual sciences: and on each of these levels too, no number of afterlives could exhaust the experience.

Complexity and size

We can summarise the way the advance of science has transformed our understanding of the nature of life – plants as well as animals – and of our relationship with other living creatures under four inter-related headings. First of all, *complexity*. On every level of organisation: biochemical, physiological, morphological, genetic, all are comparably complex.[10] Second, a recognition that *size* is no measure of that complexity. Third, the dawning of the shocking realisation that all forms of life are genetically related; and fourth, the degree of diversity of living species.

Size is irrelevant when it comes to complexity in multicellular creatures. It is relatively easy for us to understand that all the complexity of a large mammal such as a whale or an elephant – or ourselves – is present in the tiniest of mammals (the bumblebee bat of Myanmar, which weighs two grams and can sit comfortably in a teaspoon). And relatively easy for us to accept that it lives a life of scarcely believable wonder, almost unimaginably different from that of the elephant, only not of a size convenient to the more immediate appreciation possible to the human eye or mind. But it is far harder for us to accept – because it takes us outside the comfort zone of our direct experience of things – that all the complexity present in the body of a really big insect (such as a dragonfly: and long, long ago, during the Carboniferous period of Earth history there were dragonflies with wingspans of a metre or more) is to be found in the smallest midge.

As we get to learn ever more and more about the real scale and wonder of the living world it becomes increasingly difficult to believe that the brief account of how it all came about provided by the Bible is an adequate or accurate description. According to that account, it was a mere week's work for a God imagined as an all-powerful maker of things, who had called these creatures into being from nothing, and placed them in position on the stage of creation, each in its allotted station, each with its part to play in the Great Drama about to unfold as the curtain of history was drawn across for the first time, and in which we humans were to be the *dramatis personae*. God is the author of the play, withdrawn to the wings, intervening from time to time to tweak the action if it seems to be heading in the wrong direction.

The niche – the individual ecological role of a species, peculiar to itself – can be extraordinarily specific: at times incredibly so, awesomely so. Edward Wilson quotes as a favourite example the life of a fairyfly (*Caraphractus cinctus*) that lays its eggs in those of diving beetles.[11] Fairyflies include the smallest of all insects; many are only fractions of a millimetre in length. They are so small it is hardly surprising that we know next to nothing about them. In actual fact they are not really flies; they belong to a family of parasitic wasps (the Mymaridae) with frilly, feathery-looking wings with which they can swim underwater – in spite of their tiny size. The female fairyfly scouts for a likely pond and then lands on the surface; when she gets her bearings and finds what she is looking for she digs her way through the surface film with her legs, then swims to the cache of eggs which the female has laid under characteristic incisions beneath the skin of water plants; she lays one of her own eggs in each of the beetle eggs, and resurfaces. Another species lays its eggs in those of the demoiselle dragonfly (*Calopteryx virgo*), whose eggs are deposited in the cellular tissue of the leaves of white water-lily: and this is what the fairyfly is in search of when she enters the water, in which her frilled wings allow her to swim with ease. The tiny larvae pupate in a few days, and have a pupal life of ten to twelve days.[12] Or consider a more familiar example of niche specificity: familiar because we all carry them as passengers! *Demodex folliculorum* is just a third of a millimetre long and spends its entire life in the oily hair follicles of human eyelashes. The mites mate in these little caves, in which there are sometimes as many as twenty-five of the tiny creatures. And think how many others there are of whose lives we know nothing – yet.

'I would guess that existing biology is under one-millionth of what will eventually be known,' wrote Edward Wilson.[13]

> Let us be careful not to speak as if our little plummets had sounded the depths of the universe. Those who have surpassed their fellows in the improvement of natural knowledge, have always been the first to admit that what they have come to know is lost in the infinitude of the unknown.[14]

> This leads me to recommend to you the practice of examining minutely the different plants and animals you meet with. Let your magnifying-glass be no day idle, for it is in the miniature world that most variety, most beauty, most elaborate mechanism, most wonderful displays of creative wisdom are to be found.
>
> **James Lawson Drummond** (1832), *Letters to a Young Naturalist*, p. 102

The diversity of life on Earth

One of the earliest attempts to compile a catalogue of living animals was Albert the Great's *De Animalibus* ('of man and the beasts'). This is a most extraordinary book, full of information, especially in relation to the *uses* to which particular animals could be put in the light of the belief that they were created in the first place primarily for our use and service.[15] Albert relied wherever possible on his own observations and information he had been able to gather himself at first hand: in keeping with his insistence (which he learned from Aristotle and passed on to Aquinas, on whom it exercised an equally profound influence) that *true knowledge must start with the data of our own senses*. In a work of such scope however, he had to rely on the word of others for creatures of which he had no direct experience, and in these cases, he generally sounds a note of caution when something appears incredible to him, but without dismissing it outright, such is his awe at the many other natural wonders that appear improbable to the common sense of our limited personal experience.

Albert's tally comes to something over five hundred species. For all its claim to encyclopaedic status, it deals only with those creatures known to Europeans in the Middle Ages, when there were no microscopes, and our knowledge of tropical and marine biodiversity was negligible. It is a most instructive exercise for those who have not studied biology to leaf through the pages of one of the standard reference catalogues that summarise the diversity of life on Earth today. By the time of John Ray in the seventeenth century, the estimate total of insect species alone had grown to ten thousand:[16] 'The consideration of these appearances might induce us to believe, that variety itself, distinct from every other reason, was a motive in the mind of the Creator, or with the agents of his will.'[17] But this was only the beginning.

For all the intimacy of acquaintance with familiar animals it shows, there is something *missing* in Albert's *De Animalibus*. It is profoundly utilitarian, rooted in a literal interpretation of the meaning of Genesis 2:15: all that lives was created for our use. There is no sense that there is something deeper here, something deeper of God to be experienced through contemplative encounter with other creatures, no sense of the worth of other creatures to be obtained through such encounter. With the advance of science from the seventeenth century we begin to see the living world with new eyes: extensions of our own eyes given to us with the invention (discovery) of the microscope. We begin to realise the true scale of the beauty, complexity, intricacy, wonder of even the smallest creature; we begin to realise that they are not just a bundle of provisions for our use, but that in some sense beyond comprehension, there is something of God in them.

In R.S.K. Barnes' modern textbook *The Diversity of Living Organisms*, vertebrates merit only eight out of a total of three hundred and forty-five pages, and mammals only get half a page.[18] In Margulis and Schwartz' *Five Kingdoms* only five out of a total of five hundred and twenty pages are devoted to vertebrates.[19] The rest is given over to similarly concise descriptive accounts of all the other groups of equally complex organisms. A few of these are familiar to be sure – molluscs, crustaceans, annelids, for example – but most are likely to be unfamiliar, even to many biologists: Gnathostomulida, Rhombozoa, Orthonectida, Nematomorpha, Acanthocephala, Kinorhyncha, Priapulida, Gastrotricha, Loricifera, Entoprocta, Pogonophora and Onychophora to name at random a dozen of the thirty-seven phyla of animals out of the thirty-seven listed in Margulis and Schwartz.

Linnaeus composed a marvellous metaphor to represent biodiversity. He envisioned it as an enormous mansion with countless corridors and rooms, each the home of a particular group of plants or animals:

The museum of nature, like a palace, has an enormous number of connected chambers, filled with the stupendous contrivances and wonders of the Creator, to each of which a place is assigned according to its kind; to the greatest amphitheatres of nature the first entry is open to every one, but the smaller ones are usually shut; here there is need of skill to unclose by slow degrees the doorway of each chamber, within which a new world, as it were, displays itself before our eyes … The chief key for unfastening the bars of this palace that has been for all the ages closed is afforded by the microscope, which gives us the same help in examining minute bodies that are close to us as astronomers get from the telescope in the investigation of distant bodies in the heavens.[20]

The microscope (or indeed, just a hand lens) provides the key, and those who venture through any one of Linnaeus' doors with one in their possession – with full sensory and intellectual awareness – are likely to be so caught up in the wonder of what they encounter that they would be happy to spend the rest of their lives in that one room. They have taken a step closer to seeing them as they really are, independent of us, and towards understanding how overwhelmingly greater the reality of their being is beyond our human embrace. It matters little which particular room of the ninety-five or so we enter – and many of these doors lead into hallways off which a multitude of other doors lead to subsidiary chambers. The corridor you enter through the doorway labelled 'insects' for instance has around twenty-five doors. One of them bears the name 'Moths and Butterflies', and this is where you encounter some of the one hundred thousand living exemplars of this particular mode of being-in-the-world, each worthy of a volume in celebration of its unique achievement.[21] A human lifetime can do no more than sample the wonder of it. And so it is for the other rooms, those that house other modes of being-in-the-world. However significant our invitation to enter, their *existence*, what they are about, is entirely independent of ours.

Albert the Great wrote his *Man and the Beasts* in the same age in which Thomas wrote his *Summa Theologiae*, the latter grounded in an apprehension of the living world essentially based on the former. There is almost nothing about *what life really is* in Albert's great compendium: but the blossoming of understanding that has taken place in the centuries since should have transformed the reach and depth of theology but failed to do so: because the achievement of the *Summa* was taken to be the last word in theology, reflecting a failure to see that theology too, like other sciences, must itself be a growing, living thing, *the very life blood of which is the evolution of human understanding.*

These considerations are taken into another dimension entirely when we realise that the biodiversity of our age is but a still frame in a moving narrative. There has been comparable diversity during every period of geological time, always different, the glorious biodiversity of any one period of geological time – which few but palaeontologists are privileged to wonder at – an efflorescence of hitherto unexpressed embryonic possibility.

CHAPTER 3

THE WONDER OF THE OTHER LIVES

Whenever I can, early in the morning or as dusk approaches, I sit outside. Sitting here alone and in silence I am visited on occasion by squirrels, hedgehogs, shrews, wood mice. A young fox comes by at dusk most evenings, her timetable regulated by the sun and an intimacy with the geography of her world that needs no GPS. I realise, when I look deeper into myself, that the countless evenings I am not visited are spent in the hope I may again be given the grace of touching, however superficially, their lives. Among the most memorable experiences of my life have been those other all-too-few occasions when badgers and seals, foxes and bats have allowed me to be in their presence, in the presence of the God their different lives acclaim.

We come to know more and more about the variety of life on Earth with each passing year: not only in taxonomic detail, but about the ways of life of different creatures: although we know much less about this, because it takes more time and effort to shed light on the daily lives of small creatures than it does to describe their bodies in the meticulous detail required of taxonomists. But even so, the number of people sufficiently skilled to properly describe new species in most groups of plants or animals is an infinitesimally tiny fraction of the number that would be required to describe the flora and fauna of Earth adequately.

In spite of this, each year sees the publication of more and more descriptive manuals that make what we do know available to a wider readership than has ever before been possible. This availability of information is greatly augmented by the power of the internet. And yet, although the knowledge garnered by scientists is more readily available than at any time in the past, there is no effective mechanism that distils this mass of detail and makes the essence of it available to society at large. This is a great failure of education curricula, and particularly of religious education. The results of surveys carried out to ascertain people's understanding and appreciation of biodiversity are depressing.

The richness of the lives of other creatures, the fullness of those lives, has hitherto been hidden completely from us, but with the progress of science is beginning to come into focus for charismatic birds and mammals, less so for trees and flowers, hardly at all for the equally if not more mesmerising lives of invertebrates and less conspicuous plants, or fungi. It is extraordinarily difficult for us to appreciate the evolutionary achievement individual species represent. We must always start by remembering that this species before me stands at the end of an evolutionary journey as long as our human journey; that if we follow the path of that journey backwards through geological time it will meet with ours, because the mesmerisingly complex network of the paths they trace is a family tree. We are all, every species of us, brother and sister to different degrees of consanguinity.[1] The differences that define us are always related to the demands of the different ways of life to which we have become adapted during that long journey.

Each species looks out upon, and presents itself to, a world centred on its self, focused through senses that apprehend those elements and dimensions of reality that are relevant to it. Each is therefore, in essence, a life made possible and supported by a unique combination of the material and energetic resources present in the world. It is the *embodiment* of these resources, exploiting through them a unique mode of living possibility presented by the evolving cosmos. But when we observe the lives of other creatures we inevitably see them through our own human eyes. We cannot appreciate the fulfilment their being brings, feel as they feel, think as they 'think', enjoy as they, each in its unique way. What then, of what we can know of God?

Time and again in my growing acquaintance with the lives of particular creatures I have been so overwhelmed by the wonder of their lives: but *more* than this, as I have meditated on each in turn, sucked into their lives, every time mesmerised, at the realisation of how each is as fully the centre of its world as we think ourselves to be. The list of the creatures whose lives I have shared in this intimate way extends to several hundred now, and I never lose sight of the fact that this is the smallest fraction of all there is or was. And how dare I use the word 'intimate' for a mere acquaintance, for it is in truth no more than that. And how must my appreciation pale beside that of the God *whose ideas they are*: 'intimations of things which for their greater part escape our sensual experience, but which to an increasing consciousness may yield their secrets.'[2]

The sensory achievement of other animals

So extraordinary are the adaptations that equip individual species of plants and animals for their particular, unique mode of life you might well wonder sometimes if what you read is being made up, so *unusual* does it appear. For indeed it is unusual: no species of life is usual. Each is different, unique, exploiting a way of living no other exploits.[3] Our ever-increasing awareness of the capacities of different creatures – often so far superior to our own – opens for us a deeper awareness and appreciation of their dignity: of what their being in the world *represents*. Ecological description, for all its complexity and sophistication, and the enormous detail with which it can describe individual other-than-human lives, does not have the words – the letters even – to touch the *quintessence* (for which, indeed, there *is* no descriptive language). The questing intuition however acts as a lens to split this quintessence into component visible colours that illuminate all the rest, as it were, from behind.

Our sight is the sense through which we experience the nature of the world, the beauty of the world, most acutely. Unlike most mammals, we see the colours of the rainbow. The magnificence of the visual arts is a celebration of what we see with our eyes, and of what our mind and spirit intuit behind our perception. But our visual acuity is the merest fraction of that of other creatures.

We are in awe before the lives of birds.[4] We don't have to be ornithologists or members of bird clubs to find tears for the dawn chorus, but the more we come to know about the lives of birds the more our awe and wonder grow, and continue to grow. The reason we can all respond in this way is because birds are big enough to see with our eyes. We don't need binoculars or a microscope. Of course, they vary greatly in size, from hummingbirds to albatrosses, but we can enquire about and see into much that goes on in their lives just by looking and paying attention.

There are North American owls that can pinpoint a mouse at a distance of half a mile even when the intensity of illumination is no more than that of a single candle.[5] Raptors have two foveae (focal points) in their eyes. This is like having a camera that has both a telephoto and a macro lens. Some birds, for example blue tits, can see ultraviolet.

Some owls excel not so much in their visual acuity, but in their auditory acuity. The ears of these owls are positioned asymmetrically, so a sound reaches the two ears at slightly different times or at slightly different volumes, enabling them to pinpoint the source with extraordinary precision. This enables the great grey owl, for instance, to locate rodents beneath the snow, then power through the surface with pinpoint precision to grab hold of them. Ducks a-dabbling seems the most banal of activities, but they have sensitive touch receptors in the beak tips. The sensitivity of a duck's bill may rival that of our fingertips. Birds probing in wet sand can set up a pressure wave whose shape enables them to detect bivalves.

Some snakes (the family that includes pythons, boas and pit vipers) have good 'standard' eyesight (humans setting the standard of course), but they can also 'see' in infrared (the sense receptors for this are pits that lie near their nostrils). This enables them to pinpoint prey in the dark from its body heat. And they are able not only to see in infrared and visible light at the same time, but to switch from one to the other. Not only do bees have the unimaginable capacity to see ultraviolet light, they can detect the polarisation of light in a way analogous to the way we distinguish blue from red, an ability to navigate by the position of the sun even when it is cloudy. But some insects and birds have four, five or even six colour receptors – compared to our three – which enables them to experience a riot of colour it is impossible for us not only to experience, but even to imagine.

The sense of smell may be thousands of times stronger in dogs than in humans: inside their nose there are up to three hundred million olfactory receptors, compared to our six million, and the part of their brain that processes the information they gather (the olfactory cortex) accounts for 12.5 per cent of their brain mass compared to less than 1 per cent in us. But this is not simply a case of more of the same, a difference of degree. It has different 'levels' to it as it were, enabling the animal to pick up different layers of information. Some birds also have a very acute sense of smell. Albatrosses and petrels have been described as living in an 'olfactory seascape', using their refined sense of smell to find their way around and locate food.

The tiny predatory wasp *Microplitis croceipes* uses smell to locate the caterpillars of the corn earworm on which it lays its eggs. It can pick up the smell of its prey at concentrations of one in a thousand billion – one hundred times weaker than the lowest concentrations detectable by artificial, commercial 'electronic noses'. They can be trained to respond to other smells, and are now being trained to react to narcotics, neurotoxins and explosives by the US military.[6] Silkworm moth males can pick up the scent of a single female at a distance of several miles. The male of the emperor moth can detect the pheromonic perfume of the female half a mile away. Midges can detect carbon dioxide in human breath at 200 m. The ability of many insects to survive atmospheric pressure change or oxygen depletion beggars belief, our notion of what is possible under such conditions limited as it is by what we ourselves can tolerate.[7]

The discovery of the echolocation capacity of bats is startling, but we have come to take it for granted, no longer awed by this extraordinary sensory ability, so superior to ours. The signals bats emit would sound like a cacophony of extra-loud screams, clicks and squeals to us if we could hear them, but they are emitted in ultrasound, beyond the range of human hearing. The echoes they cause enable the bat to pinpoint the position and speed of the target with extraordinary precision; some bats can detect the distance between themselves and their prey with an accuracy of as little as 4 mm. So individually distinctive are these sounds that bats can recognise each other from their voices.[8] Birds too can echolocate, but – unlike bats – they use low-frequency audible clicks.

Whatever about imagining how animals see in unimaginable colours, how are we to imagine how it feels to detect magnetism? There is good evidence that many species, including pigeons and chickens, sea turtles, naked mole rats – and possibly cattle – can detect the Earth's geomagnetic field, sometimes with astonishing accuracy. The magnetic receptors are probably in their heads, based on crystals of magnetite, which align with the Earth's magnetic field and pull on some sort of stretch receptor or hair-like cell as it changes polarity. Another possibility is that pigments in their eyes called cryptochromes can detect the magnetic field chemically and provide a visual cue the animal can use as a compass.

Birds have a variety of navigational mechanisms, including star and sun compasses and olfactory cues. They can also detect the direction of the Earth's magnetic field using microscopic crystals of magnetite located around their eyes and in the nasal cavity of the upper beak. They detect the strength of the field by means of a chemical reaction.[9] Birds also have nerve endings inside the upper beak that have lots of bullet-shaped structures rich in iron. These beak magnetoreceptors respond to changes in the intensity of the magnetic field rather than its direction, enabling the bird to build a mental map of the magnetic hills and valleys it 'perceives' in its surroundings.[10]

Many other animals are also sensitive to magnetic fields, each in its own particular way: lobsters, fish and mole rats, sharks and rays, bats and turtles, and many insects – including ants, bees, beetles and butterflies.[11] The simplest organic compasses are found in certain bacteria that live in the anoxic mud on the sea floor, and whose cells contain chains of crystals of iron compounds that align themselves with Earth's magnetic field, which enables them to swim away from oxygen-rich water, to which they are ill-adapted.

The achievement of individual species

When we look closely at the lives of creatures we are overwhelmed by the intricacy and beauty of what we see. This is what the great naturalists of the eighteenth and nineteenth centuries were starting to say: in England perhaps especially, for reasons that had to a great extent to do with the theological perspective of the Established Church at this time.[12] And look attentively they did, with eye and microscope, at everything in the natural world about them. This stream of enquiry was to become a tide as the nineteenth century advanced. Early Darwinism placed great boulders in its path, but this scarcely stemmed the tide, which has ever since continued and indeed swollen immeasurably in terms of the volume of enquiry, but increasingly devoid of attribution to the hand of a designer God: no longer thinking in terms of what philosophy calls 'final causes' that is. It is only when we introduce such a *force* into the Equation of Meaning, however, that everything snaps into meaningful, exhilarating, focus.

The deeper your acquaintance grows the closer you come to a real appreciation of this vast truth: that we are all made with the same loving care, the harlequin fly with the same care as myself, and the frog in its pool, the rotifer in its pond, the tardigrade in the cushion of moss that is the forest in which it spends all of its life. There are encyclopedias of the human body that extend to many volumes. There are medical libraries filled with books on the ailments to which every organ is subject and how we are to deal with them in our inevitable encounters with pain and disintegration of the body.

Some decades ago a book on the miracle that is the human body appeared, under the title *Fearfully and Wonderfully Made*: a phrase lifted from Psalm 139; and endless volumes describing every organ and cell in the human body in minute detail line the shelves of medical libraries the world over.[13] There could be comparably voluminous encyclopaedias on every other species were everything there is to know about them to be written down, were healing and keeping them healthy to be any part of human concern. A book like *Fearfully and Wonderfully Made* could be written, supported by comparably endless volumes of detail, for each and every species: for each of the tens of millions of species for which we have invented names: as for each of the tens of millions for which we have not, both in our age of the world and in every geological era gone by. 'Every creature is a book about God,' wrote Meister Eckhart. The entire history of the universe is condensed in the being of every single species, yet differently in each. A philosophical exposition of the exuberant inventiveness, the inexhaustible wonder of life's diversity (Thomas Aquinas' 'myriad hues of being') is found in what Arthur Lovejoy called the 'Principle of Plenitude', according to which 'No genuine potentiality of being can remain unfulfilled ...' 'Their abundance is as great as the possibilities of existence'.[14]

Empathy

There is an episode in the early life of John Muir which describes the response of a sow to the killing of one of her litter.[15] The sow had given birth to a large litter, which she took into the woods to forage for roots and acorns when they were old enough. On one occasion a wandering Indian shot one of the little pigs, causing the mother and her remaining offspring to hurtle in terror back to the farm shanty for protection.

> The solemn awe and fear in the eyes of that old mother and those little pigs I never can forget; it was as unmistakable and deadly a fear as I ever saw expressed by any human eye, and corroborates in no uncertain way the oneness of all of us.[16]

Muir *knows* how the mother hog feels. This knowledge is not based on dissection or genetics or comparative biochemistry. But neither is it *fictitious*. It is intuitive in this sense. It assumes all the information that science presents us with and evaluates it in terms of a broader picture that brings in the totality of human experience and value.[17]

This extended empathy is all-important, because it brings to us the realisation that we have in common with other creatures not only a common ancestry, sharing genes and all that implies, but that with those creatures that are closest to us we share in common an emotional life.

Nor is consciousness confined to vertebrate animals such as primates, dolphins and whales, and certain birds such as crows. Recent and continuing research shows that cephalopods (octopuses and their kind) have a complex brain organised along lines strikingly similar to ours, and have comparable learning abilities, memory and spatial awareness, displaying many mental skills that rival the cleverest mammals. It is even thought by some researchers that molluscs may have been the first to evolve a brain that could make sense of the world we all live in.[18] Yet these creatures are anatomically and morphologically so different from us, having diverged from a common ancestor some half a billion years ago.[19]

With other vertebrates we do not have sensory clues to which we can empathically relate as readily as we can with our close furry kin. But birds are feathered dinosaurs: an astonishing fact that helps us to appreciate that reptiles also, and the amphibians and fishes that are close to them in evolutionary terms, are not as devoid of emotion as our desperately limited ability to perceive it, and the assumptions to which this gives rise, lead us to believe. We must not take this too far though, and impute our human emotions of love and hate, pleasure and the joy of being alive: but strive to take hold of the reality that on the level of *emotion* life exhibits a kaleidoscope of diversity that is comparable to – and indeed develops from – the more material expressions of diversity among life forms.

> Even frogs and toads and fishes may be tamed, provided they have the uniform sympathy of one person, with whom they become intimately acquainted without the distracting and varying attentions of strangers. And surely all God's people, however serious and savage, great or small, like to play. Whales and elephants, dancing, humming gnats, and invisibly small mischievous microbes – all are warm with divine radium and must have lots of fun in them.[20]

With creatures further removed from us in evolutionary terms the expression of emotion is less evident to us. The very nature of that emotion has less in common with our human experience first of all, and the greater anatomical and physiological difference makes it more difficult for us to see or hear its actual expression. Nevertheless, the joy in life of the few birds whose lives are lived close to ours is sometimes abundantly *in evidence*. Nobody who has watched and listened to swallows in the shared space of a farmyard over the summer can have any doubt of their emotion, even though we might *see* little of it as we stand face-to-face with beak and feather and eyes that focus the world so much more sharply than ours.[21]

The emotions of invertebrates are forever closed to us, their joys and sorrows so far from ours, arising from lives so different, that we can never empathise with them. What possible point of entry can I find into *their* hidden lives, our families have grown so far apart in the hundreds of millions of years since we shared a common ancestor?[22] But the God whose creatures they are, each acclaiming something unique about what it means to be alive must, on some remote metaphorical level, empathise: understand and indeed be ultimately, albeit at an incomprehensible remove, the source of it.

But the further we move away from where we are on the Tree of Life, as we approach modes of existence more remote from ours in evolutionary terms (when for example 'we walk with the lone worm, wandering in the twilight of consciousness'), the more difficult this becomes, because their anatomy and physiology are very different from ours, and because their sensory perceptions, and what emotional responses these generate or facilitate, are often beyond anything we can touch with fellow feeling.[23] Our sympathy and empathy with them therefore must go beyond shared emotions to reside in our understanding and the behaviour towards them that understanding dictates. And, of course, 'how little we know as yet of the life of plants – their hopes and fears, pains and enjoyments.'[24] In William Paley's day two centuries ago we were only beginning to understand the function of organs present in other creatures but lacking in us:

> For instance, insects, under all their varieties of form, are endowed with *antennae*, which is the name given to those long feelers that rise from each side of the head: but to what common use or want of the insect kind, a provision so universal is subservient, has not yet been ascertained: and it has not been ascertained, because it admits not of a clear, or very probable comparison, with any organs which we possess ourselves, or with the organs of animals which resemble ourselves in their functions and faculties, or with which we are better acquainted than we are with insects. We want a ground of analogy.[25]

And that behaviour must now, in the light of our new understanding, be governed by an ethical imperative that rests first of all on our appreciation of other species as living self-expressions of God, each species a different note in that stupendous orchestra, a unique hue in the super-psychedelic rainbow of life; second, on our ever-growing understanding of our shared history, our family connections, our common destiny on Earth; and third, because we now see so clearly that without them and the biosphere they constitute, our human life is, in proportion to our neglect and abuse of that biological diversity, diminished and ultimately smothered.[26]

> The universe would [indeed] be incomplete without man; but it would also be incomplete without the smallest transmicroscopic creature that dwells beyond our conceitful eyes and knowledge.[27]

Should we, then, fall in love with worms and beetles? We cannot. But we can and must use our capacity to reason in order to appreciate how inadequate our everyday reaction to such creatures is in the light of what we now know of the *reality*. We must try to take those human lenses off: which will not necessarily change our emotional response, but it will *change our perspective*; it will change our intellectual and ultimately our ethical and spiritual response.

In more highly evolved forms of life the being of creatures manifests as personality and our encounter with them is a relationship that becomes ever richer the more intimately we come to know them. It is akin to the relationship that develops between myself and other human beings but different. We are familiar with the relationship that can develop with the pet animals we invite to share our lives, but it can extend so much more deeply into the taxonomic branches of the tree of life than that. We get to see something unique in the individual animal – beyond what we see in the species – when we devote to it the attention of the pet owner – or parent. Of his relationship with his pet geese, Paul Theroux wrote:

> I often thought: if only people knew what my geese are like when I am alone with them – the solitary pleasure only the pet owner is privileged to know. It is impossible for anyone except the owner to see the creature as it actually is, because in the presence of others the animal behaves differently – fusses, gets nervy and loud or silly or hostile, playing the fool as children often do in the presence of strangers. No one knows except the parent, or pet-owner, what a marvel the creature is, in repose, and that when you're alone you are nearly always at peace – such intelligence and serenity and mutual understanding the visitor never sees. I often sat with five silent geese as though I was one of the flock; they took little interest in me, or in one another, and were patient and calm.[28]

A story is told of Richard Martin – the 'Humanity Dick' so influential in the setting up of the RSPCA – 'as a benign old gentleman strolling on the beach, picking up the undersized fish the fishermen threw out of their nets, and putting them back into the sea.'[29] Martin is a character whose history is intertwined with myth, even though he lived less than two centuries ago. That anecdote reminds me of Francis of Assisi, of whom it was said he picked earthworms out of the way lest they be trodden underfoot. The madness is the same, if madness it is, but it is a madness that resonates still and continues to root itself into our evolving consciousness.

The minuter parts of creation

It is in the minuter parts of creation that the works of the Almighty proclaim most clearly to us the wonders of his hand, and that man cannot be entitled to the appellation of wise who dares to contemn or asperse them.

JAMES LAWSON DRUMMOND (1832),
LETTERS TO A YOUNG NATURALIST, P. 22-23

In the standard who's who of life on Earth, insects occupy a mere five or six pages out of the total of 345, even though they account for the great majority of the living species that have been described.[30] The rest is taken up with the remaining eighty-eight groups of plants and animals on Earth: each as deserving of its few pages as the next.[31] Insects are divided into thirty-four groups known as 'orders', the common names of some of which are familiar – butterflies, beetles, dragonflies – others less so. But we know little about the lives of the overwhelming majority, even of those that have been formally described and named – never mind those that have not, and in all likelihood never well be. Yet each represents a unique and marvellous achievement of living possibility. It is difficult to convey in words any real impression of the *ingenuity* with which every possible mode of existence is exploited through this kaleidoscopic natural diversity. Every possible source of energy and material is utilised: and most of this is hidden from us. The more deeply you can immerse yourself in these wonderful creatures, the more you come to understand their complexity and their beauty, the adaptations each of them has developed on its unique evolutionary journey – which fit each of them to its unique mode of living – the closer you appreciate them as the Divine Mind appreciates them.

In the Book of Job, we only hear the voice of God five chapters before the end, when he asks Job whether his limited understanding of the true wonder of creation qualifies him to question: 'What do you know?' he asks; and the examples he picks are wondrous creatures of which the people of that time knew next to nothing: hippopotamus and crocodile. In our day, hundreds of books have been written about hippopotamus and crocodile. Countless theses have been written about particular aspects of their morphology, physiology and ecology. But for smaller creatures such as insects it is a different matter. A little over a century ago the great entomologist L.C. Miall wrote in awe about how little was then known of the lives of flies: and few people were more qualified than he to make that observation because few knew more than he did about them.

I have made it my business for some years to hunt out the larvae of our common insects. I have searched the waters, both stagnant and flowing, and have pried into all accumulations of decaying organic matter that I have come across. I have particularly attended to the early stages of the Diptera. But I have to confess that nineteen-twentieths of the Diptera now buzzing about in my garden are known to me, if at all, only as items in a catalogue. No doubt a large proportion have been reared close at hand. But they are so well hidden, and the naturalist is so blind, that it is only when he sees the swarms of winged insects that he becomes conscious of the multitude of larvae and pupae which he has overlooked.[32]

At that time there were books about mosquitoes and silkworms, and Miall himself had written a book about a species of midge, but very few people studied flies in any sort of dedicated way, and microscope technology was, by comparison with today, at a relatively primitive stage.[33]

Every year I potter about the garden in late winter, looking and listening for signs of spring: an early violet or primrose perhaps in some sheltered corner or the spring song of the robin. But spring has already come in the lives of others. Swirling in the air, now above my head and in the blink of an eye later among the branches of an apple tree, in a dance choreographed in a way I understand less even than I understand the choreography of murmurating starlings, are swarms of midges, so tiny I can make out no detail of their bodies individually, even when they are still. At least I call them midges, but actually – if by midge I mean the biting nuisances of warm summer evenings – they are something different. These are chironomids, a family of midge-like flies that pay no attention to us, and this is a mating swarm. They have spent the winter as larvae or pupae in some corner of the garden: some corner that ecologically is utterly their own, as unique to them as the course of the stream is to the life of the kingfisher or the fringe of Antarctic ice to the penguin. Only with the eyes of the microscope, and all the extensions of our senses that advanced optical and chemical technology put at my enquiring fingertips, can I appreciate it in the way I can appreciate a bird or a flower, or peer into the intimate corners of its life as I can into the life of the wren with my binoculars: so utterly different, but as tuned to the tiny facet of reality to which its being-in-the-world is the ultimate living response to the possibilities and challenges of that one corner.

And that is *this one species*, which only three or four people in Ireland are expert enough to identify by the unique name that sets it apart from all the others in the taxonomic catalogue of the Chironomidae.

Chironomids are among the most successful of insects. The adult flies are familiar to most people as the swarms of dancing midges above streams and other freshwaters, which are the males awaiting the arrival of females. The juvenile stages of these little flies – and so, much the greater part of their lives, for their adult life lasts no longer than a week or two – is spent in watery places: freshwater bodies of every conceivable size, and such wet terrestrial habitats as rotten wood and other decaying vegetable matter, dung and moss. The great diversity and numerical success of the group is indicative of the great range of microhabitats they have learned to exploit over the course of their evolution. There are some fifteen thousand species worldwide, 1,273 of them in Europe: of whose lives, for all our tools of enquiry, very little is known. Under favourable conditions they can often reach population densities of several tens of thousands per square metre.

By 1950 only fifty species of chironomids had been recorded for Ireland; since then the number has gradually and steadily risen as the result of the dedicated studies of a handful of specialists, to the present figure of five hundred and twenty or so species. These are listed in a recent publication of 420+ pages: which is exclusively concerned with taxonomic detail, and in particular with the subtle character differences that enable the species to be distinguished one from another. And yet, each of these is unique, occupying a distinct ecological niche of its own, different from every other, between them occupying every conceivable body of water, however small, however polluted. Carmel Humphries, who pioneered the study of chironomids in Ireland, described them as 'one of the most, if not the most, important group of freshwater organisms'.[34]

In running waters they occupy habitats in rivers, streams, waterfalls, thin water films on vertical rock surfaces, seepages and glacial meltwaters. In standing waters they are found in lakes, ponds, pools, a variety of temporary water bodies (including garden barrels and rain-filled containers), phytotelmata, tree rot-holes and in the leaf-axils of pitcher plants and bromeliads. Some inhabit saline lakes and marine coastal brackish water habitats while a small minority occur in coastal waters to a depth of thirty metres. A minority are terrestrial species that are associated with moist soil habitats rich in organic matter, in leaf litter in woodland, in grassland and tillage soils and in fungi, rotting wood and cow dung.[35]

Black-flies (*Simulium*)

> *Natura in minimis maxime miranda* (Nature is at its most-to-be-marvelled-at in the smallest creatures).
>
> LINNAEUS

Every summer I take my students to the nearest stream to meet *Simulium*, whose tiny larvae live in their myriads attached to stones in swift-flowing water. They are as wonderful as any creature on God's Earth in terms of their fitness to be here, in the way tens of millions of years of evolution have shaped them for life in the torrent. Each is attached to a little pad of silk to which it clings by means of a rosette of tiny hooks. Thus firmly anchored it sways in the current, stretching its head into the stream, from which it filters its food using a delicately feathered fan for the purpose. If the larva is dislodged – whether by the force of the water or a curious naturalist – it releases its hold and disappears into the stream. But watch closely and a minute later you will see the little creature hauling itself back to its pad by means of a slender thread of silk which it spun the instant the current carried it away, and which still anchors it securely to its home pad.

When the larva has reached its full size it pupates, firmly attached to a stone or stem. It has an elaborate bunch of filaments at its front end which function as gills, extracting oxygen from the water so that it can be taken into its body via the spiracles, which are the special breathing openings at the base of the filaments. Now it faces a particular problem, because the adult fly that will emerge from the pupal case is entirely terrestrial, unable to survive in turbulent water if it crawls out of its submerged pupal case. But tens of millions of years of evolution have perfected a solution for the little fly. As the adult develops, a film of air builds up inside the pupal skin, so that when this splits and the fly emerges it does so in a bubble of air which immediately floats to the surface, and as the bubble bursts, the fly takes wing straight away and flies to nearby vegetation to pause and take its first look at the world that lies beyond the water.

Is it any surprise we are filled with admiration, amazement, wonder? We often feel this way when we look a little closer at these creatures we can hardly see, whose lives are their own business, often entirely unknown to us. Is not their right to their place in the world as great as ours, as the Jains and Deep Ecologists believe? However, there is another side to these wonderful creatures, for *Simulium* has the most painful bite of any fly. The creature whose larva so stirs our imagination can attack animals in such numbers as to cause death from loss of blood and the poisonous effect of their bites. In 1923, nearly twenty thousand domestic animals were killed in this way by the Golubatz fly, a species of *Simulium* that breeds in a particular part of the river Danube. Other species are so numerous and venomous that they make life a misery for reindeer in the tundra and muskeg, and render large tracts of country there more or less uninhabitable during the summer. Certain tropical species carry the worm that causes river blindness, and all the misery that goes with it for millions of people.

Our health and well-being demand that we raise our hand against these pests, but our understanding of their complexity, of how perfectly they are adapted for life in their particular corners of the Earth's ecosystems, requires that we do so with regret. This is the perspective that informed the great Albert Schweitzer's reverence for life:

> To the truly ethical man, all life is sacred, including forms of life that from the human point of view may seem to be lower than ours. He makes distinctions only from case to case, and under pressure of necessity, when he is forced to decide which life he will sacrifice in order to preserve other lives.
>
> The man who is guided by the ethics of reverence for life stamps out life only from inescapable necessity, never from thoughtlessness. He seizes every occasion to feel the happiness of helping living things and shielding them from suffering and annihilation.[36]

Plants with flowers

It is the same for flowering plants. No words can begin to convey the utterly dazzling variety of their most numerous families: especially perhaps the orchids (Orchidaceae), asclepiads (Asclepiadaceae) and the Asteraceae, the family to which daisies and dandelions belong. There are maybe twenty-five thousand species of orchids – a family of enormous complexity, diversity of shape and form, and beauty – five times as many as mammals, and at least as many composites (the daisy-dandelion family). There are maybe three thousand asclepiad species. And the most amazing aspect of all this is that the variety and beauty appreciated by us is accidental: in the sense that each and every one has evolved to occupy a particular mode of living unique to itself; every detail of its design is *functional* and, as far as ecology goes, for itself.

The call of Jesus to 'consider the lilies' (Luke 12:27) is of course intended as an exhortation to us to rely on Providence for our important needs: the most essential qualifying gloss on which is the necessity to extend the meaning of the word to include responsible management on our part of the Earth resources through which Providence is exercised. But there are two other things we might notice about this brief injunction. First, it is an appeal to our aesthetic response to wild flowers: to natural beauty and harmony; and second, there is the call to attention: *consider*.

In those days, two millennia ago, as it had been for as long as there had been a human presence in the world, our capacity to respond to this injunction was limited to sensory perception. In its relation to the life of plants this is an area in which we can see with particular clarity that progress in understanding we discussed in chapter two. A great deal can be discovered by sensory encounter: through taste and smell, sight and touch: and needed to be, if we were to answer such questions as: can I eat it? For what purpose is its timber best suited? Does it have medicinal or other practical use?

We have looked at flowers with wonder ever since self-reflective consciousness awoke in us. What are they? What role do they play in the world? This is less transparent than it is in animals which, for all their differences – which raise all sorts of questions of their own of course – share so much in common with us that from the very dawn of humanity we have been conscious of a deep affinity we cannot comprehend. But why are *flowers* so varied: in form and size, colour and smell, and in the vegetative structures that produce them?

As with the more general creation myths (a subset of these indeed) different cultures attempted to explain the appearance of different flowers on Earth in mythological terms. In Greek mythology for instance, the flowers familiar to everyone were conceived as floral incarnations of various mortals caught up in liaisons of one sort or another with the immortal gods.[37]

A concept that became deeply rooted in the western tradition was based on the belief that God – since he had made everything else in the living world to be at the service of mankind – would have left some clue as to what that purpose might be. This became known as the Doctrine of Signatures. Familiar examples are the various plants whose names refer to some part of the body. For example, herb Robert enjoyed a considerable reputation in the herbal tradition of the Middle Ages, especially as an astringent in the treatment of skin conditions: it, tutsan and a few others were the great *vulnerary* herbs – used for healing wounds. In exposed situations, especially where water is scarce, the stems and leaves of herb Robert take on a bright red colour. This was interpreted as a sign from God that the plant could be useful in treating skin conditions (where the skin often becomes inflamed), and in 'regenerating' the blood.[38] Another example is provided by the several species of 'figworts' ('Fig' is a now obsolete word for haemorrhoids). The 'figwort buttercup' *Ranunculus ficaria* (lesser celandine) has clusters of tubers just below ground level that bear some resemblance to haemarrhoids or piles; in the case of the figworts (certain species of *Scrophularia*) the fancied resemblance is in the fruits.[39]

There are numerous other examples of attempts to understand the purpose of flowers in spiritual terms. Especially striking is the elaborate explanation for the highly exotic form of the flower of a plant the first Jesuit missionaries encountered in South America, utterly unlike anything found in Europe. In this strange new flower the European missionaries saw a living synopsis of the passion of Christ. Passion flowers (*Passiflora*) are a diverse and very successful genus of plants (mostly vines), with some five hundred species found throughout the tropics (except Africa), and especially characteristic of South America and south-east Asia.[40] Accounts of their extraordinary structure began to filter back to Europe with missionaries returning from New Spain in the late sixteenth and early seventeenth centuries: at around the time the monastic scholar Jacomo Bosio was working on his extensive treatise on the Cross of Calvary. (By this time also a tradition had developed in Europe of recording symbols of the Passion on the tombstones of prominent people.) Bosio was slow to believe what he was seeing at first, but in time he came to believe that the flower had been created by God to represent the mysteries of the Passion: 'It may well be that in HIS infinite wisdom it pleases HIM to create it thus, shut up and protected, as though to indicate that the wonderful mysteries of the cross and of HIS passion were to remain hidden from heathen people of these countries until the time preordained by HIS highest Majesty.'

The five petals and five sepals were interpreted as the ten apostles (conveniently minus Judas and Peter, who had thrice denied that he knew Jesus). The crown of thorns was represented by the twisted and plaited filaments of the corona, its blood-red fringe suggesting the scourge with which Jesus was tormented (its imagined seventy-two filaments were taken to represent the exact number of thorns in the crown). The prominent stigmas are the three nails with which he was crucified, and the five stamens are 'of the hue of blood evidently setting forth five wounds received by our LORD on the cross'. The chalice-like ovary and receptacle were interpreted either as a hammer or the Holy Grail. The pointed leaves are 'shaped like the head of a lance or pike like the spear that pierced the side of our Saviour', their tendrils resembling the whips used to flagellate him, 'while the underside of the leaf is marked with dark round spots signifying thirty pieces of silver', that Judas was paid to betray Christ. The flowers remain open just for a day (the time Jesus spent on the cross), after which the petals fold over the ripening ovary, symbolising Jesus enclosed in the tomb, and the Hidden Wisdom that constitutes the Mysteries of the Cross.[41] In fact the extraordinary structure is a uniquely successful device for pollination: in most species by large bees, but others are pollinated by bumblebees, wasps and bats: and a few are self-pollinating.[42]

It was only in the eighteenth century that the nature and function of the different parts of flowers came to be understood for what they really are *in themselves*. The realisation that the stamens and carpels are the male and female reproductive organs of the plant was an amazing, not to say shocking, discovery. It was first expounded in a book in which Linnaeus classified flowering plants in terms of the number and arrangement of these organs, and in language that was provocatively erotic.

The first botanist to realise the true functional significance of the form and size, colour and scent of flowers was Christian Konrad Sprengel (1750-1816). In 1787 he undertook a meticulous study of the wood cranesbill (*Geranium sylvaticum*), and realised for the first time the extraordinary elegance and detailed precision with which it is adapted for pollination by its insect visitors. In the light of this new insight he went on to look at the structure of other flowers: a six-year study that culminated in the publication of his great work on insect pollination in 1793, which begins as follows:

> In the summer of 1787, while I carefully watched the flower of the wild geranium (*Geranium sylvaticum*), I found that the bases of its petals were provided on the inner side and on both edges with fine soft hairs. Convinced that the wise Creator of nature has brought forth not even a single hair without some particular design, I considered what purpose these hairs might serve. And here it occurred to me that if one starts with the supposition that the five drops of nectar, which are secreted from as many glands, are destined for the nourishment of certain insects, one must at the same time find it not improbable that there should be some provision for preventing this nectar from being spoiled by rain, and that these hairs may have been placed here for the attainment of this purpose.[43]

Over the course of their evolution the structure of flowers has become adapted, often with the most amazing intricacy and ingenuity from our human perspective, to attract the particular insects that pollinate them, and to maximise the chances of effective transfer of sperm-containing pollen to egg-bearing carpels. 'Nature', Sprengel concluded, 'appears not to have intended that any flower should be fertilised by its own pollen.'[44] Countless botanists since Sprengel have been captivated by the mesmerising beauty, intricacy and diversity of the structures of flowers, and there is now a vast literature on this subject of floral biology.

INTERLUDE
Consider this leaf ...

How then has the plant stored up this energy? Chiefly by the chlorophyllian function, a chemicism *sui generis* of which we do not possess the key, and which is probably unlike that of the laboratories.

HENRI BERGSON, *CREATIVE EVOLUTION* (1911), P. 276

A thousand years ago we looked and could see only so far in terms of seeing what is really there. All you can see is green. It is a green sheet. It's just a leaf after all. You can see no structure here apart from veins and the texture. But it's not – as you might think – some sort of green fabric, with the dye uniformly distributed. With the development of good light microscopes, we were able to see that the green was confined to little bean-shaped dots, the chloroplasts, which is where the sugars are made. Because they are so small, that's all you can see with a light microscope. The average chloroplast is about 3µm (micrometres) across (a micrometre is a thousandth of a millimetre). In one square millimetre of the surface of a leaf, there are about half a million chloroplasts.

Only in the 1960s with the advance of electron microscopy did we begin to see that there is a complex micro-architecture in the chloroplast. It is a capsule inside which is what looks like a futuristic housing estate, with skyscrapers that look like circular discs stacked on top of one another, and connected by tunnels and passages: all in this little space, a few thousandths of a millimetre across.

But the most awesome developments of all have only taken place in the last forty years or so, when using biochemical techniques of the most extraordinary ingenuity we have been able to peer into the chemical machinery of the chloroplast, which captures photons of light energy from the sun and uses these to split water; and then, by means of a sort of molecular bucket brigade, the energized electrons produced in this way are passed along a chemical chain until it can be packaged in the sugars and other things that ultimately provide the energy that powers everything we do. You speak with the voice of the sun. Your smile is sunlight. To really appreciate all this though you really have to understand something of the language of chemistry, and the warmth of that language is somewhere around freezing point.

For a metaphor that might carry the faintest glimpse of what is going on in the chloroplast, think of what it might be to be an observer inside a beehive, but a billion times smaller, surrounded by all that purposeful movement, but in this case the bees are atoms and molecules.

As amazing as what is actually going on here is the fact that we can have the capacity to look through the door and see what is going on in those tiny, dark rooms.

We now suspect that the almost inexplicable efficiency of plants at capturing and storing the radiation that hits the leaf is due to the way the vibration and dynamics of the array of molecules at the leaf surface utilise quantum capacities. In other words, in some scarcely comprehensible way the leaf is able at a macroscopic level to harness the super-efficiency of quantum processes.

CHAPTER 4

NATURE AS REVELATION

The ages of the world

James Ussher was perhaps the foremost biblical scholar in the English-speaking world of his day. Born in Dublin in 1581, he was one of the most influential figures in the Irish Protestant Church, for which he drew up the Articles of Doctrine in 1605, and in which he became Archbishop of Armagh in 1625. He left Ireland just before the Rebellion of 1641, and spent the remainder of his life in England, where he died in 1656. Such was his reputation for scholarship, honesty and piety that he managed to remain on good terms with all sides in the turbulent years of mid seventeenth century England, losing the trust of neither King nor Parliament. He was allowed to act as an advisor to Charles I during his confinement on the Isle of Wight in 1648 (he was beheaded the following year), and yet, when he died in 1656, such was Oliver Cromwell's respect for his integrity and reputation he ordered he be buried in Westminster Abbey.[1]

Ussher was passionately interested in history and antiquities, in the history of Christianity generally, and in particular in Britain and Ireland: and in the Old and New Testaments. At this time the Bible was universally believed to be the revealed word of God: a historical record of all that had happened since the creation. Ussher was an unsurpassed mine of information on the Bible and an outstanding textual scholar, and went to great pains to secure as many early versions of the Old and New Testaments as he could, not only in the great libraries of England, but through his numerous contacts with biblical authorities on the European mainland and further afield. So, after decades of research, Ussher produced in 1650 his monumental *Annals of the Old Testament*, in which he gave dates to every event recorded in the Bible right back to the beginning, when God began his week-long work of creation at nightfall (6 p.m. to be precise) on the evening of Saturday, 22 October, 4004 BC.[2]

But although our modern retrospective scorn is generally reserved for Ussher in this regard, his attempt represents our earliest European attempt to provide an accurate chronology, using the only methodology available: 'an honourable effort for its time ... our usual ridicule only record[ing] a lamentable small-mindedness based on mistaken use of present criteria to judge a distant and different past.'[3] Isaac Newton (who was fourteen when Ussher died) differed by only four years (4000 BC) from Ussher in his estimate of the age of the Earth, and Johannes Kepler by twelve (3992 BC).[4] Such were the limits of our understanding of the nature of the biblical books in their day, and such our interpretation of what *revelation* means.[5]

Our earlier notion of God saw him (for it was a He) as a great artificer, who had fabricated all creatures ready-made and finished in the beginning, and who resided somewhere outside, from where he watched the drama of creation unfold through history. We now know that the image of God as a benevolent ruler conceived in our own image belongs to our intellectual and spiritual adolescence. 'If God made us in his image, we have certainly returned the compliment,' as Voltaire wryly put it. The progress of human understanding has also allowed us to see that the drama is enacted not merely through history in the narrow human sense, but involves a plenitude of other creatures of a diversity and complexity unsuspected in earlier times: because we did not possess, as we do today, the tools to see this.

Today we probably have a much deeper appreciation than Nicholas of Cusa of the impossibility of a human grasp of the infinite. And again, we owe this *theological* advance to the advance of 'science':

> A human being cannot judge except in a human way. When a person attributes a face to you [God], one does not seek it outside the human species since one's judgment is contracted within human nature and in judging does not depart the passivity of this contraction. In the same manner, if a lion were to attribute a face to you, it would judge it only as a lion's face; if an ox, as an ox's; if an eagle, as an eagle's.[6]

Two books

What do we mean by 'revelation' then, in view of this impossibility? How does God *reveal* himself to us; how does God enable us to come to know him, to see him in so far as our human eyes *can* see God? Traditionally the manner of revelation more familiar to us is 'scripture', written in human words and concepts by human hands, and a product of history. And requiring therefore the tools and devices of hermeneutics to interpret what they mean, what they meant to say, to discover the truth in them; and so, potentially misleading.

Then there is creation itself, the 'other book', the 'magnificent book in which God speaks to us and grants us a glimpse of his infinite beauty and goodness'; 'God has written a precious book, "whose letters are the multitude of created things present in the universe".'[7] This theme is echoed repeatedly through Pope Francis's 2015 encyclical:

> This contemplation of creation allows us to discover in each thing a teaching which God wishes to hand on to us, since 'for the believer, to contemplate creation is to hear a message, to listen a paradoxical and silent voice.' We can say that 'alongside revelation properly so-called, contained in sacred Scripture, there is a divine manifestation in the blaze of the sun and the fall of night.' Paying attention to this manifestation, we learn to see ourselves in relation to all other creatures: 'I express myself in expressing the world; in my effort to decipher the sacredness of the world, I explore my own.'[8]

At the start of the modern period (towards the middle of the sixteenth century) Sir Thomas Browne distinguished these two books of revelation: 'besides that written one of God, another of His servant Nature, that universal and publick Manuscript, that lies expans'd unto the Eyes of all.'[9] But this fundamental idea goes back much further. In the fifth century St Augustine wrote:

> Some people read a book in order to discover God. But there is a greater book – the actual appearance of created things. Look above you and below you, and note and read. The God that you want to discover did not write in letters of ink, but put in front of your eyes the very things that he made. Can you ask for a louder voice than that?[10]

Reading the 'other' book

There have been many variations on that theme in the several centuries since. William Paley, writing in 1802, believed that – as the true wonder of the living world was beginning to be uncovered through the more detailed exploration of natural history that was properly beginning in his day – we had entered a new era of revelation. 'The world henceforth becomes a temple,' he wrote, 'and life itself one continued act of adoration. The change is no less than this: that whereas God was formerly seldom in our thoughts, we can now scarcely look upon any thing without perceiving its relation to him.'[11]

This is not to deny the validity or truth of 'that written one of God', as long as we realise that *this latter is born of the Presence and Word of God in human history*: and in the history of life, Earth and cosmos out of which this is born[12] ... and that this written Word needs to be interpreted in that light: a process which began in earnest with the biblical hermeneutics being developed in the nineteenth century.[13]

In a way it is better to think of the other 'book' as a scroll rather than a paginated text in which you can readily turn at will to whatever page you like. With the rolled-up scroll you can only read the text sequentially, line by line, paragraph by paragraph. This idea is beautifully expressed by Robert Boyle, whom we met in our earlier discussion of Robert Hooke and his microscope:

> The book of nature is a fine and large piece of tapestry rolled up, which we are not able to see all at once, but must be content to wait for the discovery of its beauty, and symmetry, little by little, as it gradually comes to be more and more unfolded, or displayed.[14]

The distinction we make between the 'two books' of revelation parallels that between mind and spirit, or matter and energy. On the level of our everyday experience they appear to be different 'things', but ultimately and *essentially* I believe they are the same. In a similar way, the word of God in scripture comes out of the experience of communities in history, and that experience is part and parcel of our *primary* encounter with material reality: the things of everyday life. The complexity and immensity of human experience in history can only be expressed verbally in the most tenuous fashion. It is different for different cultures, a part of the intimate encounter over millennia between each of them and the particular place in which it forges its particular geographical identity. The only word of God that is written in God's own language rather than the languages of creatures is the Creation itself: and our personal and communal encounter with that Creation is the kernel that germinates into our relationship with God – whatever theory of knowledge we apply to the process by way of explanation.

The metaphor of the unfolding tapestry or scroll applies not only to the advance in human understanding of the nature of reality, but also to the progress of our human role in the story. Here too there are key events where new insights come into focus: and here the variety and geographical spread of human ethical advance mirrors as it were the efflorescence of the living world. As with that efflorescence of living beauty and diversity, much of this cultural variety is a product of the interaction between human and environment in all the different parts of the world in which humans found themselves. Other facets, however, are more catholic in significance, with implications for the direction of human evolution.

The origin of such insights in particular cultures is accidental. Individual human beings, at critical moments in the search for meaning, begin to catch glimpses of the *Way*, and attempt variously to articulate its outlines. So far beyond all comprehension is the Great Attractor that their feeble attempts may appear contradictory of each other in many respects. But it becomes possible, in due course, to see that the faint light that picks out the direction of the Way in all its different experiences is always the same. We are called in a New Direction, the following of which is most immediately seen in how we act towards each other, and to the world around us, as we take our early steps in this New Direction. Each of us is born into a particular culture at a particular time in history. Our individual starting point must of necessity be where we find ourselves.

The new perspective we develop as a result of our understanding of evolution requires of us a critique of the cultural perspective into which we are born, but good human behaviour does not depend on the extent of our knowledge of the workings of the world, however uniquely our individual experience augments and deepens that appreciation. We are not better human beings because we are experts on orchid pollination or protein metabolism. We are better human beings because we are determined to live our lives in accordance with God's plan for the world.

Responding to beauty; creation unfolding

The incarnation of the Divine is ubiquitous.

MARK JOHNSTON (2009), *SAVING GOD*, P. 121

We read the book of creation through *sensory, intellectual and spiritual encounter*. That requires *attention* of us. The first and most essential ingredient in developing the appreciation that fuels the affirmation that lies at the root of religion is attention. We find this hard, so much has distraction become part of our lives. Indeed, it has taken over the lives of many of us. (That word 'distraction' comes from the Latin word *dis-trahere*, which means 'to draw in the wrong direction': outwards, away beyond, rather than on that which is close up, to which I can relate with body, mind and heart in this place.)

The more we attend to the beauty in the detail that is about us the more attuned we become to what God is about. It is through their beauty, St Augustine wrote, that creatures praise God: through being what the unique aspect of the unfolding of living possibility in the universe each embodies has enabled them to be. When Augustine questioned creatures to reveal to him what they could tell him of God, 'they cried out with a loud voice: "He made us."'[15] *What they are* is the only answer they can give. But they can only cry out in a loud voice when we listen, when we *attend* to what is being said to us *by their very being*.

A growing awareness of the dignity of living creatures other than ourselves gives rise to a sense that there must be something deeper to their presence in the world. In many cultures creatures are divinised; in some, as in certain forms of esoteric religion today, nature is seen as divine. This pantheism was anathema to traditional Christian thought, which saw it as somehow distracting from the divine. But in a sense beyond the capacity of any words to convey, with the progress of understanding, the meaningfulness of the notion of God as outside of creation begins to fade as the face of the Cheshire Cat faded before Alice, only its smile remaining; and begins to come into focus instead through all of creation as (when we were children) faces would appear from the branches and trunks of trees in puzzle books once we had adjusted our eyes to what until then had remained hidden.

It is inspiring beyond our human conception, beyond our ability to grasp, endlessly beyond word, that all this has *unfolded* from the tiny kernel of the beginning: that every possibility was wrapped up in that seed, all that has eventuated into reality (and so much that did not). It is the progress of science that has revealed this to us, and its theoretical elaboration is best discussed (if with difficulty grasped) in the work of Thomas Kühn, with his concept of 'implicate folding'. But we find ideas that are very similar in earlier thinkers, even if these do not rest on the weight of evidence and detailed observation our modern concept does. Nicholas of Cusa has this wonderful image of creation as *explicatio Dei*, which is almost synonymous with the phrase Kühn uses: the unfolding of God. All that lives – and ultimately all that is – is the unfolding of One Reality, and the distinction between every living thing is the distinction between cousins.

Vast quantities of ink have been expended in trying to decide whether God's action in creation should be described as pantheistic or panentheistic. Both viewpoints agree that God is 'present' in nature, but in pantheism the identification is absolute. Panentheists argue that although God is present in creation, he also remains outside of it; 'panentheism affirms that although God and the world are ontologically distinct and God transcends the world, the world is "in" God ontologically. In contrast, classical theology posits an unqualified distinction between God and the world: although intimately related, God and creatures are always and entirely other than one another.'[16]

Whatever word or school we use to refer to it, this is the thrilling, shocking truth of it: that every instant of my life, as of every human life, is a moment in the Becoming of God and I am called to express my appreciation, I – we – alone able to do so with understanding: and called also to deepen that understanding to whatever level I am capable of. Every walk, every reflective hour reading Natural History (God's history), becomes prayer: which underlines the theological importance of taking natural history seriously. The approach of William Paley and other earlier divines such as the Victorian naturalists may be dated, but not the direction of their journey of the mind and spirit.

Our excitement and joy in creation has to be the faintest glimmer of God's own. The more appreciative our eyes, the more are they the eyes of God. Appreciation, say of a piece of craftsmanship in wood or metal, involves understanding all that has gone into its making, the contribution of all the hands and minds involved in that process. So too with the species of creation. When I immerse myself in this act of becoming acquainted more intimately with birds or flowers, mosses or spiders – at however far a remove from source – I experience the breath of the divine as fully as human capacity is able to. The deeper my intimacy grows the more I come to appreciate the inexhaustible nature of such experience, and the more I sense how infinitesimal a portion of it any one person can embrace: that it is so inexhaustible its depth could not be plumbed even if everybody on Earth embraced the privilege of peering into a corner of it.

We must preface every attempt to speak of this with acknowledgement of the utter inadequacy of the words we must use to do so, most of all of course the word 'God' itself. Creation is the embodiment of God. This is not to say creatures are God, who is Other and Beyond – though not in any spatial sense because dimensionality enters the picture only with the coming into being of material things. Creation is the appearance of God in materiality: the things of creation on the one hand and the unfolding process that is cosmic evolution on the other. When we respond to beauty, truth, joy, intelligibility in any facet of creation we are in tune with that something of God at the heart of it. No wonder we stumble over ourselves here in our attempts to find words that will fit. *Something* of God, but the tiniest scintilla, and touched only when we reach, heard only when we listen. We pick it up with our senses, with our mind, with our spirit. We may perhaps not recognise it for what it is if our reception is sensual only, or if it is emotional only, or only intellectual: we receive it *through all that we are*.

We still don't have a word for *what* we respond to at the heart of experienced reality, for what it is that catches us. Beauty, truth, harmony are aspects, but not the thing itself. Thomas Aquinas' word for that 'something' at the heart of the forms of creation that we respond to 'intuitively' is its light: 'the measure of the reality of a thing is its light.'[17]

We thrill to the *manifestation* of creatures: to what they present in themselves when we encounter them. At times, those rare times when we see with a greater clarity of receptivity, it can be heart-stopping. Here is Alfred Russel Wallace's description of his first encounters with the butterfly *Ornithoptera Croesus*:

> The beauty and brilliance of this insect are indescribable, and none but a naturalist can understand the intense excitement I experienced when I at length captured it. On taking it out of my net and opening the glorious wings, my heart began to beat violently, the blood rushed to my head, and I felt much more like fainting than I have done when in apprehension of immediate death![18]

It is this same thrill of which W.H. Hudson is speaking when he quotes Thoreau's response to the song of the robin:

> The cry of the wild bird pierces us to the heart; we have never heard that cry before, and it is more familiar to us than our mother's voice. 'I heard,' says Thoreau, 'a robin in the distance, the first I had heard for many a thousand years, methought, whose note I shall not forget for many a thousand more, – the same sweet and powerful song as of yore. O the evening robin!'[19]

It is Gerard Manley Hopkins' awe before the hovering kestel:

> My heart in hiding
> Stirred for a bird, – the achieve of, the mastery of the thing.
>
> Brute beauty and valour and act, oh, air, pride, plume, here
> Buckle! AND the fire that breaks from thee, then, a billion
> Times lovelier, more dangerous, O my chevalier![20]

It is the *achieve* of the thing, and what comes through to us in our encounter with that achievement, to which we are invited to respond; the achieve: the sheer wonder of the way in which it is adapted to its particular world (which the progress of scientific enquiry elucidates ever more deeply), and the mesmerising complexity that underpins it all: 'the flooding, overwhelming experience that could not be denied.'[21] This is what enthrals naturalists: those who devote appropriate attention to the things of creation. What group is chosen for the encounter scarcely matters: the same beauty is manifest, incarnate, in all, a beauty that rises through every level of its complexity to explode through in the sensory and intellectual encounter of our mind, body and spirit with its being-in-the-world:

> Here is beauty – whatever the philosophers and art critics who have never looked at a moth may say – beauty that rejoices and humbles, beauty remote from all that is meant by words like random or purposeless, utilitarian or materialistic, beauty in its impact and effects akin to the authentic encounter with God.[22]

Some groups are particular favourites: birds and flowers, charismatic carnivores and their prey, whales and dolphins, butterflies and sharks. The list lengthens as our imaging capacity grows: and so now we can be mesmerised on our screens by spiders and beetles, ants and microbes. In recent years bats have come to the fore – of particular note because for all of human history they were viewed with such ignorance and fear, and mindlessly persecuted accordingly – but for anybody who knows anything about them among the most wonder-inspiring of all animals.[23]

In nearly every major group there are species of comparable sense-stopping beauty: wherever the possession of such a quality is an important element of being what uniquely they are. Certain groups are especially rich in such species; among plants orchids and stapeliads most strikingly perhaps, but a visit to a botanic garden or a trawl through the internet will show there are many other families to rival these. Among animals, countless groups of insects and other invertebrates, not to mention birds and mammals. In all such cases our appreciation is a fraction of that of the creatures at which this beauty is targeted: pollinating insects or birds in the case of flowers, other members of its own species in the case of birds and mammals.

But we might equally be overwhelmed by any other creature, if the angle of perception presented it in such a way that our human reception permitted comparable clarity of vision. This 'heart-stopping' is the extreme of course: there is a spectrum of response, and where I am on that spectrum depends on my individual capacity, each of us differently endowed in this regard.

We are thrilled also by the *doing* whereby this creature acts out who and what it uniquely is. Becoming is what it is all about. Creation is first of all a verb rather than a concatenation of nouns. The very first words of Genesis, usually translated 'In *the* beginning God created …' actually read 'In *beginning* God created …' And indeed, what follows is more a re-creation than a making *ex nihilo*, from already existing material; indeed, if we take the Bible at face value, Earth was already in existence when God started his work: 'In the beginning when God created the heavens and the Earth, the Earth was a formless void and darkness covered the face of the deep, while a wind from God swept over the face of the waters.'[24] Subsequently, the waters above are separated from the waters below, the waters under the sky are gathered into one place, the Earth 'puts forth' vegetation, the waters 'bring forth' living creatures of all kinds.[25] In other words, all life develops from inanimate matter, once the Earth has evolved to a state where this can happen.[26] It is all action in other words.[27]

We are most intimately aware of this among ourselves, within our own species: in the performance of sport, music, drama, the intercourse of physical, mental or spiritual intimacy. God touches me through Ronaldo's goal, Queen on the stage in Budapest, in my own exhilaration at crossing the line, in meeting the deadline, at being the best at what we do. God is experienced not only in liturgy and prayer, but in the ecstasy of aesthetic achievement, sex, food, any aspect of goodness (*gustando vivimus deo*).[28] And what can I ever know of what that thrill is like within any other species? Except to know that it is by means of this *performance* that it worships its creator?

> And áll trádes, their gear and tackle and trim. …
> He fathers-forth whose beauty is past change:
> Praise him.[29]

This harmony the Pythagoreans and their mathematical disciples in our own day understood in terms of proportion, of measure; the musician hears it as sound, the naturalist in what is seen and understood: people in every walk of life experience the consonance which is ecstasy, whether sexual or athletic, intellectual or spiritual: all different facets of the same Something that is beyond sense or human understanding, but in which all these are at once embraced.

Without the reach of the mind and spirit, without stretching out our hand to try to touch the mystery that moves us in a way that leaves us lost for words; without the search for God, as we have been satisfied to call it traditionally, life is without meaning.

The only possible response to Richard Dawkins is that, Darwin or not, you feel compelled to accept that our understanding of nature, of living things, is changed and illuminated and made complete by your acceptance of the existence and creative power and sustaining nature of God.[30]

It is in light of all this that Michael Ruse argues for a new theology of nature:

> that sees and appreciates the complex, adaptive glory of the living world, rejoices in it, and trembles before it. I argue for this even though the people who reveal it to us today in its fullest majesty may be people for whom Christianity evokes emotions ranging from bored indifference to outright hostility. This is irrelevant, especially to those of us who know professional Darwinian evolutionists. As Ernst Mayr once said to me: 'People forget that it is possible to be intensely religious in the entire absence of theological belief' (interview, March 30, 1988). Theologians working on the science/religion relationship, few of whom have actually had hands-on experience with nature, let the hostilities of atheists like Dawkins, or their embarrassment with the Intelligent Design enthusiasts, blind them to the genuine love and joy with which today's professional evolutionists respond to their subjects. We should strip away the pseudo-arguments in the way of a full appreciation of the argument to complexity and start sharing what moved the natural theologians of old and what still moves the evolutionists of today.[31]

The voice that is our intuition touching lighter than any feather the Reality that is at the heart of it all, is not in the whirlwind, but (metaphorically of course) is a small still voice. We must not expect that if we listen long and hard enough the trees will speak to us, or that God (or the Blessed Virgin) will appear to us over a bush (even if for earlier cultures this was the only way, as they understood it, to find words for the numinous in what was happening in their lives).

Science demonstrates with stunning conviction how we are all made with the same loving care. There is a wonderful passage in Nicholas of Cusa where he arrives at the same conclusion, but only conceptually or intuitively: without the concrete sensory and intellectual evidence we have. In his fifteenth century there were no microscopes to help us see how wonderful each species of living being is.

> You, who are the absolute being of all, are present to all as if you had concern for no other. And for this reason there is nothing which does not prefer its own being to all others and its own way of being to all other ways of being, and it so upholds its own being that it would rather allow the being of all others to perish rather than its own. For you, Lord, so look on anything that exists that no existing thing can conceive that you have any other care but that it alone exist in the best manner possible for it and that all other existing things exist only for the purpose of serving the best state of the one which you are beholding.[32]

And the mode of praise of each species is commensurate with this.

Inside and outside: where is God?

Insofar as God exists – i.e. has material expression – God *is* in creation; God is *in* creation. But every word in the simple sentence 'God is in creation' is fraught. We have already discussed our use of the word 'God' to stand for an Ultimate Reality that cannot be denoted. We cannot conceive of 'is-ness', of Being, other than through our biological lenses, and the Is-ness appropriate to an Ultimate Reality unrestrained by our conceptual limits does not admit the distinction in space or 'location' implied by our use of 'in' or 'transcends'. God is also 'before' creation insofar as that means anything since we have no way even of thinking of 'before' time, before the existence of material things. Friedrich Schleiermacher touches on this very point: 'The distinction (always rather a curious one, and, if I may say so, roughly drawn) between a God who is outside of and above the world, and a God who is in the world, does not particularly meet the point.'[33] Finally, no advanced consideration of any of this is possible without an understanding and appreciation of reality (creation) that is fully informed by the advance in our knowledge of it provided by science.

The progress of physical science shows us that there *is* no outside to the cosmos. At the level on which all reality is ultimately constituted, the distinction between inside and outside and all such dimensional opposites, breaks down. If we use 'outside' in relation to creation (in the light of what we now understand of the nature of matter and energy) we use it in a sense we cannot *imagine*. 'That which is named is small. That whose magnitude cannot be conceived remains ineffable,' wrote Nicholas of Cusa.[34] What also breaks down is any real distinction between immanence and transcendence.

God therefore is not outside or above Creation. Modern cosmology can envisage no above or outside. The emphasis we give to different parts of the sentence is important here. There is nothing outside: no *thing*, i.e. no material reality outside of the cosmos of our experience. God is not outside or above creation: God *is* not outside. But that which is the ultimate force at the heart of it all has its 'being' 'beyond', at the heart of, but so Other is this being that all our words, born as they are of our material being, are inadequate almost to the point of being meaningless when it comes to understanding what 'beyond' in this sense can mean. It is this sort of inadequacy that lies at the heart of all our disagreements as to the nature of this Ultimate, including the verbal tug of war between those at opposite ends of the rope of belief in God, atheists at one end and theists at the other.

God is beyond then, in that sense that leaves us lost for words. And because this is the way it is, we also have to remember that all our attempts to talk about 'what happens next' after it all started are the babblings of children. But since human discourse is all we have, let us use it as best we may, though we know its limitation to be unlimited (as Nicholas of Cusa would say); knowing too there are other languages we cannot speak, of lion and ox and eagle and of all the other countless expressions of material life, both those with us on today's Earth and those whose duration here has expired (to say nothing of angels and aliens!).

On one occasion when St Augustine was out walking (engaged in peripatetic pondering: this was a time when he was deeply engrossed in trying to work out exactly what the doctrine of the Trinity was supposed to mean) he encountered a child playing on the shore, where he was emptying buckets of sea water into a little pond he had dug in the sand. On being asked what he was doing, the child replied that he was in the process of emptying the sea into his pond. When wise old Augustine informed him that this was impossible, the child replied that he had a better chance than the saint had of understanding the Trinity:

> We know God most of all as the unknown, because the mind is found to know God most perfectly when it is known that his essence is above everything it can apprehend in the state of this life; and so, although it remains unknown what he is, it is however known that he exists.[35]

> Since we are not able to know what God is, but only what he is not, we are less likely to make mistakes when discussing what he is not than what he is. We should therefore first discuss what God is not; then, how it is possible for us to know him; and thirdly, how he is to be named.[36]

'Poor little talkative Christianity.'[37] But we stumble on nevertheless, children learning to speak with more meaning and better articulation as the centuries of augmented understanding pile one on the other. The progress of science increases our capacity incrementally and progressively to see and appreciate more and more the awesome complexity, the sheer wonder, the terror, of Creation. When we ask today 'where is God' it is the same question the disciples of Jesus asked, the same question the medieval scholastic or Chinese sage asked, the same question asked in the language of palaeolithic peoples: but the answer we can now comprehend is of a different order to anything before. And once what we call 'Faith' allows all of this to come into focus for us, we find ourselves at the centre of the most wonderful insight we can have. *Created reality is the embodiment of God*, and this embodiment, this realisation of God, is something that unfolds gradually over the time of the cosmos.

Earlier intimations of God's presence in creation

Just as there are intimations of evolution in the way people thought about creation much earlier than the nineteenth century, so too this new way of thinking about incarnation is presaged in earlier theological speculation. There is always a great deal in the writings of the early theologians we can re-interpret in the light of our modern understanding, but in order to find these passages we have to trawl through a vast amount of speculative theology of little relevance to us today. And when we do interpret the selected passages in the light of our modern understanding we have to remember that the new meaning is something we have added: not a kernel of truth that was there all the time: the conceptual framework is simply congenial to this new meaning with which we invest the old words.

For the early Greek theologians such as Gregory of Nyssa, 'Christ is a cosmic principle, immanent in the world, though not confined by it; and the scheme of salvation [is] regarded as part of the constitution of the universe, which is animated and sustained by the same Power who was fully manifested in the Incarnation.'[38] One of the foundational concepts of neoplatonism, seen in a more developed Christian way in the writings of Thomas Aquinas, is that all the different forms of being we see in creation are embodiments of 'ideas' in the 'mind' of God: but in the mind of God they are perfect: the *archetypes* of the beauty to which we respond in creatures. As we have seen, it was part of the thinking of the philosophers who pondered the Great Chain of Being that, God being what He is, every *possibility* would have to be realised, embodied in creation: and indeed this conviction was behind the search to discover new forms and patterns; and the more deeply continued search penetrates, the closer we come to an appreciation of the archetypes in the mind of God – or as close as it is possible for our human mind and body to do so.

God *expresses* himself in the diversity of creatures, Thomas Aquinas tells us: as though creatures are words, sentences, paragraphs in a great narrative. But it is so much more than this. In the early Christian centuries theology came to understand 'Christ the Word' as the utterance of God, the embodied Thought of God through whom the world has come into existence. The utterance of God: creation as the discourse of God, and what scientific enquiry is all about is *decipherment* of that discourse, a progressively deeper entering into its intelligibility and beauty in the course of which we discover that each form of life requires an entire volume, a library indeed, in order even to *describe* the fullness of its achievement: and we can scarcely *read* it without learning the language of biology.[39]

Just as we can find intimations of an understanding of evolution in earlier thinking we can also find intimations of this way of understanding the Presence of God in creation in earlier philosophy. But whereas these earlier intimations were speculative, advances in cosmology and biology provide concrete evidence, clothe these speculations in historical truth. Science, it can be argued, is the child of Faith, but can only grow to maturity as long as that Faith remains open to the unrestricted reason through which God allows us to glimpse his distance and his closeness. Otherwise it becomes orphaned and grows into troubled teenage years.

Nowhere is this more clearly seen than in the writings of Friedrich Schelling (1775-1854), who introduced a radical evolutionism into theology and metaphysics, although he was writing long before Darwin's time.[40] A very similar understanding is found in the writings of Schelling's friend and disciple, the naturalist Lorenz Oken (1779-1851). 'The philosophy of Nature', he wrote, 'is the science of the eternal transformation of God into the world.' Although all things may be said to pre-exist in God, they do so 'not in a real but only in an ideal manner, not *actu* but only *potentia*'.[41]

Thus, at last, the Platonistic scheme of the universe is turned upside down. Not only had the originally complete and immutable Chain of Being been converted into a Becoming, in which all genuine possibles are, indeed, destined to realisation grade after grade, yet only through a vast, slow unfolding in time; but now God himself is placed in, or identified with, this Becoming.[42]

As we saw in chapter two, awareness of the way in which all understanding is grounded in our experience of reality recurs over and over through the history of western philosophy and theology. Different stages in the development and expression of this core insight act as waymarkers to which we may return periodically, even as we recognise the need to move forward and place our own markers of trust in reason along the Way. Immanuel Kant believed that we cannot conceive of God in himself apart from our *experience*. Schleiermacher argued that there is no basis for asserting that God in himself exists beyond the world; 'Like Spinoza, Schleiermacher asserts that divine causality is entirely immanent and never supernatural. We cannot even form a concept of God apart from the world, much less affirm its truth. And we cannot affirm the reality of supernatural miracles.'[43] 'Divine activity does not occur over and apart from natural causality; God is not found outside of the totality of finite things.'[44]

Equally we can find intimations of this way of understanding the Presence of God in other cultures, but articulated in the different language and idiom of those cultures. What science does is provide a scaffolding to hold our human advance towards the Infinite in the right direction, a lens that keeps that direction in focus: a correction to superstition.

Nature not for us primarily

What is creation for? We struggle to find anything like the right *theocentric* word. We look for the most serious words we can find, knowing this to be the very deepest of theological conundrums. We used to say 'for God's own glory', but that scarcely means anything to modern ears. The principle of the

Tao is spontaneity: perhaps as good a word as we will find for the explosive efflorescence of possibility into ever-changing being that is the Great Story, what Hindu mythology describes as the Cycles of Brahma-Brahman. Maybe the Hindu concept of *lila* is as close as words can get. *Lila* is the Sanskrit word for *being at play*. This is how God (Brahma now of course, at the Brahman stage of the cycle!) *becomes* (materially) what/who He is (essentially). Our acclaim echoes His. 'Alleluia' (as Alan Watts remarked) means 'whoopee!'[45] We will only 'get' creation when the 'alleluia' with which we acclaim it is not the staid and reverent monotone at suitably modulated decibels but the 'whoopee' it started out as! *We join in* when we say 'wow' as we take in the beauty of the flower of eyebright, the weirdness of water bears, the flow of water over rock, the smile of the beloved. 'The song of the angels is the laughter of the universe.'[46]

There is a striking illustration of this growing awareness that the ineffably awesome diversity of life on Earth is not about us (not in the first place, *not necessarily at all*: if at the same time, in the end, not incidentally) in a passage in Alfred Russel Wallace's account of his travels in the Malay Archipelago, in which he reflects on the fact that paradise birds – among the most evidently beautiful creatures on Earth – live in such remote places that we might never get to know of their existence: a consideration 'that must surely tell us that all things were *not* made for man.' Here is the passage (He has just obtained a specimen of the King Bird of Paradise):

I knew how few Europeans had ever beheld the perfect little organism I now gazed upon, and how very imperfectly it was still known in Europe … I thought of the long ages of the past, during which the successive generations of this little creature had run their course – year by year being born, and living and dying amid these dark and gloomy woods, with no intelligent eye to gaze upon their loveliness – to all appearances such a wanton waste of beauty. Such ideas excite a feeling of melancholy. It seems sad that on the one hand such exquisite creatures should live out their lives and exhibit their charms only in these wild inhospitable regions, doomed for ages yet to come to hopeless barbarism; while on the other hand, should civilised man ever reach these distant lands, and bring moral, intellectual, and physical light into the recesses of these virgin forests, we may be sure he will so disturb the nicely balanced relations of organic and inorganic nature as to cause the disappearance, and finally the extinction, of these very beings whose wonderful structure and beauty he alone is fitted to appreciate and enjoy. This consideration must surely tell us that all things were *not* made for man.[47]

This truth is of course magnified beyond calculation by our realisation that only a fraction of the species alive today are known to us, and only the tiniest fraction of that again of those species that have lived in earlier geological epochs – and these we know only in the most superficial fashion.

––––––––––

Daniel Dennett once wrote that if he could give an award for the single best idea anyone ever had, he would give it to Charles Darwin: ahead of Newton, or Einstein – or anyone else.[48] As we will see in a later chapter, Darwin's role was not quite as original as is generally believed; his contribution was to kindle into flame ideas that had been around for a century before his time. And certainly, it was publication of *The Origin of Species* that brought evolution to the centre of human attention.

The concept of evolution revolutionised biology, and its gradual extension to embrace the entire cosmos in the twenteeth century revolutionised the whole of science. It is no less true that it is transformative of spirituality: nor less true to say that that critical transformation has yet to take place. Here is what John Haught has to say about it.

> To a great extent theologians still think and write as though Darwin had never lived. Their attention remains fixed on the human world and its unique contents. The nuances of biology or, for that matter, cosmology have not yet deeply affected current thinking about God and God's relation to the world.[49]

––––––––––

One area in which this paradigm change is potentially transformative is in our understanding of what relationship means, and the ethical and moral consequences of that change. When Jesus was asked by one of the Pharisees what he considered to be the greatest commandment in the Law he replied: 'You shall love the Lord your God with all your heart and with all your soul and with all your reason. This is the great and first commandment. The second is like it: You shall love your neighbour as yourself. All the Law and the prophets depend on these two commandments.'[50]

There are two points here. The first (in relation to the second commandment) is that all that lives is related to me genetically; my family extends to the limits of life and beyond, and this must become the foundation upon which the argument for custodianship is built. The second point (this in relation to the first commandment) is that *the second commandment is not different* from the first: it is 'like to this'; and with our new understanding we can see what this means in an altogether different light. It is like unto this because there is something *of* God in every creature. Each is a facet of the material embodiment of God's Reality; they are aspects of God's incarnation as it were. We don't need theological language to feel all of this, or to feel the need to respond, or to talk about it. Indeed, theological language, in its attempt to nail it down, loses sight of that essential kernel at the very heart of it.

Whatever the differences between the different perspectives from which we view the meaning of things, the starting point is the same for us all: that bare encounter with creation: sensory and emotional first, then intellectual, and then (in all its different ways) spiritual. We need to maintain – or restore where (as is so often the case) this is needed – the sensory encounter. It is not enough to live with the memory of it except when it is withdrawn beyond our reach. 'Only in what remains of Eden, teeming with life forms independent of us, is it possible to experience the kind of wonder that shaped the human psyche at its birth.'[51] You don't need a rainforest, or to go on a cruise to see penguins in the Antarctic, or take up scuba diving. On our own doorstep there are wonders that can evoke in us the awe the young Charles Darwin felt on stepping into the rainforest of the Amazon for the first time.

In philosophical terms this, I think, is what the theologian John Cobb in his discussion of F.S.C. Northrop's pioneering contribution to discussion of the possibility of developing common ground between Christianity and Buddhism is trying to say.

> The basic visions of East and West are complementary. Both necessarily begin in the sheer immediacy of experience, which Northrop calls the differentiated aesthetic continuum.[52]

But:

> The East has attended more than the West to the primary experience that is not yet shaped by ideas or concepts … Instead of seeking the best conceptuality available, as the West has done, the East stays close to this continuum, experiencing it as a flux of sensa. Like the West, the East goes beyond this flux, but whereas the West transcends it though ideas, the East probes beyond it in a different direction.[53]

In recent years many – probably most – religious congregations have adopted a 'care for the Earth' section in their constitutions and regulations. In part this represents the growing awareness of the seriousness of the environmental challenges we face, and especially of the issues of social justice they present: the 'preferential option for the poor'. But in part also because of the way in which the burden of the Works of Mercy the various orders and congregations were established to engage in has passed onto secular shoulders. It is not enough however to sing to a different tune. We need to feel for what is at stake with the same vocational intensity as we responded to that earlier Call. It has to be said, and the implications pondered upon, that an example is being set for us in this regard by many who devote themselves to the work of secular environmental organisations that have no overt religious agenda.

In spite of that formal adoption of an environmental agenda, we often fail to realise in our lives the kind of ecological conversion *Laudato Si'* calls for (*Laudato Si'*, 5). We think it is somehow peripheral: but 'The ecological crisis is a summons to profound interior conversion.'

> It must be said that some committed and prayerful Christians, with the excuse of realism and pragmatism, tend to ridicule expressions of concern for the environment. Others are passive; they choose not to change their habits and thus become inconsistent. So, what they all need is an 'ecological conversion', whereby the effects of their encounter with Jesus Christ become evident in their relationship with the world around them. Living our *vocation to be protectors of God's handiwork is essential to a life of virtue; it is not an optional or a secondary aspect of our Christian experience*.[54]

This conversion calls for us to examine how we have acted or failed to act, and for us to change our lives accordingly.[55]

The conversion called for is not just personal – on its own this can never be enough – 'The ecological conversion called for is also a *community conversion*.'[56]

> Living our vocation to be protectors of God's handiwork is essential to a life of virtue; it is not an optional or a secondary aspect of our Christian experience.

> The ecological conversion called for is also a community conversion.

Creation as Incarnation

Those of us who are theologically inclined may wish to reflect on the way all of this deepens and extends the meaning of incarnation.

The science of cosmogenesis elucidates in ever greater detail the earlier stages in the unfolding of creation, in the process giving us a picture that is breathtakingly greater, more awe-inspiring, than anything any earlier age could even envisage, calling for the human response that finds expression in acclaim and worship.

What makes this blossoming possible is that progress of scientific understanding, which is itself a process of evolution, part of that broader process of unfolding which is how God works in the world. Our spiritual development then, is an evolutionary process. *Dogma* is useful in anchoring our slow progress in the vertiginous process of ascent, as useful and necessary as the pitons hammered in bedrock by a climber, but needing to be replaced by others higher up as we climb.

The progress of scientific understanding is now beginning to do the same for the way in which we may think of how God incarnates in the world, giving the same sort of articulation to what that means in material terms, bringing the dim theological notion of the Cosmic Christ into something that begins to come into focus, begins to make the kind of sense we can actually understand – without getting any closer to the mystery of it: insofar as our human grasp is up to it: in the way cosmogenesis does for the earlier phases, *creation and incarnation being the same process, not isolated, time-separated events.*[57] What this means is that incarnation did not begin with the conception of Jesus. Incarnation – the embodiment of the divine in material form – begins at the beginning of time, with the calling into being of that seed from which all material reality subsequently unfolds. The profound insight at the heart of this re-envisioning of incarnation brings us close to the core Hindu mantra *Isha vasya idam sarvam*: God is immanent; the divine pervades all; all our lives, plant, animal and human are its embodiment.

If we can attain this way of seeing in all of reality the manifestation of God, our relationship with Creation – and with all the particular existents in which it is embodied – must be essentially characterised by *fundamental reverence*. It cannot be merely instrumental.

Thomas Aquinas attempted to condense his understanding of why God had created such extravagant diversity of life on Earth into a single paragraph, in every phrase of which immense depth of meaning is condensed. In his *Mysticism for Modern Times*, Willigis Jäger attempts to do the same for modern creation mysticism:

> God incarnates in the cosmos. He and his incarnations are inseparably connected with one another. He is not *in* his incarnation; He manifests himself *as* incarnation. He reveals himself in the tree as tree, in the animal as animal, in the person as person, and in the angel as angel. They are not creatures in addition to which there is a God who slips into them. God is each and every one of these creatures and yet he is not them, since God never exhausts himself in any single creature, but is always all the others as well. It is precisely this that is the experience of the mystic. The mystic apprehends the cosmos as the meaningful manifestation of God, while many people behave towards the cosmos like illiterates toward a poem. They count the individual letters and words but are unable to understand the meaning that gives the entire poem its form.[58]

CHAPTER 5

THE THEOLOGY OF BIODIVERSITY IN *LAUDATO SI*'[1]

In the fabulous compendium of Irish Early Christian lore and practice known as the *Martyrology of Oengus* there is an anecdote about the mysterious St Molua, who lived in the second half of the sixth century, which recounts how on one occasion St Mael Anfaidh was out for a walk when he encountered a small bird wailing and sorrowing by the side of the road; and as he wondered what this could mean an angel informed him, 'Mo Lua son of Ocha has died, and that is why the living things bewail him, for he never killed a living thing, great nor small; not more do men bewail him than the other living things do, and among them the little bird that you see.'[2]

Readers may be familiar with the wonderful tale in the life of Ciarán of Saighir, whose first monks in the wilderness of south-west Offaly in fifth century Ireland where he made his hermit's home were fox and badger, deer and wild boar. And of course, we all know about Francis of Assisi, who spoke of Friar Wolf and made nests for his little sisters, the wild turtle doves.

> When St Ciarán arrived at Saighir, the first thing he did was sit under a certain tree, in whose shade a ferocious wild boar was lying. At first when he saw the man, the boar fled in terror, but then he was made gentle by God, and he came back to Ciarán as if he had known him all his life: and that boar became a disciple of Ciarán in that place just like any monk. And he assiduously rooted up bushes and hay with which the holy man could make his cell. At this time no man lived with Ciarán, because he had escaped from his disciples to his remote place on his own. But afterwards other animals came out of their lairs in the wilderness to Saint Ciarán: namely a fox, a badger, and a wolf and a deer:

they remained tame in his presence, and obeyed him in everything, just as though they were monks.

But the day came when the fox, being shiftier and more sly than the other animals, stole the sandals of his abbot, holy Ciarán himself, and abandoning his vocation, took them away with him to his former lair in the wilderness, wishing to eat them there in peace. Knowing this, holy father Ciarán called another of his monks to him, namely the badger, and sent him into the wilderness after the fox, so that he might bring back his erring brother. The badger, because he was a creature skilled in the ways of the woods, obediently headed off in search of the thief, quickly picked up the trail and arrived at the lair of brother fox. Finding him about to eat his lord's sandals, the badger cut off the fox's two ears and his tail, and beat him up, and then compelled him to come back with him to his monastery, so that he might atone for his theft. The fox, having little choice in the matter, accompanied the badger, and they arrived back at none with the sandals undamaged. And the holy man said to the fox, 'Brother, why have you done this evil thing which does not become a monk. You know that the water here is sweet and free to us all, and likewise we all eat the same food? And if you had a yearning for flesh, almighty God would have provided it from the trees of the wood for us to give to you.' So then the fox, begging forgiveness, did penance for his deed, and from then on he only ate what he was told to eat, living out his days as one of the brothers.

In the vast and colourful tapestry that is the history of Christianity we find here and there these flecks of green thread that represent occasional intimations of kinship and compassion between ourselves and animals, but these threads contribute nothing to the great pageant of creation, salvation and redemption depicted there. The tapestry is abundantly adorned with plant and animal life, but only as the backdrop to the great drama that is being enacted centre stage, in which the actors are human beings, made in the image of God. These others were created in the first instance to be at the service of mankind, 'the most perfect of the animals, since in the order of perfection it ranks highest', as St Albert describes us: a view of the relationship rooted in the traditional and mistaken understanding of the infamous verses in Genesis 1 in which God confers mastery upon us.

Let us make man in our image, after our likeness: and let them have dominion over the fish of the sea, and over the fowl of the air, and over the cattle, and over every creeping thing that creepeth upon the Earth.[3]

This view of the relationship between God, ourselves and other forms of life – ourselves alone, it would appear, created in His image – is copper-fastened in traditional mainstream theology. 'Reason has not been given to [animals] to have in common with us,' wrote St Augustine, 'and so, by the most just ordinances of the Creator, both their life and their death is subject to our use.' In the opinion of Thomas Aquinas: 'It is not wrong for man to make use of [animals] either by killing them or in any other way whatever.'[4] In a more modern vein, the Jesuit theologian Joseph Rickaby – echoing the traditional view of what creation is *for* held as firmly by Martin Luther and John Calvin as by Thomas Aquinas – wrote: 'Brute beasts, not having understanding and therefore not being persons, cannot have any rights ... We have no duties of charity, nor duties of any kind to the lower animals, as neither to sticks and stones.'[5] And, as recently as 1994, the Catholic Catechism stated that 'God willed creation as a gift addressed to man ... Animals, like plants and inanimate beings, are by nature destined for the common good of past, present and future humanity.'[6]

Down the centuries this understanding of the relationship between God and his creatures has been graphically represented by images of the Great Chain of Being, which ranked other creatures below us at intervals that reflected their similarity to us humans, just as it ranked angels and saints at intervals above, between ourselves and God in his heaven.

But, just as the progress of scientific understanding of how creation actually works has transformed the way we see the cosmos, and our human understanding of the fabric of reality: so too, and indeed as part of that broader expansion of the human horizon on cosmic reality in its quest for God, has it transformed our biological appreciation of what God is about, of how God is at work in the world.

Central to this advance was the technological progress that made the microscope possible, and which began to give us new eyes: eyes that can see what has always been before us, but hidden: we the first privileged to see what (as Thomas Browne put it) had been hidden from all the ages before us: central also was the technological advance that enabled us to visit the deepest recesses of the oceans, the outermost horizons where life is possible.

The two axes around which our biological understanding has been utterly revolutionised can be described under the headings of complexity and affinity. All that lives is comparably complex biologically. The cells of other creatures, the building blocks of the body, are no less complex than our human cells. But just stating it like that gives no sense of how mesmerisingly complex, on every level that description is possible, every living creature, plant no less than animal, is. But to be truly overwhelmed by this requires knowledge of biology, the deeper that knowledge the greater the depth to which you are overwhelmed, and few of us are so privileged.

The diversity of life on Earth

Our modern understanding of the theological significance of life on Earth begins with the work of the great English naturalist John Ray (1627-1705), who is best remembered today for his monumental contribution to the description and cataloguing of the diversity and complexity of plant and animal life at a time when the *scale* of diversity and the *nature* of complexity (and particularly the ways in which plants and animals are adapted for their particular ways of life) were *beginning* to be appreciated. For him what this demonstrated was the greatness of the God who was behind it: the 'Wisdom of God' as he calls it in the title of his seminal summary of his reflections in this area.[7]

We must not forget the profound antithesis between the natural and the supernatural, the material and the spiritual, that had led Christianity between the third and the sixteenth centuries – in both Catholic and Protestant spirituality and theology – to a scorn and depreciation of nature. John Ray's open delight in the beauty, order and complexity of the natural world: on a sensory, aesthetic level first of all, augmented by growing understanding and appreciation on an intellectual level, and constantly alert to its spiritual significance, is 'in striking contrast to the philosophy and religion both of the Catholic and the Protestant traditions'. To Augustine, as to Luther, nature belonged to a plane irrelevant if not actually hostile to religion. Its beauty was a temptation, its study a waste of time, its meaning so distorted that there is a radical difference between Nature and Grace. But the direct insistence upon the essential unity of natural and revealed, as alike proceeding from and integrated by the divine purpose, had not found clear and well-informed expression until Ray's book was published.[8]

Ray's *Wisdom of God* was profoundly influential (going through four editions in his lifetime, and many more after) most immediately perhaps through its influence on William Paley's *Natural Theology*, to which Charles Darwin acknowledged his indebtedness.[9] In the preface to the definitive edition of his book, published in 1826 (and so just before organic evolution moved to centre stage in biology, just before our human capacity to focus on that fourth dimension of time began to come properly into focus) Ray attempted 'to run over all the visible works of God in particular, and to trace the footsteps of his wisdom in the composition, order, harmony, and uses of every one of them, as well as of those that I have selected'. But to do so, he wrote, would be a task not only 'far transcending my skill and abilities; nay, the joint skill and endeavours of all men now living, or that shall live after a thousand ages, should the world last so long.'[10]

In John Ray's day the number of species – in his words 'known to science, as the saying goes' – was under forty thousand.[11] But while he acknowledged that this was an underestimate ('How many of each genus remain yet undiscovered, one cannot certainly nor very nearly conjecture; but we may suppose the whole sum of beasts and birds to exceed by a third part, and fishes by one half, those known.'[12]) he can have had no idea whatever of the extent of that underestimate.

To date, something like 1.7 million species have been described. Half of these are insects, some 250,000 are vascular plants and bryophytes, 41,000 are vertebrates; and then the rest. But this is only the number of those that have been *formally described*. The true number of multicellular species is likely to be between ten and thirty million. Whether the figure is five or thirty million scarcely matters as far as our human ability to get our head around such numbers is concerned: to comprehend even a million is beyond us.

> Astronomical sums of time are so great that they bankrupt the imagination. We listen to the geologists and physicists wrangling over their accounts and compounding vast historical debts with the relish of usurers, but it is all one to us after the first million years.[13]

Whether ten or thirty million species, it is impossible to get our heads around these numbers. And as we struggle to identify order within this bewildering diversity, there is a danger implicit in taxonomy that we think of them in terms somewhat analogous to a vast, colourful stamp collection to be sorted. And here, perhaps, we face the greatest challenge. For every one of these millions is biologically as complex as I am, made with the same loving care, unfolded from the same seed of being at the beginning of things, has travelled an evolutionary journey similar to mine, from the same starting point, but in a different and complementary direction.

Actual numbers of *species* are only one aspect, one measure, of the diversity of life. The other is diversity at the level of groups or organisms. To get a sense of this, consider two of the most popular university textbooks on biodiversity: Barnes' *The Diversity of Living Organisms* (which we met in chapter three)[14] and *Five Kingdoms*, by Lynn Margulis and Karlene Schwartz.[15] These are a sort of who's who of life, a taxonomic equivalent of our human biographical dictionaries, in which each group is allocated space proportional to its biological stature, just as in these dictionaries the number of words is (supposedly) proportional to the significance of the individual in question.

In the three hundred or so descriptive pages of Margulis and Schwartz (third edition), vertebrates and their relatives merit a mere five out of a total of five hundred and twenty pages.

No more than we can relate visually to particle physics can we relate fully to this, but to the extent we can, we touch the hem of God's own self-fulfilment in being.

The structures of the insect's body exhibit a perfection that, from a mechanical point of view, is unsurpassed, while the external beauty of some of the creatures makes them fit associates of the most delicate flowers or no mean rivals of the most gorgeous of the feathered world.

David Sharp, *Cambridge Natural History*, vol. 5

Biodiversity and *Laudato Si'*

An appreciation of all of this is the essential foundation for the remarkable passages in *Laudato Si'* on the meaning and worth of individual species. It is precisely its rootedness in this essential biological foundation that gives these passages their unprecedented colour and depth: and it is only against this background that we can properly appreciate the conversion to which the encyclical calls us in this regard.

> Together with our obligation to use the Earth's goods responsibly, we are called to recognize that other living beings have a value of their own in God's eyes; 'by their mere existence they bless him and give him glory'. (*Laudato Si'*, 69)

> Each of the various creatures, willed in its own being, reflects in its own way a ray of God's infinite wisdom and goodness. Man must therefore respect the particular goodness of every creature, to avoid any disordered use of things. (*Laudato Si'*, 69)
>
> Creation is 'God's loving plan in which every creature has its own value and significance.' (*Laudato Si'*, 76)
>
> Even the fleeting lives of the least of beings is the object of his love, and in its few seconds of existence, God enfolds it with his affection. (*Laudato Si'*, 77)
>
> Each creature has its own purpose. (*Laudato Si'*, 84)
>
> Everything is, as it were, a caress of God. (*Laudato Si'*, 84)[16]

Our meditation upon the meaning of it all is deepened as the progress of understanding of the nature of creation's diversity makes it ever clearer to us that creation is *not* in the first instance *for* us. 'Each creature has its own purpose,' *Laudato Si'* reminds us;[17] 'The ultimate purpose of other creatures is not to be found in us. Rather, all creatures are moving forward with us and through us to a common point of arrival, which is God.'[18] Only such meditation will bring home to us the depth of truth in which such phrases in the encyclical are rooted.

This meditation begins with *attention*. Pope Francis speaks of the 'mystical meaning to be found' in the smallest detail (the example he chooses is a leaf).[19] He quotes Patriarch Bartholomew: 'It is our humble conviction that the divine and the humble meet in the slightest detail in the seamless garment of God's creation, in the last speck of dust in our planet.'[20] The passage continues:

> The ideal is not only to pass from the exterior to the interior to discover the action of God in the soul, but also to discover God in all things. Saint Bonaventure teaches us that 'contemplation deepens the more we feel the working of God's grace within our hearts, and the better we learn to encounter God in creatures outside ourselves.'[21]

Read this again carefully. Traditionally we might perhaps have registered the first part of this sentence with greater force: 'contemplation deepens the more we feel the working of God's grace within our hearts'; but now we need to register the second part with equal appreciation: 'contemplation deepens the better we learn to encounter God in creatures outside ourselves.'

But this calls on us to stop where we are and to look, and in the engagement that follows, sensory, rational and conative, to *attend*. When Jesus says, 'Consider the lilies ...' he is saying, in so many words if we think deeply enough about it, drop everything for a time and come, follow me in this direction, along this other dimension that takes me through and beyond time. The injunction to consider the lilies can be a little misleading since for us 'lilies' are exotic, flamboyant flowers in gardens and florists, fit for the altar. But in the Middle East they are the weeds of the wayside – the Palestinian equivalent of dandelions and daisies and primroses on the edge of our cultivated fields.

Evolution in *Laudato Si'*

A profoundly important aspect of biodiversity that can easily escape our first reading of the encyclical – and indeed our second or hundredth reading of it – is that this wondrous 'web of life', this rainbow of living diversity, cannot be described in the three dimensions of space. Indeed, to confine it to these dimensions of the present, and although as such it defies beyond measure our human capacity to take it all in, is to miss something absolutely central to its ultimate meaning.

The biodiversity of our age is but a still frame in a moving narrative. We now see that the mesmerising abundance of life on Earth is not defined by the tiny fraction of it that we humans experience or can experience: the still frame in this moving narrative which is all that we can experience, our time on Earth confined as it is to the last one hundred thousand years. Although it is possible to argue that living diversity had reached a peak around the time humans first appeared on Earth, there has been comparable diversity during every period of geological time, always different, the mesmerising biodiversity of any one period of geological time – which few but palaeontologists are privileged to wonder at – an efflorescence of hitherto unexpressed embryonic possibility.

The touch of *Laudato Si'* on this fundamental fourth dimension and its implications is of the very gentlest: in Paragraph 80 God's divine presence '*continues* the work of creation'. 'The universe *unfolds* in God, who fills it completely' in Paragraph 233; 'Faith allows us to interpret the meaning and the mysterious beauty of what is *unfolding*' in Paragraph 79. The gentle touch of a feather: for all that this is explosive in its spiritual significance it is explored no further, essentially for reasons of ecclesiastical diplomacy, guaranteed as it is in this age of our theological infancy to stir up a hornet's nest of conservative outrage in the Church, particularly in those quarters where Pope Francis is trying to wrestle with conservative opinion in other, more immediately pressing, issues equally critical to a mature understanding of how God is at work in the world.

Saint Albert wrote his magisterial work on the natural history of animals – the first encyclopaedia of biodiversity – during the lifetime of Thomas Aquinas (between 1258 and 1262).[22] In this fantastic book – fantastic in both senses of that word – he gathered together everything that was known about animals in his day. It's full of direct observation, in keeping with his dictum that man's knowledge must begin with an apprehension of reality obtained from direct encounters with nature itself.[23]

The total number of species in Albert's catalogue of all God's creatures ran to just five hundred, overwhelmingly dominated by the ones we could see with our own eyes.[24] And how much more might we expect to know? In one of his sermons, St Columban wrote (I suppose this would be around AD 600) of how little we should expect to know of God's creatures; 'Our small minds are not made for that,' he wrote; 'Think of this world our familiar Earth and sea: familiar indeed, and how much we know of them, and how little. What do we know of the teeming life beneath the waves, or even on much of the surface of the Earth?' The answer is that today we know an absolutely incredible amount. We know of creatures he could never, ever, have imagined.[25]

There is no more magisterial statement of the theological meaning of biological diversity than that found in St Thomas' *Summa*: 'God cannot express himself fully in any one creature: and so he has produced many and diverse life-forms, so that what one lacks in its expression of divine goodness may be compensated for by others: for goodness, which in God is single and undifferentiated, in creatures is refracted into a myriad hues of being.'[26]

But in 1250 our direct encounter with the rest of creation was limited by the fact that it was effectively confined to Europe and the lands just beyond its borders. As for what we knew of the life of the ocean, it scarcely extended beyond paddling depth; and limited not only by that, but by the limits of vision of the un-extended human eye (the microscope is several centuries into the future) just as until the early seventeenth century our experience of celestial creation above the atmosphere was limited to what the eye could see without the fabulous extension provided by the telescope: and our speculations about what ultimately lay Behind and Beyond and Beneath it All could only be the lisping of a child in its conception of what That could possibly mean, spelled out in the syllables of intelligent apes, conjured out of human ideas of Might and Majesty (with the imaginative addition of such novel features as human creatures with long dresses and wings and a life after death spent beyond the clouds).

And perhaps the simple, beautiful words of the Angelic Doctor *were* an adequate articulation of our thirteenth-century understanding of what God is about in creation. But nothing less than an endless symphony, sounded with all the harmony the advance of musical sensibility makes possible, will do in response to what the progress of modern biology allows us to see of the nature and genesis – and familial kinship – of life on Earth, of which we are the one chosen species in whose hands is placed the responsibility for its preservation and continuance.

Encounter

The deeper our *appreciation* – the more closely we come to God's own delight in his embodiment in material being: if 'close' can ever be an appropriate adjective in discussion of our relationship with God. This appreciation is always in the first instance sensory and aesthetic, only subsequently enhanced – and immeasurably so – by the penetrative gaze and grasp of the intellect and spirit: in its hold upon us making us aware of a longing deeper than deep within us for what is taking possession of us *through* this presence in my life.

As our appreciation of the beauty and diversity of life grows, so does our understanding of the utter *complexity* of every other life form – that each of them is as physically, chemically and biologically complex as we humans are, each in its unique way. The more we study a particular group the more we are drawn into the thrill of its being: *the more we are drawn into the thrill of its being*: whether it be moths, or flowers, or hoverflies, fishes or birds or snails – to mention a few of the groups we are more familiar with. The more you attend in this way the more you come to appreciate these beings as God appreciates them: and such attention is the very core of worship, and the gratitude that wells up in us is the very essence of Eucharist. 'This quality of seeing the world with attentive and loving care is profoundly religious,' writes Elizabeth Johnson.[27] The thrill I get is the faintest echo, the palest reflection of God's fulfilment in creation. And it comes to me through encounter with creation: sensory *encounter* first of all, augmented and deepened by intellectual encounter: and that is something that grows and develops through history.

When I immerse myself in this act of becoming acquainted more intimately with birds or flowers, mosses or spiders: at however far a remove, I experience the breath of the divine as fully as human capacity is able to. The deeper my intimacy grows the more I come to appreciate the inexhaustible nature of such experience, the more I sense how infinitesimal a portion of it any one person can embrace: that it is so inexhaustible it could not be plumbed even if everybody on Earth embraced the privilege of peering into a corner of it.

———————

The *koan* is not a literary form we associate with the literature of the West: but there are some.[28] One of the most profound is in the poetry of Tennyson:

> Flower in the crannied wall,
> I pluck you out of the crannies,
> I hold you here, root and all, in my hand,
> Little flower – but if I could understand
> What you are, root and all, and all in all,
> I should know what God and man is.[29]

'If I could understand'; but all of us, in our various ways and to varying degrees, are like the Peter of Wordsworth's poem of that name about a man of limited sensibility at the start of the poem, whose eyes are opened during the course of the narrative; but for whom to begin with:

> A primrose by a river's brim
> A yellow primrose was to him,
> And it was nothing more.[30]

We don't see ourselves in the Peter of the poem's early stanzas; but then, when did you last meet someone who sincerely identified with the Pharisee rather than the Publican of Jesus' parable?

Incarnation[31]

In theology, we are held fast in a formulation of what incarnation means that was welded together to still the speculative theological turmoil that was rife in 325 CE, even though that formulation is steeped in a child's grasp of what creation means. We are reminded of something Charles Raven wrote more than sixty years ago:

> We as human creatures limited by our status cannot speak with knowledge of what transcends our experience: we may lay down certain propositions about the nature of the Godhead, we may support them by inference and analogy, but it is sinful pride, and great foolishness, to talk as if we could define the infinite or formulate absolute truth. We must beware of claiming for our words an ultimate wisdom, an inerrant authority.[32]

How sweet to muse upon His skill displayed,
(Infinite skill!) in all that He has made;
To trace in Nature's most minute design
The signature and stamp of Power Divine;
Contrivance exquisite expressed with ease,
Where unassisted sight no beauty sees;
The shapely limb and lubricated joint,
Within the small dimensions of a point:
Muscle and nerve miraculously spun;
His mighty work who speaks, and it is done;
The invisible in things scarce seen revealed;
To whom an atom is an ample field.

William Cowper

And other eyes than our's
Were made to look at flowers,
Eyes of small birds and insects small:
The deep sun-blushing rose
Round which the prickles close
Opens her bosom to them all.
The tiniest living thing
That soars on feathered wing.
Or crawls among the long grass out of sight,
Has just as good a right
To its appointed portion of delight
As any King.

Christina Rossetti, 'To what purpose is this waste?'

Therefore have I uttered that I understood not; things too wonderful for me, which I knew not ... I have heard of thee by the hearing of the ear: but now mine eye seeth thee. (Job 42:3, 5)

The world in which man today leads his ordinary life is becoming more and more a purely technological one. The things with which he is concerned are artificial; they are artefacts, not creations. The danger inherent in this situation is that man might, erroneously, come to regard the world as a whole and the created things with it – above all, man himself – in the same manner in which he regards, correctly, his own artefacts belonging to the technological sphere; in other words, man is beginning to consider the whole world of creation as completely fathomable, fully accessible to rational comprehension, and above all, as something which it is permissible to change, transform, or even destroy.[33]

What is the nature of this 'something' at the heart of the forms of creation that we respond to 'intuitively'? Saint Thomas' word for it is its 'light': 'the measure of the reality of a thing is the measure of its light.' *Ipsa actualitas rei est quoddan lumen ipsius*: the reality of a thing is itself its light.[34] But it is utterly beyond our capacity to know the source of that 'sound' in itself: 'We have no power of perceiving this correspondence by which the formal truth of things is constituted.'[35]

When we look at the beauty (in all or any of its dimensions: aesthetic or intellectual) we do not see a reflection of a Creator that is Other, an absent artificer. We see – experience – something of God. We are in the presence of God. I *am with* God. I am *in* God. And God is in me: as He *is* in the buttercup or the butterfly – or the spider – my experience encounters and attempts to embrace. For Thomas each is an *expression*, an *embodiment*, shaped by matter and energy, of an aspect of the beauty of the creator: not merely a reflection in a mirror of some aspect of the divine.[36]

We must preface every attempt to speak of this with acknowledgement of the utter inadequacy of the words we must use to speak of it, most of all of course the word 'God' itself. Creation is the embodiment of God. This is not to say creatures are God, who is Other and Beyond – though not in any spatial sense because dimensionality enters the picture only with the coming into being of material things. Creation is the appearance of God in materiality: the things of creation on the one hand and the unfolding process that is cosmic evolution on the other. When we respond to beauty, truth, joy, intelligibility in any facet of creation we are in tune with that something of God at the heart of it. No wonder we stumble over ourselves here in our attempts to find words that will fit. *Something* of God, but the tiniest scintilla, and touched only when we reach, heard only when we listen. We pick it up with our senses, with our mind, with our spirit. We may perhaps not recognise it for what it is if our reception is sensual only, or if it is emotional only, or only intellectual: we receive it *through all that we are*.

This is what ultimately lies behind the excitement of Margaret Mee's vigil as she waits in darkness for the blossoms of the Amazonian moonflower (*Selenicereus wittii*) to open, 'transfixed by its spectral beauty and extraordinary sweet perfume.'[37] It is the compulsion to fall to your knees at the shock of seeing furze in riotous bloom for the first time, as Linnaeus is reported to have done on his brief visit to England in 1736.[38] It is my own, never-to-be-forgotten, heart-stopping amazement at finding bee orchids for the first time when I was thirteen. So overpowering is the response flowers can arouse in us that John Ruskin refused to believe there could be anything functional about their beauty: or if there was, it was surely secondary.

For pre-literate peoples this was the first and only scripture; and it was 'read' in the open cathedral of the natural world. For people in pre-Christian

Ireland, for example, this was the cathedral of the forest. When Christianity came to Ireland in early fifth century, it wasn't coming into a spiritual vacuum. There was an ancient native spiritual tradition that was deeply imbued with the *lived experience* of the Divinity imminent in creation: an Ultimate that defied definition, defied the embrace of words. This lived immersion was not some sort of glorified nature study. The life of the people – rural people all – was intimate with nature, absorbed in the reality of the encounter. The spiritual leaders who embraced Christianity had all grown up with this, and been trained in its practice. These were rural societies, without cities or towns, and their belief was essentially animist, a nature religion in which sacred places in the wilderness, usually associated with forests, water or mountains, took the place of temples.[39]

Closer to our own time, Thomas Berry often recalled words spoken in the great Cathedral of St John the Divine in New York by the Sioux elder Lame Deer in 1975: 'It made an overwhelming impression on me and lingers in my mind still and causes me often to reflect on what we have gained and what we have lost in the life style that we have adopted, on the encompassing technocratic, manipulative world that we have established, even on the sense of religion that we have developed.'[40]

> After lifting his eyes to survey this vast cathedral, [Lame Deer] turned to the audience and remarked on how over-powering a setting this cathedral was for communication with the divine reality. But then he added that his own people had a different setting for communion with the Great Spirit, a setting out under the open sky, with the mountains in the distance and the winds blowing through the trees and the earth under their feet and surrounded by the living sounds of the birds and insects. It is a different setting, he said, a different experience, but so profound that he doubted that his people would ever feel entirely themselves or able to experience the divine presence adequately in any other setting.[41]

Nature is much more than the art of God. It is the embodiment of an Artist who is otherwise incorporeal, immaterial. The materialisation of reality that is creation provides the medium through which God becomes visible. Something of God 'materialises' in every species. In the words of D.H. Lawrence (no less!):

> When from a world of mosses and of ferns
> at last the narcissus lifted a tuft of five-pointed stars

and dangled them in the atmosphere,
then every molecule of creation jumped and clapped its hands:
God is born! God is born perfumed and dangling and with a little cup![42]

The dimming of the rainbow of life on Earth

As we come to better understand God's purpose in creation in this light – the same light with which Thomas Aquinas saw it, but ours is a brighter light by far – it becomes clearer to us that creation is at its most fundamental about God's own self-fulfilment in Being and not therefore for us or about us in the first instance, however central we are to its continuation into the future God intends; as we come to better understand God's purpose in creation in this light, we begin to see that the haemorrhaging of the living abundance and diversity of life we are bringing about in our time, the greatest ecological extinction the Earth has ever experienced, has a significance that goes way beyond our concern for its impact upon our human welfare.

We evaluate the critical nature of the biodiversity crisis in terms of its effects on the human situation. But now that we come to see – are beginning to see – Earth alive as the very embodiment of divine purpose, everything in that human-centred perspective changes. This dimming of the rainbow of life's diversity is not merely inconvenient and potentially disastrous. It is denial of God's purpose. If we truly believe, and bring our understanding to bear upon what we are making of the world, we should be horrified. God's mind and heart and word to us are in all the species that weave life's diversity. Just as we look back appalled at the venality and cruelty of the advance of Christianity over the centuries, so (a thousand years into the future) we may look back on our moment of custodianship of the Earth as the time we lost our way – again.

It is given to us, our unique privilege and responsibility, to care for the Earth not as we would care for a garden in which we grow the vegetables that sustain us, but because it is the garden God walks in, and we have been invited to walk with him. We are placed in this Garden of Eden to share in God's own wonder and delight at his creation; ourselves alone endowed with that gift of Mind that enables us to tend and nurture it as God wants us to tend it.[43]

If we can attain this way of seeing in all of reality the manifestation of God, our relationship with Creation – and with all the particular existents in which it is embodied – must be essentially characterised by *fundamental reverence*. It cannot be merely instrumental. This is the mysticism to which we are, all of us, called. We find an intuitive sense of it in primitive religions which see in nature something numinous, whether identified with the things of nature themselves – trees, streams and mountains and so on – or distinct from them, sometimes assuming personality and the mantle of divinity on some level. *Our* reverence is informed by our vastly greater understanding of *how* they have come to be, of how their history is entwined with ours, of the wondrous complexity whereby their existence is maintained.

––––––––

When I step over the threshold I am in that Presence. If I can clear my mind of the clutter of distracting thought I free myself of things that prevent it sinking into me, and allow myself to *redirect* my sensory awareness of what is around me: to the beings through which and in whose (lesser) presences this greater Presence is mediated. This is the essential core common denominator of spiritual experience, prior to thought or word. It is the seed that crystallised in the rational mind all those tens of thousands of years ago, whose slow and progressive growth over the ages since draws us forward, into a future where what is essentially human in us will come to the centre.

Part of that process of progressive crystallisation is the redirection of thought to the beings about us, through which we become in time overwhelmed by the awe of their achievement. This is the essential contribution of natural history, endless and myriad-faceted, to the growth and maturation of spirituality. And while it may appear that its end is knowledge per se, that knowledge is but the medium that takes us beyond itself to its source: 'The highest that we can attain to is not Knowledge, but Sympathy with Intelligence ... Nature is a personality so vast and universal that we have never seen one of her features.'[44]

––––––––

On several occasions Pope Francis calls for 'profound ecological conversion'. The phrase is lightly skipped over but it is not lightly meant; there is no aspect of the encyclical where the depth and extent of that 'profundity' is more likely to be underappreciated. Conversion is a metamorphosis of meaning, and in no other facet of the conversion called for here is this more demanding or more difficult to get our heads and our hearts around than the *true meaning* of life on Earth. Nor is it accomplished in a flash; it is not something that is effected once and for all by being struck from the horse of our complacency, but merely initiated by that dawning of new insight. It must grow in us from there, in me as an individual over my lifetime, in the community in which we hold each other's hands on this new path we can scarcely see, in humanity at large on this pilgrimage into a distant future where, as only Faith can comfort us, on some level deeper than our understanding can compass, the lion will lie down with the lamb and all tears will be wiped away.

But in the practice of our everyday spiritual lives it gives new meaning to the conservation and restoration of biological diversity. It provides us with an agenda within which our new awareness is nurtured and advanced, and it has the advantage that it is a *secular* agenda which we can share with the broader community and in the process perhaps advance ecumenical understanding in a way the narrower focus of the churches in this direction might otherwise fail to do.

What this involves will vary from place to place, but its territorial focus should be the parish (for reasons I have reflected on elsewhere), and perhaps beginning with a new inventory and assessment of its natural diversity.

CHAPTER 6

PURPOSE, DESIGN AND MEANING

If the *weltstoff* is not basically 'loaded', how could it afford any opportunity for natural selection?

TEILHARD DE CHARDIN[1]

Chance and necessity

Fred Hoyle wrote that the likelihood of the random emergence of even the simplest cell from the raw materials to hand in the early Earth four billion years ago – atoms and simple molecules consisting of up to thirteen atoms – was about the same as the likelihood that 'a tornado sweeping through a junkyard might assemble a Boeing 747 from the materials therein'.[2] In 1982 he wrote:

> If one proceeds directly and straightforwardly in this matter, without being deflected by a fear of incurring the wrath of scientific opinion, one arrives at the conclusion that biomaterials with their amazing measure of order must be the outcome of intelligent design.[3]

John Hands concludes that, 'As with the emergence of matter, it is very probably beyond the ability of science to explain the origin of life.'[4] Which doesn't mean that it is beyond explanation, but that it is beyond the reach of human intelligence.

Over the last two centuries there has been a revolution in the way we understand the purpose of creation. We used to think – because this is what the first chapters of Genesis tells us – that all plant and animal life was created for us, to be at our service. Many plants are edible, others useful for building and for making tools and implements. Some are poisonous, but many of these have medicinal virtue, and in medieval Europe it was widely believed that God had left signs in the plants as to what that virtue was (see chapter three).

The thing about all this though, is the belief that there is a *purposefulness* in nature that reflects an Ultimate Agency behind and beyond creation, a purposefulness the lineaments of which we can decipher. People in the Middle Ages had an instinctive sense of harmony based on the totality of their encounter with creation. They tried to explain this for a time in terms of a harmony of the concentric spheres of which they conceived the universe to be made: they didn't expect to *hear* or otherwise sense this harmony – they didn't think you could: but they believed you could understand, articulate it, through mathematics.[5]

The essential confrontation between science and religion today is not over evolution (see chapter eight). Alfred Wallace was at least equally responsible for the theory of evolution by natural selection which is generally credited to Charles Darwin, and throughout his long life was one of its most articulate and unwavering advocates.[6] But it is profoundly significant that he believed that Ultimate Purpose, Supreme, Immaterial 'Mind' or Spirit had to be behind everything. (On the other hand, he also believed that spiritualism provided the evidence for the reality of life after death.) This latter 'heresy' – anathema to the scientific community of his day – is largely responsible for the way in which Wallace's central role in formulating, elaborating and defending the theory of evolution was so diminished after his death. While he lived, it was very different. He loomed large, profoundly esteemed and respected by the great names we remember – Darwin, Huxley, Hooker and the like. But his spiritualism was discomforting. Darwin ended one of his letters to Wallace (in which he responds to the latter's 'little heresy' that natural selection alone cannot account for the evolution of the human mind) with: 'Your miserable friend.'[7]

In fact, evolution is essential to modern faith and it is transformative of that Faith in something of the way the reluctant shift to a heliocentric faith was transformative of medieval faith, and we haven't fully managed that transformation yet.[8] The essential confrontation is over *purpose*. The scientific understanding of the world that gives us the Good Life we enjoy has no need of this ultimate purpose. This scientific way of knowing, which bankrolls our affluence, seems suffused with 'godlessness' so to speak.

Evolution – our descent from a common ancestor of all living things – is incontrovertibly true, and the natural selection of random variation a key mechanism in its progress. We are awed by the mesmerising diversity of life that results: but does it not (argue the proponents of 'intelligent design') require a directing divine hand, a super-natural tweak at appropriate intervals, to steer it through the improbable shoals to arrive at the results we see? 'Intelligent design' theory states *a priori* that certain evolutionary events are not naturally explainable, *thus ruling out the possibility of an explanation if there is one.*[9]

But it is a non sequitur to say that because a particular characteristic now exists, it must have originated through random mutations – no matter how unlikely this appears: simply because this is the only process we are prepared to consider. Yet it has proved impossible to account in these simple terms for many of the key developments in the evolution of life, among the most fundamental being the origin of life itself,[10] and the evolution of the fully fledged genetic system from simple chemical precursors.[11]

However convincing it may have seemed in Darwin's day, the argument that the complexity we see in living things arose through natural selection only, blindly and without direction, has become increasingly problematic as our understanding of the mesmerising complexity we see at the molecular level has grown. The most famous exponent of the idea that biochemical complexity could not have come about just by the natural selection of random variation – that it is *irreducible* in this sense – is Michael Behe, whose book *Darwin's Black Box* provoked furious attack when it first appeared. Fury is all very well, but as Behe argues with conviction in his most recent return to the fray, the stunningly complex molecular machine of the cell is no closer to receiving a Darwinian account today than it was back in 2006.[12] For Behe himself, 'like all other complex functional, purposeful arrangements, the stunning sophistication [of the cell] is best explained by an intelligent cause'.[13]

But we simply do not have the conceptual framework to articulate what is at work here. Talk about 'design' simply won't do, so woven is it with human conceptual limitation. How can something be designed and at the same time be free to evolve in different directions? *Something else* is involved in the progressive achievement of complexity: but that something else is also implicate in created reality from the moment of creation, and in principle open to rational scrutiny, however invisible to the eye of the human mind at this point in time.

There is a process of *unfolding* at work. We cannot know where it is going, but we can look back and try to see where it has taken us so far. We can identify key moments of *advance* in that unfolding: the origin of life, of the cell, of heredity, of mind, and most recently of soul. Might it all have gone differently, in a different direction on a billion planets elsewhere in the universe? These have now become biological (and indeed theological) questions rather than just the imaginative speculations of space fiction. However infantile the maturing of our ability to comprehend, some things are clear to our minds, if only in elementary outline. All that evolution has achieved under the perhaps unique circumstances of our world was enfolded as *inherent possibility* from the first moment, however many directions its unfolding might otherwise have taken. The orthodox 'intelligent design' proponent will prefer to collapse the process of our incremental understanding at this point and say that there are moments which require the hand of God to intervene from outside. Once we reach for words at this point, however, the ascent of our reach for the Ineffable Other falters and fails.

The argument for 'intelligent design' began with William Paley's famous and now familiar 'watch on the heath' example, in which the 'watch' (the most complex human artifact Paley could imagine in his mechanical era) is a metaphor for the complex individual species, and the reader is invited to think of this in relation to the creatures he or she encounters in his or her own however-limited experience of the world. (On this level in our day the most complex computer imaginable might be a somewhat more adequate exemplar.)

In crossing a heath, suppose I pitched my foot against a stone, and were asked how the stone came to be there; I might possibly answer, that, for anything I knew to the contrary, it had lain there forever: nor would it perhaps be very easy to show the absurdity of this answer. But suppose I had found a watch upon the ground, and it should be inquired how the watch happened to be in that place; I should hardly think of the answer I had before given, that for anything I knew, the watch might have always been there. ... There must have existed, at some time, and at some place or other, an artificer or artificers, who formed [the watch] for the purpose which we find it actually to answer; who comprehended its construction, and designed its use. ... Every indication of contrivance, every manifestation of design, which existed in the watch, exists in the works of nature; with the difference, on the side of nature, of being greater or more, and that in a degree which exceeds all computation.

William Paley (1802), *Natural Theology*

Michael Behe's examples are taken from the microscopic world of biochemistry: but his 'watches' are not metaphors – they are actual instances of biochemical structures and processes that could not possibly come about by accident. I won't attempt to summarise this here: the reader who feels confident enough to cope with basic chemistry should read them for him or her self.

The wonder of these examples from the world of molecules and cells does not take away from the wonder of the macroscopic world. Indeed, it magnifies and elevates that wonder to an altogether higher plan, just as Paley's mechanical example attempted to elevate everyday human experience of the natural world to a different plane. The more intimate and familiar our acquaintance on that everyday level with other creatures, the more awe-inspiring that experience becomes: and the more rationally inadequate and superficial our juvenile attempts to account for it all by, for example, natural selection appear.

When we hold steadfastly to what our human encounter with the natural world reveals, we may be content to use the simple, unadorned (however culturally elaborated) language of 'Faith' as our starting point:

> The real, which is perfectly simple, and supremely beautiful, too often escapes us, giving way before the imaginary, which is less troublesome to acquire. Instead of going back to the facts, and seeing for ourselves, we blindly follow tradition.[14]

All that evolution has achieved is the outcome of natural processes we can understand: even if we have not yet arrived at the fuller understanding that is possible for human comprehension; and although – wonderful as it is – our human understanding of what is going on is, even today, of the most superficial kind. The unfolding that is evolution consists of the coming into material, existential reality of potentialities built into matter in its very essence at the inception of things, but 'intelligent design' seems too meagre a term for this, laden as it is with the taint of divine intervention and even were that absent with the mechanical imagery of human design. There is no need for the 'hand' of God (and in some inevitable sense that is how we picture his intervention) because 'He' is within it from the beginning and the entire drama is *the gestation of an implicate potentiality*.

So we do still have to grasp the nettle of design, but in order to redefine it in this sense. We are paranoid about not being seen as 'creationists', or being tainted with the heresy of 'irreducible complexity'. On the basis of the totality of our experience (not a selection of isolated events and processes) it is more rational to speak of Ultimate Purpose of some kind. And since we worship rationality as the ultimate arbiter of knowledge, to reject this is to defy our own supreme faith in reason. What the source of that Ultimate Purpose might be is utterly beyond our human comprehension, and in our attempts to get our heads around it our primate intelligence inevitably flounders or drowns.

The question of a supreme entity is quite beyond the current level of scientific study and may remain so into the indefinite future. Since the universe we can see and detect is still beyond a full scientific explanation, the possibility of understanding its creator, should there be one, is so remote as to be discarded.[15]

The ultimate question, the question that matters above all else, is that of whether it All *means* something. We cannot doubt that a story is unfolding before our eyes across cosmic and geological time, but is this just a coincidence or is there some direction to it; does it have something to it we might think of as 'design', working towards an end? This most radical of all questions immediately gives rise to two further questions if the answer is 'yes'. What is the nature of whatever is the source of this design, this Ultimate Mind; and what is my small role in all of this? How should I order my life if I want to live in accordance with this 'Ultimate Mind'?

An answer to the first of these two further questions can only come to us through the personal encounter of our individual life with the universe about us (which we may call 'creation' if our experience and reflection leads us to believe that Ultimate Mind is at work). So too any answer to the second question can only be arrived at through that encounter, and becomes progressively clearer as our understanding of the nature of things evolves and matures over time, as we saw in chapter two.

The unfolding of the universe to this point has been characterised at every stage by an almost-infinite succession of coincidences that just about pass as statistically possible if all we are talking about are numbers rather than the *real things* of creation, elevated onto a different level of complexity after each coincidence. More than *mere* chance is required. Evolution is characterised at every stage by a fine-tuning without which intelligent life could never have come about, and which appears to have *intended* its ultimate appearance:

> There exist a number of unlikely coincidences between numbers of enormous magnitude that are, superficially, completely independent; moreover, these coincidences appear essential to the existence of carbon-based observers in the Universe.[16]

Freeman Dyson, one of the greatest theoretical physicists of the last century, famously summed the position up in 1979 when he wrote:

> The more I examine the universe and study the details of its architecture, the more evidence I find that the universe in some way must have known we were coming. There are striking examples in the laws of nuclear physics of numerical accidents that seem to conspire to make the universe habitable.[17]

Even a brief summary is beyond the scope of these pages, but here are a few examples. Conditions were so hot for the first 380,000 years after the Big Bang that only sub-atomic particles – protons, neutrons and electrons – could exist: only when things had cooled (somewhat!) did it become possible for them to combine to form atoms of hydrogen. But if the relative masses of proton and electron had been in the tiniest degree different, atoms could never have come into existence.[18]

The laws of nature form a system that is extremely fine-tuned, and very little in physical law can be altered without destroying the possibility of the development of life as we know it. Were it not for a series of startling coincidences in the precise details of physical law, it seems, humans and similar life forms would never have come into being.[19]

If gravity were a *bit* stronger than it actually is, 'the Big Bang would have been a squib ... A bit weaker and it couldn't have made stars and galaxies. If the charge on the electron differed by just a few per cent, stars could not have created the heavy elements needed for Earth-like planets to form. Carbon would not exist if the strong force varied by half a percent. And so, no life. And if the cosmological constant had been even slightly different, the tiny dose of dark energy that is the source of the accelerating expansion of the universe would be lacking.'[20]

Perhaps the most staggering example of this ultra-fine-tuning – but difficult for the non-physicist to understand – is the precision of the difference between the positive and negative values of what is known as the vacuum energy involved in controlling the expansion of the universe. If this differed by as little as 0.00000000000000000000000000000000000000000000000000000 0000000000000000000000000000000000000000000000000000000000000000 00000000000000000001 the universe would have expanded too quickly for galaxies to form.[21]

Galaxies, for example, could never have formed without the perturbations that produced the inhomogeneities necessary to get them started. Likewise with the formation of the precursor molecules for life. The building blocks in the primordial soup were simple compounds: CO_2, NH_3, CH_4 and H_2O. But when they interact under the appropriate conditions (such as early Earth provided) the end products are not a random assemblage of assorted molecules, but the two dozen amino acids and the nucleotide bases necessary for the coming-to-be of all life on Earth.

> The point is that if the original reactants were reforming into larger molecules by chance alone, the products would be among billions upon billions of possibilities and would likely vary each time the experiment was run ... Some factor other than chance is necessarily involved in the prebiotic chemistry of life's origin, though one need not resort to supernatural phenomena. That other factor we reason to be the microscopic electric forces naturally at work among the molecules – forces that guide and bond small molecules into the larger clusters appropriate to life as we know it, thus granting the molecules some specificity and stability.[22]

Much the same can be said for the way in which these amino acids combine to form proteins. Insulin is the simplest protein (by far). The likelihood of this forming by chance from its component fifty-one amino acids is $1/10^{51}$ (10^{66}). This means that to get insulin by random combination, by chance, the amino acids would have to combine 10^{66} (a million trillion, trillion, trillion, trillion, trillion times). In other words, we could randomly assemble the twenty amino acids trillions upon trillions of times *per second for the entire history of the universe* and still not get insulin.

> The laws of the universe are cunningly contrived to coax life into being ... If life follows from [primordial] soup with causal dependability, the laws of nature encode a hidden subtext ... which tells them: 'Make life!' ... It means that the laws of the universe have engineered their own comprehension.[23]

The only way out of this for those who reject meaning in the universe is to postulate the Multiverse: the idea that there are countless billions of parallel universes, so many in fact that one of them was bound to be ours![24] This is a purely theoretical construct, without the slightest evidence to support it, as extreme an example of turning one's scientific back on Ockham's Razor as it is possible to imagine: 'To invoke an infinity of other universes to explain one is surely carrying excess baggage to cosmic extremes.'[25]

By way of comment on the reality or otherwise of the multiverse, it is tempting to quote Ionides' sarcastic dismissal of the last great chimera of this kind: the ghostly ether that was the medium deemed necessary for the propagation of waves; as Clerk Maxwell said, 'Ethers were invented for the planets to swim in, to constitute electric atmospheres and magnetic effluvia, to convey sensations from one part of our body to another, till all space was filled several times over with ether.'[26] 'Whatever science failed to explain in any other way', wrote the Ionides, 'was at once attributed to this marvellous substance.'

> In addition, ether was supposed to have the great merit of furnishing an absolute gauge by which the rate of motion of all other bodies could be reckoned. Whether the ether itself moved rapidly or slowly was beside the point.' ... Of course an unknown and unproved substance of this sort may act as a valuable hypothesis, but in itself it explains nothing; and the temptation to explain everything by an addition which explains nothing has always been irresistible.[27]

Einstein showed that there was no need for the assumption that there needs to be a gauge for absolute motion.

> Through my scientific work I have come to believe more and more strongly that the physical universe is put together with an ingenuity so astonishing that I cannot accept it merely as a brute fact. There must, it seems to me, be a deeper level of explanation. Whether one wishes to call that deeper level 'God' is a matter of taste and definition. Furthermore, I have come to the point of view that mind – i.e. conscious awareness of the world – is not a meaningless and accidental quirk of nature, but an absolutely fundamental facet of reality. That is not to say that we are the purpose for which the universe exists. Far from it. I do, however, believe that we human beings are built into the scheme of things in a very basic way.
>
> Paul Davies (1992), *The Mind of God*, p. 16

Scientific theories that try to explain away the appearance of design in the universe as the result of 'chance and necessity' are not scientific at all, said John Paul II in 1985, but an abdication of human intelligence:

> To all these indications of the existence of God the Creator, some oppose the power of chance or of the proper mechanisms of matter. To speak of chance for a universe which presents such a complex organisation in its elements and such marvelous finality in its life would be equivalent to giving up the search for an explanation of the world as it appears to us. In fact, this would be equivalent to admitting effects without a cause. It would be to abdicate human intelligence, which would thus refuse to think and to seek a solution for its problems.[28]

Part of the reluctance on the part of so many scientists to accept that design/purpose is at work in evolution is that they appreciate more acutely than the rest of us that these words are defined by our narrow human experience of them. Yet even Darwin exclaimed, 'Have we any right to assume that the creator works by intellectual powers like those of man?'[29] (He is commenting on the imperfections in the design of the eye.) The narrowness of even the great Thomas Huxley's definition of 'purpose' as it applies to the structure of plants is instructive in this regard. 'Who has ever dreamed', he wrote, 'of finding an utilitarian purpose in the forms and colours of flowers, in the sculpture of pollen-grains, in the varied figures of the fronds of ferns?'[30] And this just a few years before Darwin's great book on the almost incredible sophistication of orchid pollination, which elaborated on this very 'purpose' in spectacular fashion.[31]

Whatever its end may be, it cannot be doubted that there has been a direction to evolution. One of its characteristics is the realisation – the becoming real – of maximum diversity in what is materially possible: most evident to us in the diversity of life. The other is progressively increasing complexification and cooperation.

> It can be said that the history of evolution is the history of increasing sociation and community. Not only is community an example of complexity, but the more complex you are, the more sociable, cooperative and apparently altruistic you can be. If the only force pushing the biological world onwards is Darwinian natural selection, the natural selection is pushing it constantly in a direction that favours community, cooperation and altruism.[32]

The course of cosmic evolution is often said to be characterised by increasing differentiation, greater integration and communion and the progressive appearance of greater self-creation possibilities (autopoiesis) – all three in harmonious but necessarily dialectical balance – a formulation that is probably always traceable back to the philosophy of Whitehead.[33] Perhaps the easiest way to think of it is in ecological terms. For *differentiation* think not only of biological diversity, the mesmeric diversity of life, but chemical diversity on one side of it, and cultural diversity on the other. We see *communion* on each of these three levels as an essential binding and driving force. Without the inbuilt, part-of-the-essence-of-what-they-are tendency and capacity of cells to bind into tissue, and for them to differentiate into multiple tissue types, multicellular life would not be possible.[34] *Autopoiesis* is the development of individual identity, characterised by some quality of being unique to itself: in pre-biotic being that of the different elements and compounds, in biology of species, each a unique mode of living possibility; at the level of the human *in each individual.*

Evolutionary advance is steered by natural selection of characters, features that have a genetic foundation in random mutation, but are held in place by subsequent behaviour: the interaction between the individual, the species, and the environment: and this behaviour is a spectrum that extends from antagonism and conflict through to various forms of cooperation, to affection and love at the other end.[35] It has been fashionable to reduce the entire process to a blind struggle by genes to perpetuate themselves, the phenotypes that carry these genes being seen as little more than sophisticated robots manipulated by genes, but more recently the learned behaviour of individuals is seen as a key factor influencing the selection of those genes best able to perpetuate favourable learned behaviours: that is, 'changes in the phenotype that emerge from developmental processes ... are converted to genetically fixed characters;' in other words, genes following development, not the other way round.

There are several striking examples in our own species from the development of farming, where the adoption of cereal- and milk-based diets triggered the evolution of extra genes for starch-digesting enzymes, and of genetic changes that allow adults to digest milk sugars. In a more general sense, the more nutritious diet provided by cooking may have made available the energy that permitted the evolution of the large, energy-expensive brains necessary for the development of human consciousness. In a fundamental way therefore, organisms are able to direct evolution in the direction best suited to their continued progress.

It is possible to reconcile these apparently contradictory views. We all clearly make decisions on the level of everyday action, and although whether I cut the grass or let it grow for another week is influenced by all sorts of considerations, the decision can go either way. All the same, it is the cumulative interaction of individual decisions as uncountable as stars in the universe that constitutes history.

But is its direction predetermined? 'Progress', in the sense of movement in a certain direction, may be inevitable, but is it progress in a direction that brings improvement? There is undoubtedly improvement over geological time in the sense that life has – given the nature of the Earth it inhabits, that constrains it and presents opportunity – inevitably evolved in the direction of ever-greater awareness and increasing complexity, with the concomitant efflorescence of beauty that accompanies it, achieved at incalculable individual cost.

But can we say the same of human history? Few historians today set much store by Tolstoy's view that there is a thread at the heart of human history that directs or pulls it along a predetermined course. According to Tolstoy the idea of individual free will as 'something capable of influencing historical events ... is the same for history as the recognition of a free force moving the heavenly bodies would be for astronomy.' Surely its course argues strongly against a benevolently ordained guiding thread?

As we survey the world around us it is difficult to see evidence of human care and custodianship. It is hard not to be sympathetic with those Deep Ecologists who see us as a blight upon the face of the Earth. Our use of energy and material resources is profligate and unsustainable. No words can describe the extent of our uncaring reduction of the natural world and the hundreds of millions of different life forms it sustains. On the other hand, there are the tremendous advances in human understanding that have led to technological progress that could enrich human life and possibility immeasurably, were they to be applied in ways the balance of reason and virtue that constitutes wisdom should direct.

At any time in human history we would have seen a comparable balance of darkness and light, and struggled to see a direction to it all. One hundred and fifty years ago no less saintly a figure than John Henry Newman surveyed the world of his time with despairing eyes:

> To consider the world in its length and breadth ... the tokens so faint and broken, of a superintending design, the blind evolution of what turns out to be great powers of truth, the progress of things, as if from unreasoning elements, not towards final causes, the greatness and littleness of man, his far-reaching aims, his short duration ... all this is a vision to dizzy and appal; and inflicts upon the mind the sense of a profound mystery, which is absolutely beyond human solution.[36]

Where is the guiding light? What thread can there be, what star ahead that draws us on towards what is better, more beautiful, more true? For Newman himself it was his Faith, the spar from the foundered ship to which he clung in a raging sea.

The human world of today is profoundly different from that of Cardinal Newman in three ways: there are now nearly eight billion of us compared to 1.5 billion in his time; technological advance in the intervening one hundred and fifty years has placed at our disposal tools of change and destruction unimaginable in his day; and the retreat of the wild has left us with no more than a fraction of the natural world and its resources. To take but one example, the Atlantic Coastal Rainforest that so enchanted the young Charles Darwin is believed to have covered between one and 1.5 million km² when the Portuguese first arrived and began to cut it back for agriculture and pasture. Today only some 4,000 km² remain, no more than a fraction of which is primary forest. And yet that fragment is home to twenty thousand species of plants, 40 per cent of them endemic.[37]

Science underpins conservation not only by demonstrating our dependence on the integrity of environmental functions, and our *need* of the natural world for which our being is programmed. It now also enables us to see a core of meaning at the centre for which we may wish to use the inadequate word 'religious': that the universe is meant, that in Einstein's phrase, the universe means us to be here:

> It is true that we emerged in the Universe by chance. But the idea of chance is itself only a cover for our ignorance. I do not feel like an alien in this universe. The more I examine this universe and study the details of its architecture, the more evidence I find that the universe in some sense must have known that we were coming.[38]

All of this confronts us with another version of the Great Question. What kind of God? To which no morally acceptable answer is to be found within the confining framework of human understanding. To the limits of the nature of possibility being stretched by discoveries in modern physics and biology we must now add Deep Future Time: deeper than geology. Between the Alpha of our origins and the Omega of our final destination we may perhaps still have to traverse and decipher most of the letters in the alphabet of human possibility.

> The advances that the human race has made in understanding the Universe have been immense but, this notwithstanding, it is quite likely that, in the not too distant future, learned human society will look back at our present construction of the Universe in the same way as we now look back on that of Aristotle.[39]

A deeper signature

There are two sorts of explanations for what is going on in nature, for what is at work in creation. There is the infinity of explanations of *how things work*: on the mechanical, chemical, physiological, molecular, evolutionary levels, and all of these, as well as being *particular*, are ultimately reducible to number, to what can be measured with rulers and clocks: or at least that is the hope and intention. But it *is* reduction, and in the process the realities explained in this way are progressively *bled* of colour and vibrancy and immediacy: the qualities by which they relate to us.

But there is something deeper in knowing – something deeper in what is known – that defies definition of this kind. And so, there is another kind of attempt to explain – which also is part of the rational appropriation of sense experience – which tries to reach deeper, to see behind all these particular explanations: but here words and equations fall *immeasurably* short. This 'something deeper' in knowing, which reaches toward and seeks to touch the vivifying essence of things (the 'almost mystical, creative, organising force' Ernst Haeckel saw behind the endless beauty and forms of the tiny radiolaria and other life forms he studied and, mesmerised, drew), is usually referred to as 'intuition'. Some few of us have a psychological disposition that augments that glimpse, that sense, into physical ecstasy – or a sense of the intellectual beauty.

> We have a sense of its presence; it is there, somewhere ahead, just out of sight, just beyond our reach. As we look at life, we have an uneasy sense of the communication of some universal truth that lies just beyond our grasp. ... The meaning haunts and ever eludes us, and in its very pursuit we approach the ultimate mystery of Life itself.[40]

For example, I can take a piece of music and analyse its structure but fail to catch its meaning. Music 'is brimful of meanings which will not translate into logical structures or verbal expression' (George Steiner). Or consider Schumann's response to being asked to explain a difficult étude. All he could do by way of answer was to sit down and play it a second time.[41] We might describe these as experiences of transcendence, but that word suggests something outside of them, beyond and other than, rather than something aflame at the material heart of what is experienced.

'Intuition leads us to prehend ideas; to grasp them all of a piece,' wrote Colin Tudge. It is part of the rational appropriation of sense experience: its deeper part:

> If we take on board the idea of universal consciousness then we can say more grandly that the receptive mind seeks to engage directly with that universal consciousness. This I am sure is what mystics do. This is the reason why prophets and gurus throughout the ages have sought quiet places – mountain tops and deserts and the shade of trees.[42]

Pope Francis touches on this notion in his reference to the Islamic mystic Ali al-Khawas in *Laudato Si'*. The paragraph that begins, 'The universe unfolds in God, who fills it completely. Hence, there is a mystical meaning to be found in a leaf, in a mountain trail, in a dewdrop, in a poor person's face', goes on to say:

> The spiritual writer Ali al-Khawas stresses from his own experience the need not to put too much distance between the creatures of the world and the interior experience of God. As he puts it: 'Prejudice should not have us criticise those who seek ecstasy in music or poetry. There is a subtle mystery in each of the movements and sounds of this world. The initiate will capture what is being said when the wind blows, the trees sway, water flows, flies buzz, doors creak, birds sing, or in the sound of strings or flutes, the sighs of the sick, the groans of the afflicted ...'[43]

Faith is about seeing the miraculous in the everyday, not about waiting every day for the miraculous.

Jonathan Sacks (2012), *The Great Partnership*

Over-confidence in the science of the age

In his annual report for 1858, the momentous year in which the Linnaean Society of London published Darwin and Wallace's brilliant account of evolution and natural selection, their president Thomas Bell famously reported that 'the year which has passed has not, indeed, been marked by any of those striking discoveries which at once revolutionise, so to speak, the department of science on which they bear'. Forty-five years later, Albert Abraham Michelson – an extraordinarily brilliant scientist, who won the Nobel Prize for physics in 1907, the first American to do so – wrote:

> The more important fundamental laws and facts of physical science have all been discovered, and these are now so firmly established that the possibility of their ever being supplanted in consequence of new discoveries is exceedingly remote.[44]

This, only a few years before Einstein discovered relativity (building indeed on Michelson's work to do so) and Max Planck steered physics into the entirely new and bewildering quantum world.

As a particular instance of how little we understand, consider how little we actually *comprehend* of the transmission of information about reality. Never mind for the moment the fact that the *essence* of what happens when we *see* things is as mysterious as ever it was, in spite of our extraordinarily detailed insight into the physical and biochemical mechanisms by which it is achieved: and in spite of the carelessness in the use of language in a textbook account that can begin: 'In essence what happens is this ...' Consider more basically how little we grasp the way space is filled with subatomic particles in motion, pulses, waves, carrying all the information about what is happening throughout the cosmos at every moment, including the maelstrom of data transmission that binds our digital civilisation: and yet each message remains distinct, does not interfere with any other message. What a miracle it is – still – that when I answer my mobile phone to speak to you, your voice has a moment ago travelled into the upper atmosphere to be picked up and resent via satellite to me: and if the satellite had been a thousand kilometres away it would still have picked up the same message. And yet the message has travelled clear and without interruption at the speed of sound or light through all the billions of messages being transmitted at the same instant equally without interruption.

The danger of an increasingly narrow perspective in modern scientists is elegantly summarised by John Hands. He quotes E.O. Wilson:

> The most productive scientists, installed in million-dollar laboratories, have no time to think about the big picture and see little profit from it ... It is therefore not surprising to find physicists who do not know what a gene is, and biologists who guess that string theory has something to do with violins. Grants and honours are given in science for discoveries, not for scholarship and wisdom.[45]

The primacy of reason

Trust in reason is the only foundation upon which the human enterprise can securely build: but it is important that we should not identify 'reason' with what we have come to think of as 'science'. The critical use of reason is the bedrock of rationality, but only that. It is, if you like, the rooting system of rationality upon which to build our *evaluation* of experience: of what is beautiful, what is good, what is true. This is an absolute, an ethical imperative. It is what the atheist Jacques Monod called the 'Ethics of Knowledge': an absolute respect for truth, pursued 'with utter honesty, rigor and integrity'.[46] This is where people of Faith often fall down in the eyes of those committed to such an ethical imperative:

> Only in the last two millennia or so have first, philosophy and, later, the sciences, started to pursue the quest for understanding by a new approach based on the use of reason, logic, observation, and experimentation, under the guidance of intellectual rigour and honesty. This new form of search has gained few adherents so far. By and large, a majority of religious believers, often encouraged by their leaders, have failed to follow the scientific approach, in spite of the spectacular practical achievements – nuclear power, space travel, genetic engineering, the cure and prevention of many diseases, to mention only a few – it has made possible. In much of the world, the power of 'faith' remains supreme and religions maintain a largely unquestioned authority. A perverse aspect of this situation is the feeling of certainty that goes with it.[47]

Those who would speak of God without fully embracing the enormously richer picture of creation uncovered by scientific progress are forced into lay-bys off the main road along which the course of human progress streams relentlessly, the rational weakness of their discourse unable to compete with the confident intelligence that directs the computers that govern all our lives. Much of organised religion baulks at this rationality ethics, out of fear that it will bring about change: as it inevitably will, and progressively so. But this is the nature of evolution, of a piece with the change that characterises every level of creation's unfolding, each change giving rise to a new stability that itself must yield to the next advance in understanding. Indeed, this fear can be construed as a lack of true faith.

We speak of the cold light of reason. But the reason we are talking about here is not cold. *All* that is measured and modelled by the parameters of science is the reality, is what *really exists*, is embodied. *What* is measured is not defined by its mere measurement. Hence sense and value are as central to its apprehension as rationality. Socrates appreciated the limits of measurement when he criticised the *physikoi*: the very first scientists, who were intent on finding natural explanations for everything. While admiring their aim of finding *explanations*, he pointed out that they were intent only on the material aspect, without then standing back *to see the existential dimension*: the reality that comes into being as a result and exerts its presence on the world; including, in a particular way, on the world of sensation.[48]

Reason then, goes deeper than mechanical explanation. In the words of Dean Inge, it is 'the whole personality under the guidance of its highest faculty'.[49] This is what Meister Eckhart means when he tells us that 'the last appeal must be to the deepest part of my own being, and that is my reason'.[50] Eckhart doesn't abandon intellect for emotion (as Richard Rolle and Catherine of Siena seem to do). It is through the use of intellect (and so, through contemplation of creation) that we rise *above* ourselves to touch God, who is the font of intelligence and intelligibility.

Whereas science has transformed our understanding of creation, that part of it which once justly claimed supremacy over all its branches – theology – remains chained by doctrinal formulations anchored in the age in which they were formulated. It does so in order to stem the storms of debate: but it is through that very struggle to understand that we are carried forward. Our current grasp of things can only be articulated in the terms and concepts our stage of cultural evolution allows, and needs to be reformulated over and over as those concepts mature (or become less inadequate with the progressive augmentation of our understanding).

The rationality that blossoms beyond modern scientific naturalism is thus an un-eliminable foundation of Faith: but it challenges the faith many of us were brought up in on all sorts of levels. But there is no alternative to it if faith is to be able to present itself as the only truly rational response to what reveals itself in creation. This is the 'reason' on which Benedict XVI laid such fierce emphasis in his famous Regensburg address, in which he argues that a religion of reason (properly understood) has a veto on claims of other parts of 'Revelation'; 'Not to act with Logos is contrary to God's nature.' 'The scientific ethos is ... the will to be obedient to the truth, and, as such, it embodies an attitude which belongs to the essential decisions of the human spirit.'[51] ('By Logos we mean the principle of intelligibility of all that happens, a kind of pre-eminent rational intelligibility whose ends are served by the operations of the laws of nature.'[52])

The new perspective forced upon us by science also helps on different levels to loosen the bonds that bind us to our restricting intellectual conception of the Ultimate Meaning of things. The ineradicable deep-rootedness of the notion of God as King, as Patriarch, is an enormous problem, because no matter what degree of greatness we elevate it to, no matter to what power we raise it, it limits what we are reaching towards to our human capacities. Every advance of science cuts away another of the myriad cords that anchor our concept of God to the ground in this way; and yet, the utmost we can ever achieve is to touch the edge of the most distant fringe of the Ultimate Reality which the early theologian Damascius (AD 462-538) could only describe as 'That Yonder'.

> While we rejoice in the new possibilities open to humanity, we also see the dangers arising from these possibilities and we must ask ourselves how we can overcome them. We will succeed in doing so only if reason and faith come together in a new way, if we overcome the self-imposed limitation of reason to the empirically falsifiable, and if we once more disclose its vast horizons.
>
> Modern scientific reason quite simply has to accept the rational structure of matter and the correspondence between our spirit and the prevailing rational structures of nature as a given, on which its methodology has to be based.[53]

From reason to faith

That openness to *what* is being progressively revealed through the penetrating gaze of science is something that precedes our application of scientific method to it. We may think of this openness, if we like, as the essence of 'Faith'. Faith takes hold of you in advance of reason, but never divorced from it, which is why rational apologetics will always fall short. Reason is the solid ground on which the feet of Faith must stand as it lifts its eyes and its arms to heaven. In Paul Tillich's never-easy-to-understand words:

> [Faith] transcends both the drives of the nonrational unconsciousness and the structures of the rational conscious ... the ecstatic character of faith does not exclude its rational character although it is not identical with it, and it includes nonrational strivings without being identical with them. 'Ecstasy' means 'standing outside of oneself' – without ceasing to be oneself – with all the elements which are united in the personal center.[54]

How can there be doubt then? Surely Faith is all about certainty? But this doubt is on a par with the doubt that is part of the essence of scientific enquiry: and yet the certainty of science governs every aspect of modern life. This doubt is itself certainty: the certainty that every increment in understanding is but a closer approximation, taking us that bit deeper and closer to what lies at the heart of things.

Nor will humanity be able to feel solid ground under its feet in the dissolution that may await us in the centuries to come, without this Faith that absolutely suffuses reason, and is itself soaked in the unrestricted use of reason: a reason that embraces a God beyond all its anxiety, doubt and uncertainty. Freud wrote of the voice of the intellect as a 'soft' one, that would eventually – but only in 'a distant, distant, future' replace religion. And soft it is indeed, because it doesn't need to be any louder, so irrefutable is its power of persuasion: and it will indeed in the course of long, long time replace religion, not because it has conquered it, but because religion will have transformed itself through its absorption of intellect and reason.[55]

The problem with God

What Christian who has become aware of a sheet of glass insulating him from his non-believing colleagues has not asked himself uneasily whether he was not on a false tack or had not actually lost touch with the main current of mankind?

TEILHARD DE CHARDIN, *THE DIVINE MILIEU*, PP. 68-69

Is there, or is there not a Reality 'whom everyone calls God'? Does God exist or not? We have the arguments of books with titles like *God: The Failed Hypothesis* on the one side, or like Edward Feser's *The Last Superstition* on the other: written by people of comparably high intelligence, but how tenuous the arguments on both sides are is borne out by the fact that they win few recruits to their respective sides, because the root of conviction precedes intellectual argument: it has been arrived at beforehand, and by a different route.[56] Nevertheless, it should give us pause for thought that so many of those whose encounter with creation is closest, perhaps closer far than ours, have no time for religion, or at best are indifferent.

It is sometimes the case that deep conviction reached early in life becomes so deeply entrenched over time that it is increasingly difficult to review later on. When you are on a journey, if you take the wrong turn at a crossroads early on it becomes ever more difficult to correct the further you travel.[57] You are turned in the wrong direction. It is often the case that atheists see more clearly than the rest of us the inadequacy of traditional concepts of 'Ultimate Purpose', are more aware than we are that the language and practice of religion as they have experienced it, simply do not measure up to their personal encounter with the reality of the world. They are, in a way therefore, prophets of a deeper understanding. In other cases the denial of the atheist may simply be an honest refusal to acknowledge a God whose 'greatness' crumbles in the face of our accusation that it does not accord with our human notions of what greatness permits, how goodness is defined.

There is a strand of atheism, honest in its rejection of an idolatrous God, that is prepared to engage in an open-ended way reminiscent of Socrates conducting his dialogues. Julian Baggini describes this form of atheism as 'open-hearted commitment to truth and rational enquiry', so that 'hostile opposition to the beliefs of others combined with a dogged conviction of the certainty of one's own beliefs ... is antithetical to such values.'[58] Many atheists, on the other hand – including some of the most strident – simply don't *want* there to be a God: they have 'an unshakeable commitment grounded not in reason but rather in sheer willfulness, a deeply ingrained desire to *want* things to be a certain way regardless of whether the evidence shows they are that way.'[59]

In his belief that God does not exist, that there is no God, the atheist is correct in the sense that any kind of existence we are capable of comprehending cannot be predicated of God.[60] Nor can we believe in the gods our ancestors conjured up to explain, to control, to comfort. These are false gods, to worship which is idolatry. God is not great or good beyond measure, but beyond measure simply.

'Atheism' of this sort is therefore, in itself, actually no more than the first stage in rejection of a fundamental idolatry (or if you prefer, of idolatrous fundamentalism). It is well exemplified by David Attenborough and indeed by Charles Darwin himself (see below). But some who have reached this stage see no road forward; they do not see or believe that there is anywhere beyond to go, and their conviction often festers to a different fundamentalism which directs its invective at all who have not taken this first step: instead of doing all that may be done to help others to do so at their own pace.

Modern atheism is merely a branch of properly reflective apophatic theology, a branch that has chopped itself off half way, so that it is prevented from producing the flowers and fruit of its maturity that would enable us (without painstaking analysis of its philosophical DNA) to understand it for what it is. There is also a left end to the spectrum of theology itself that looks little different from atheism. All it takes is a shift of focus to arrive at this (the 'flip' we call conversion when it is in the 'right' direction). Conversion can cast us on the shores of the spectrum of Faith at any point. But wherever we are along the spectrum we live by the same Faith. ('By their deeds you will know them.')

The theological school of those god-scholars known as hard naturalists salvages a minimalist concept of God, but it is one which allows that intuition to breathe again, and it helps to clear the way for us to glimpse once more, and this time against the overwhelming evidence of the New Science, what infinity really means without rejecting our religious inheritance, in whatever cultural tradition.[61] Because all the time we comfortably conceive of the infinite that is at the heart of it all as merely 'really great': but great by our standards, whereas the measure we should be seeking is the other way round. God indeed is not great, He is beyond greatness.

––––––––

For many who are awed and overwhelmed by the beauty, complexity and diversity of the natural world and might otherwise be drawn to acclaim, an insurmountable barrier is the problem of suffering as an integral part of evolution by natural selection: an integral part of the way things are (as distinct from the different problem raised by suffering caused by human beings). It is important to remind ourselves at the outset that suffering and pain are not in themselves evil, but an essential consequence of sentience, and an increase in sentience is a central feature of the evolution of life on Earth. God's 'powerlessness' may be seen as a consequence of the fact that without pain there can be no sentience.

> What may be the solution of the mystery, and how so much benevolent foresight can be reconciled with so much cruelty, it is not for the naturalist to explain, though the mere naturalist finds it hard to shake off these thoughts when they have once come up in his mind ... But let us be careful not to speak as if our little plummets had sounded the depths of the universe. Those who have surpassed their fellows in the improvement of natural knowledge, have always been the first to admit that what they have come to know is lost in the infinitude of the unknown.[62]

We can respond in one of four ways to the immense waste and suffering we see in the living world:

1. Atheism
2. Believe that God is powerless to do things differently

3. Believe that God is malevolent

4. Believe that there is a principle of evil alongside a principle of good

1. There is no God

Atheism removes the problem, whereas belief in God makes it profoundly more acute. The problem of suffering is much greater for the believer, because he or she can no more see or accept how it can be reconciled with the notion of an all-powerful, all-good, creator than the atheist can. The all-pervasive presence of imperfection – and of suffering and evil especially – argues (on the face of it conclusively) against the idea that creation is the work of a God of whom goodness is the very essence and who is all-powerful. This conundrum is addressed by the branch of theology known as *theodicy* ('god-justice' in Greek), and it has engaged the greatest theological minds since the very beginning and will continue to do so until the end.

The more we have come to learn about biology, about the individual lives of species, the more have we come to appreciate just how *all-pervasive* waste and suffering are. Ever since Darwin this has been a tremendous stumbling block. 'What a book a Devil's Chaplain might write on the clumsy, wasteful, blundering, low and horridly cruel works of nature,' he wrote; 'I cannot persuade myself that a beneficent and omnipotent God would have designedly created the Ichneumonidae with the express intention of their feeding within the living bodies of caterpillars.'[63] For Darwin the suffering inflicted by insect parasitoids on their hosts constituted irrefutable argument against the goodness of God. Is it not more in accord with reason to assume that this is simply the way things are rather than have to reconcile it with the existence of a good and almighty God?

This uncaring god is the impossible god of which Stephen Fry recently spoke to popular acclaim (in words that echo rebellion rather than denial), of whom the agonising prose of Albert Camus speaks in *The Plague*, who is present in the concentration camps, whose nature haunts the very roots of Christian theology. When asked what he would say if confronted by God (in whom he does not believe) Stephen Fry answered:

I'd say, 'Bone cancer in children? What's that about? How dare you? How dare you create a world to which there is such misery that is not our fault. It's not right, it's utterly, utterly evil.' Why should I respect a capricious, mean-minded, stupid

God who creates a world that is so full of injustice and pain. That's what I would say … the god that created this universe, if it was created by god, is quite clearly a maniac … utter maniac, totally selfish. We have to spend our life on our knees thanking him? What kind of god would do that?[64]

Few people are more knowledgeable about life on Earth than David Attenborough, for whom the existence of a parasitic worm boring into the eye of an African child (for example) is irreconcilable with the existence of God.

When a creationist talks about God creating every individual species as a separate act, they always instance hummingbirds or orchids or sunflowers and beautiful things. But I tend to think of a parasitic worm that's boring through the eye of a boy sitting on the bank of a river in West Africa that's going to make him blind. And [I ask them]: are you telling me that the God you believe in, who you say is an all-merciful God, who cares for each and every one of us individually, are you saying that God created this worm that can live in no other way than in an innocent child's eyeball? Because that doesn't seem to me to coincide with a God who's full of mercy.[65]

Yet he is prepared to accept the possibility that he is missing something: 'Often when I open a termite's nest and see thousands of blind organisms working away that lack the sense mechanism to see me, I can't help thinking that there's someone around who created this.'[66] Accordingly, although he does not believe in God, he is reluctant to call himself an atheist.

2. Kenosis: God is powerless

One prominent theological attempt to deal with the problem is to argue that God in some sense suffers with creation.

The ubiquity of pain, predation, suffering and death as the means of creation through biological evolution entails, for any concept of God to be morally acceptable and coherent, that we cannot but tentatively propose that God suffers in, with, and under the creative processes of the world with their costly unfolding in time.[67]

This has its roots in Alfred North Whitehead's 'Process Theology', and has blossomed into what is known as Kenosis Theology, with which the name of the great theologian Jürgen Moltmann is closely associated.[68] One argument is that we could not have this wonderful world any other way:

> There are inherent constraints on how even an omnipotent Creator could bring about the existence of a law-like creation that is to be a cosmos, not a chaos, and thus an arena for the free action of self-conscious, reproducing, complex entities and for the coming to be of the fecund variety of living organisms whose existence the Creator delights in.[69]

Whitehead argued that a principle of limitation is required on God's part in order to bring this about.[70] Can it be that the world of beauty and goodness, of groping advance towards a greater awareness and achievement would not be *possible* without an essential limitation that allows and indeed requires all the inadequacy that we call pain and evil? Many modern theologians would claim this must be so, in order to counter the position that otherwise it is all *mere* chance.

Sophisticated theological answers like these are, in the first place, beyond the grasp of the vast majority of humans, *and so are irrelevant to the essence of the question*; and secondly they are purely theoretical, detached from the reality of everyday life. 'All theory, dear friend, is gray, but the golden tree of life springs ever green.'[71]

3. Faith as a response

> This word is hard; who can listen to it?
>
> JOHN 6:60

Some of the central events in the Bible have what we can describe as PC endings. But this disguises their awful meaning. Even Jesus, on a deathbed more terrible than any of us will ever suffer or would hope to witness, could not see *why* as the end approached ('My God, My God, why have you forsaken me?'). But it did not smother his faith ('Into thy hands I commend my spirit').

What are we to make of a God who orders his devotee to kill and then burn the body of his only son as proof of his allegiance? There is a two-fold horror here. There is the horror that Abraham was prepared to kill his son at God's command, and God's last-minute countermand does nothing to alleviate this command. But the greater horror – if they can be compared – is that God did intend for Abraham to be prepared to kill his son – as far as human understanding could divine: this was not just a test. We are deceived by this last-minute reprieve, by the staying of the knife at the last moment.

Søren Kierkegaard tried to square the circle: to reconcile the horror of this order with the goodness of God; but even he could not find language to articulate how this could be justified. By all that is humanly right Abraham should have refused. But the God of the Old Testament – the God of Creation – regularly allows things that are variants of the demand to sacrifice Isaac. For how many Isaacs has there been no redeeming ram caught in a convenient bush? The knife falls every time an innocent child dies in agony because his body is rooted with parasites.

In the end, we have to decide whether we believe that Creation is just an accident, is without ultimate meaning; or that if there is anything like Ultimate Meaning it is powerless to prevent evil, or is in some sense evil itself. It is beyond human comprehension that if god is all-good, all-powerful, all-loving, he could permit the evil and suffering that is built into the very fabric of the world. But perhaps in that very insight we are directed towards an answer. 'Where do atheists and agnostics acquire their often acute sensitivity to injustice, evil, suffering, and death if not from an even deeper experience of ultimate life, fulfilment, and meaning? In short, what provides the grounding for a radical experience of "what ought to be" for those who deny ultimate meaning a priority?'[72]

This, in embryonic form, is the essential message of the Book of Job. All the arguments were rehearsed here, in thirty-seven chapters of theologising, in which God is silent. Only in the last five does he appear, not to answer the charges in a voice of reason and counter-argument, because there is no answer, no justification, on our terms, but to draw us *beyond the argument*. He speaks 'out of the whirlwind', and all he talks about is the awesome wonder and terror of creation, of what he is about in the world, in all its wonder and glory, the horror and the thrill of it all. Here is your answer, he says. I don't need to add anything else by way of *apologia*. He singles out for eloquent discourse the most awe-inspiring animals known in the time of Job: behemoth the hippopotamus 'which I made with thee' and who 'is the chief of the ways of God'; and leviathan the crocodile, 'whose eyes are like the eyelids of the morning ... his heart as firm as a stone; yea, as hard as a piece of the nether millstone. Upon Earth there is not his like, who is made without fear. He beholdeth all high things: he is a king over all the children of pride.'[73]

To behemoth and leviathan we add awareness of the tens of millions of others, of whose lives we know something in our day. Beside our vastly expanded appreciation of the cosmos, of Earth, of the living world, of ourselves, the understanding of the age of Job is that of a child: and still what we know is the tiniest fraction of what is to be known. We know something of the wonder of the lives of whale and owl, caddis-worm and orchid, but of the great majority we know next to nothing: Arynchobdellida, Pogonophora, Chaetognatha, Eutardigrada, Loricifera, Paracanthoptrygii to name half a dozen at random.[74]

Proponents of the Great Chain of Being engaged with the problem in their own way. One way was to redefine evil as good, to see it as an inevitable consequence of the inherent structure of creation. It's just that we humans, so deficient in intellect, can't see how this works. The perfection of the Universal System as a whole 'in no way implied either the happiness or the excellence of the finite parts of the system':

> On the contrary, the fundamental and characteristic premise of the usual proof of optimism was the proposition that the perfection of the whole depends upon, indeed consists in, the existence of every possible degree of imperfection in the parts ... The essence of the optimist's enterprise was to find the evidence of the 'goodness' of the universe not in the paucity but rather in the multiplicity of what to the unphilosophic mind appeared to be evils.[75]

Some 'Great Chain' theologians attempted to explain the existence of evil and suffering, the evident insufficiency of the world, by arguing that God needs every imperfection in order for creation to be *complete*. For William King, the evils of existence are 'not only consistent with infinite wisdom, goodness and power, but necessarily resulting from them'.[76] King classified evils into three categories: evils of limitation or imperfection, 'natural' evils, and moral evils. He and his followers ingeniously argued that because God was infinitely good, all creatures must be less than God to varying degrees, and in this deprivation could be considered an 'evil'. If anything is to exist at all, it must be imperfect, and so be 'evil' in this sense. And since (for whatever divine reason) every possible essence is to be given existence, each according to its own kind, it is inevitable that every conceivable defect will be part of the picture. 'I am persuaded that there is something in the abstract nature of pain conducive to pleasure,' wrote Soame Jenyns; for example, 'that the sufferings of individuals are absolutely necessary to universal happiness.'[77] Spinoza was perhaps the most articulate and optimistic proponent of this notion (satirised by Voltaire in *Candide*). This is a variant of the argument for evil as 'a necessity inhering in the nature of things'.

4. There is a principle of evil alongside a principle of good

Evil in all its manifestations is so pervasive in history, and pain and suffering throughout creation, that the *dualism* of certain forms of Gnosticism and Manichaean reflection appear more convincing than monism. As well as the God who was the origin of all that is good and beautiful in the world there must also be a divinity that is the source of evil.[78] Manichaeism believed that matter and spirit had separate origins in distinct evil and good divine principles. It developed in third-century Persia, and incorporated strands of Christianity, Gnosticism, Buddhism and Zoroastrianism. Gnosticism also held that the material world was inherently evil, and escape could only be achieved through adherence to esoteric practices and concepts. Buddhism *evades* the problem of suffering by disengaging. We must accept that this is the way of things, and learn to detach ourselves.

The Manichean heresy was vigorously opposed and persecuted by the official church, but it lingered on into the sixth century. The existence of the Devil and his angels supplied a doctrinally acceptable variant of this idea: immensely powerful spirits, but creatures themselves and subordinate to God. The central theological concepts of heaven and hell, the Fall, and the Incarnation of Christ were – and continue to be – inextricably bound up with the attempt to provide a solution to this most profound dilemma.

Evil and turning a blind eye

We probably don't like to think there's much of a parallel between Sodom and Gomorrah and ourselves today, partly because we don't want anything to do with that vengeful God, faith in whom we can now rightly regard as idolatry. And partly because, again rightly enough, we don't see ourselves as 'wicked and sinners before the Lord exceedingly'. But the parallels are clear enough. We live our lives as though autonomous from the Earth and its balances and limits. Are there enough Good Men to turn the anger of 'the Ultimate One' aside: to steer us away from the brink?

The people of Sodom and Gomorrah are to us figures of caricature, of myth. But they were folk like us, with our priorities and ambitions, our concerns and fears. The legend of the now proverbial cities of sin hinges upon a conception of a God we now rightly reject as idolatrous, but it can be recast for our day. We go through life as though we have every right to use and abuse the Earth as we choose in our fickle way. It was an environmental catastrophe, one they were powerless to prevent, that destroyed the cities of Sodom and Gomorrah. We stand on the brink of environmental catastrophe orders of magnitude greater than that which befell them: but it is within our power today to so adjust our lives that we can live in harmony with such events: which are, in truth, normal episodes in the way the Earth works.

There may be little 'malice aforethought' in us – and who knows, maybe there was little enough of it in Sodom and Gomorrah: but so was – is – much else not aforethought. And who can avoid wondering how different we are, when people worldwide spend 50 per cent more on cosmetics than would be needed to provide all the women in the world with reproductive health care; when it would take £19 billion to eliminate hunger and malnutrition and people in the US and Europe spend $17 billion on pet food. Every year $14 billion is spent on ocean cruises; it would take $10 billion to provide clean water for everyone on Earth. ('Pride, greed and envy [deadly sins] are the engines that drive our modern economy.'[79])

Not divine failure but human failure

A different perspective on the problem of evil is to blame not divine failure but our human failure to control and counter its influence in society. This as I understand it is a perspective taken in Jewish theology: 'Since Auschwitz, of course, we have often asked where God was at that time, but our Jewish friends tell us that is a wrong question to ask; it is God who asks us: Adam, where were you? He asks man: What have you done with your history? Well, what have we done with our history?' 'God's name was blessed in those absurd circumstances [of Auschwitz] in which it was impossible for people to say a meaningful word!'[80]

Heresy

Sometimes it may be a long time before the glimmer of truth enfolded in embryonic form in a 'heretical' doctrine is allowed burst into flame, shedding its light and warmth on the darkness and cold of a doctrine within whose orthodoxy it had been smothered hitherto. There is no better example perhaps than the condemnation of the teaching of the Celtic monk Pelagius (AD c. 360-420), against whose essential humanism Augustine fulminated so vociferously; for Augustine, we are so fallen and depraved we are powerless to save our souls without God's intervention. For Pelagius the life and death of Jesus were not a sacrifice somehow demanded by a vengeful God to atone for an Original Sin of our First Parents, but were exemplary: the model for the fuller human life God wants of us. The teaching of Pelagius was condemned first of all by the Council of Carthage in 418 and that of Ephesus in 431. It survived in a somewhat attenuated form in Gaul and the islands of Britain and Ireland.

For all that, unknown to us, we are all Pelagians today. Hell has retreated into the doctrinal wings. Had Pelagius' views on such fundamental preoccupations as predestination, free will and the nature of Grace prevailed over the mainstream thunderings of Augustine, the subsequent history of Europe might have been different.

Outgrowing our child's notion of God

The more deeply we understand the workings of the universe, in particular the living world and especially the human mind and spirit, the more denial of Ultimate Purpose appears ever more hollow and trivial. But in parallel with that growing awareness of the Divine is a growing awareness of the triviality and inadequacy of our earlier conceptions. Atheism – the refusal to believe in the smaller gods at the heart of outmoded beliefs – is a first step towards a less immature conception. However, it is often accompanied by a militancy that attacks the cultural frameworks within which the flickering flame of our now outmoded human formulations were housed, rather than understanding itself as the modern Dark Night of the Soul in which the Real Distance between God and myself takes hold of me, and I am confronted with the challenge of the *unum necessarium*.[81] It enables me to understand and accept what the core of Jesus' saying is: give away everything that seems precious and indispensable to you and jump to affirm in my deepest heart that acceptance of the Divine is not conditional on my human understanding, is not refused because 'what God has in store' is beyond comprehension, but outside of it, and it cannot be contained in human concepts utterly limited by animal capacity. Thus, in saying that there is no 'afterlife' I am denying no more than my ability to conceive what lies behind the bewildered intuition struggling for words.

Our capacity to understand and picture cause and effect is limited by our biological limitations. The intellectual superstructures of our philosophical and theological systems are not really explanations. They are more in the nature of verbal dreamcatchers, interconnected strands of thought that we cast like nets upon the vast sea of experience.

In a recent book Christian de Duve summarises the view that personal belief about the existence or non-existence of God is, in the last resort, subjective, not objective, 'however fiercely argued and rationalised on both sides'.[82] There is of course a subjective element to 'belief' in God: but this 'belief' also has an object; so although this 'object' defies human conceptualisation it is embodied in what we experience, and 'belief' is the appropriate intuitive response. It is critically important that our response be grounded in the reality that science uncovers in ever-greater detail, but it is not the *measurement* we are responding to. It is the *embodied reality* of which the measurement provides coordinates and parameters. The measured 'objective' embodies nothing of the new existential reality embodied in the successive levels of increasing complexity that evolution produces, which is only accessible to us 'subjectively'.

The way forward?

Because we see its inadequacies, it is a mistake to assume that by abandoning the religious culture and tradition in which we were nourished, a better one will automatically take its place, made up of bright new ideas and concepts, values and practices we have gathered together from other cultural traditions not our own, all held together in a mesmerising but incoherent mesh of technological capacities. 'It is an error to believe,' wrote Konrad Lorenz, 'that after the form and content of an old culture are thrown overboard a new and better, ready-made one will quite naturally be brought into being to take its place instantaneously.'[83]

What has not kept pace with our scientific understanding of all this is an overarching *Weltanschauung* that is intellectually commensurate with that broadening and deepening in our understanding. Many feel no need to work at the development of such an overview because there is thought to be no overarching purpose that requires them to do so: the progress in our understanding of how things work is sufficient in itself: although the 'scientific' understanding of how things work is only a snapshot in time, it tells us nothing meaningful about *what is in process*: it sees no Pilgrim's Progress towards 'salvation'. What salvation there is is seen to lie in the increasing control the advance of science gives us over our lives and our destinies, and our deepest fulfilment is to be found in the application of our talents to that end.

The religious systems that earlier provided direction are seen as being up to the task no longer, and as incapable of growing in order to do so without metamorphism. We cannot use religious concepts, ideas, categories that developed out of a cosmology, a biology, a psychology, that we have left behind, that we have advanced beyond. This does not mean we cannot construct such a conceptual edifice, but that our new concepts and categories must be commensurate with our more advanced and developed understanding. 'Many of our past convictions may prove to be assumptions.'[84] *Ecclesia semper reformanda.*[85]

Eternal life

As man conceives his heaven, so he conceives his God.

LUDWIG FEUERBACH

'What resurrection means in the concrete is not seriously imaginable to us who still live within the time-space grid of our known universe,' write Elizabeth Johnson.[86] This however does not prevent theologians expounding its meaning at great length, and what follows is only more of the same. The 'resurrection of the body' is central to Christian faith. But what can *eternal* life mean? A basic understanding of biology shows us that it cannot mean the survival of our physical body, nor indeed does Christian theology intend it to, because it speaks of a 'glorified' body informed by a soul, whatever that can mean. According to Christian faith, what lives on is the soul, the spiritual essence, but corporeal in some sense beyond our comprehension.

The simple conception of individual corporeal survival stands at one end of the pendulum of belief in what lies beyond death; at the opposite end is a belief that finds expression in outright denial: nothing of us survives. For many there is a liberation that comes with letting go the expectation of 'eternal life' conceived in the narrow biological sense. It enables us to concentrate with greater attention and appreciation on the life of the short years given to us. In between these two poles all certainty fades, as any possible meaning in the words and concepts we must use drains away: words such as sur*vive*, no*thing*. At the point of swing furthest from either end in this pendulum of belief nothing remains but *faith*, the purity of faith for which Søren Kierkegaard struggled to find words: faith that is free of the need for these 'certainties' at one or other end of the spectrum. Genuine faith, as he saw it, can only come in the face of radical uncertainty. All other theological or atheistic pronouncements lie somewhere on either side of this fulcrum of swing.

Mesopotamian and early Judaic thought seems not to have needed the assistance of resurrection, or feared eternal judgement on some 'last day'. It clearly rebukes a belief in immortality that can be seen as springing merely from fear or wish-fulfilment. 'From the author of *The Epic of Gilgamesh* to Nietzsche there is a line of thought, often submerged, which holds that a belief in immortality contradicts the values that make an admirable human life possible, and should be regarded with contempt. It is a philosophy that radically opposes much that springs from late Judaism, Christianity and Islam.'[87] Amalric of Bena (c. 1200) did not believe in bodily resurrection. 'He who has the knowledge of God in himself has paradise within him.' He also believed in progressive historical revelation and a lot of other stuff that would have taken him to an early and unpleasant end in a later century.[88] Among modern theologians Charles Hartshorne rejects outright the notion of a subjective afterlife.

Regarding the future of human individuals, Whitehead declares himself 'entirely neutral on the question of immortality', allowing that 'in some important sense the existence of the soul may be freed from its dependence on the body'. Although individuals do not continue to be actual, they 'live on' in God, progressively perfected as their contributions to the world are appropriated by subsequent actualities in ways that increasingly exemplify the ideals of primordial nature.[89] John Cobb and David Griffin leave this issue open in *Process Theology*. Cobb later argues for the resurrection of the soul as a kind of existence without an earthly organism. Griffin has developed a similar case.[90] Hope, against all the odds, is born in us of this faith.

The promise of eternal life cannot be contained in the vessel of human conceptualisation or imagining. We don't have the capacity to conceive or imagine what it could mean, any more than we have the capacity to comprehend elementary particles. But that promise is contained in the totality of the Unfolding and in what it points to, and our child's babbling is, indeed, a first baby step in its direction.

> Hope is the thing with feathers,
> That perches in the soul,
> And sings the tune without the words,
> And never stops at all.[91]

We should never try to disabuse others of a belief – or a lack of belief – we consider to be immature in this regard, however we may encourage in them a faith that has no need of this reassurance. The distance between all our positions, as Thomas Aquinas once remarked, is infinitesimal compared to the distance between all our 'positions' and the Mind of God.[92] When asked on one occasion what hope there was for ordinary people if salvation depended on understanding the arguments he was making in his brilliant lectures and books, he replied that the distance between himself and the old woman in the pew is as nothing compared with the distance between all of us and God.

How can our love of God be unconditional – love of God for his own sake as we used to put it – if it depends on an 'afterlife' that merely ties us to this biological life, with all its biological limitations? The great prayer of Archbishop Fénelon is the only prayer. 'Lord, I do not know where I am going.' All I know is that there is an all-encompassing journey afoot, this unfolding efflorescence of the possibility of being, in which I am a spark of unique consciousness. Without this resignation I cannot truly shine. I need make no demands. I am only free to be myself when I can let go of the desire that ties me to demand. (In this I can perhaps be at one with my Buddhist brother.) For Fénelon, self-interest must be excluded from our love of God, for self-love is the root of all evil. Much self-love is mixed up with the early stages of the mystical 'ascent'. In the 'purgative life' love is mixed with the fear of hell; in the 'illuminative' with the hope of heaven. Even Augustine (for all his Neoplatonism) was flummoxed by what or where Heaven could be.[93]

Girded about and armoured within the certainties of an older interpretation people were prepared to devote their lives to the service of God: a God defined within the lived experience of their particular culture, with all its reinforcing richness and reassurance. The progress of scientific understanding has given altogether new depths to our human intuition of what ultimate reality is about, forcing new interpretations of the mythological nature of the stories that underpin our inherited religious traditions. But it has also undermined a *literal* interpretation of foundational concepts without which, it would appear, there is no longer any reason to devote our lives so single-mindedly to God – to the pursuit of goodness, truth and beauty in the world – or the promotion of diversity, unity and individuality: all those things evolution *is about*.

But what this also does is to lay bare our motives. I am prepared to forego pleasure (or whatever) in 'this' life because I look forward to compensation in the 'next'. My interpretation of this is purely materialistic, and if the same science that underpins the Good Life we enjoy or hope and struggle to enjoy in a future this side of the grave tells me that such an interpretation is rationally untenable, why should I forego anything? Why should I devote my life to the service of others for instance rather than attend to myself?

My genetic continuation in my descendants or the survival of my life's work through my achievements constitutes a sort of minimalist interpretation of survival after death. But clearly this is not what is meant by 'life after death' in the way we usually mean. It fudges the issue. It is evasive also to talk about the way my body changes as I get older; the body I 'inhabit' now is not the body I inhabited ten, twenty years ago. This particular body, in other words, is not an essential part of who I am. No matter what I believe, I know death will bring about a radical change of some sort. As I approach death my body may be diseased and old. How will I get up the stairs in heaven with my knees the way they are? Where will I do the shopping? If I believe literally that there will be a posse of virgins lined up waiting for me inside the Pearly Gates I have let go of that critical faculty that is the most essentially human thing in me, and the religious context that nurtures such an idea in me is deficient. My conversation with God in prayer is not the conversation of a child. It begins as such, but when I grow up, as St Paul reminds us, I put off the things of a child, and reason comes into play, eventually taking its place at the centre of the conversation. 'Prayer is a conversation of *nous* with God,' wrote the fourth-century theologian Evagrius of Pontus: not just any conversation in other words, but a conversation that involves the mind's highest activity.[94]

'God begets His only-begotten Son in the highest part of the soul,' wrote Meister Eckhart.

There are theologians who see in the fundamental physical make-up of the universe the possibility of a material embodiment of the Spirit that I Am in an eternity out of time and space. If that is so, I can have no idea, no conception, of what it means. 'Eye hath not seen,' indeed, even if that was not what Paul of Tarsus was thinking of. If Paul's words mean what we would like them to mean, they call for a radical agnosticism. But in fact this is not what he meant. It's really on the same level as, 'You have no idea how good this party is going to be.' Whereas, actually, you *can* have no idea.

If I really believe in God, in the Ultimate Purpose reason discerns in the unfolding creation, reinforcing my own deepest intuition, then I will trust that whatever happens to me is the way it should happen in order to be in best harmony with God's purpose in creation: is better than any alternative of which I can conceive. I know – in the way that science knows – that my body will disintegrate after my death, and I know that my spirit, my personality, depends on that embodiment in the way a flame depends upon the candle. I cannot conceive of any way in which it could survive that disintegration. However, so limited is our human understanding of the basic nature of reality – a limitation of which we become more aware the more deeply we understand – the more we must acknowledge that we do not know what is ultimately possible, and if holding onto a concept of life after death framed in the material terms of heaven, nirvana or reincarnation helps us to live our lives as we ought, then let us do so, knowing it for the metaphor it is.

This is the essence of quietism. Quietism is, at heart, the Taoist philosophy of *wu-wei*: not interfering in the course of events, thereby acting against *li* – the grain in wood, the lines of cleavage in crystals, the fibre of muscle, and yet at the same time being fully alert and participatory. *Li* is the natural order, the force within, behind the unfolding, the development of the Story. It is what we see made manifest in the Quintessence, the fuse that drives the flower. A form of Quietism very similar to this can be detected in the writings of Martin Luther: 'Faith does not require information, knowledge and certainty, but a free surrender and joyful bet on his unfelt, untried and unknown goodness.'[95]

This is what it is to love God for his own sake, to do what is good, to admire what is beautiful, to thirst after knowledge because we find the embodiment of God in these dimensions of reality. And while our image of one following the Way is the religious person, it is equally to be seen in the scientist straining to understand a particular corner of the working of the world (Johannes Kepler: 'I have followed with sweat and panting the footsteps of the Creator.'[96]), the painter struggling to freeze the mystical beauty of the moment, or in the dedication of a nurse taking the hand of the sick or dying: not, essentially, in the hope or expectation of reward, but for the sake of goodness, beauty, truth in themselves. This is enough. I do not need to know beyond this. Where it is coming from enfolds me, makes me a part of it. In this participation in goodness, beauty and truth I am in the presence of God, God is *in* me.

When I free myself from the chimera that I will continue unchanged after death I am freed to be truly virtuous. Now I strive after truth, beauty and goodness not because I will be rewarded, but because in doing so I am in harmony with Ultimate Purpose: because I love God for his own sake. I still live in hope, but the distinction between faith and hope is a fine one, easily lost sight of when it becomes wrapped up in theology. In hope is the confidence that *I matter* in the context of the unfolding universe in the way I matter to myself or to those who see the best in me, and that this best will be somehow – I cannot know how – enfolded into the future.

God's hand is extended to us at every moment, waiting to touch us at the limit of our upward reach: not in any generic sense, but for me specifically. I touch him in the exercise of my life's effort to be the best I am capable of becoming. The nexus of my touching the finger of God is not defined in space, by the height in inches my reach extends to, nor in time, but in the *effort*, the nature and level of which are determined for me uniquely by my physical, mental, psychological, genetic and spiritual endowment. If God's touch takes the form of visions, it is because seeing visions comes with my psychological endowment. But equally it may come through my capacity to exult in poetry or in the beauty of a mathematical formula, in dance or engineering or on the field of play or caring for the sick or fearful, or through contemplating the life of snails or sea-urchins.

The reality is greater, bigger, more complex, more diverse than we ever knew or suspected: or could have suspected. But our sense of what the Greatness/Infinity behind it all can mean can of necessity be no more than a thin membrane surrounding all this experience of ours. This forces us to expand that enclosing conceptual shell, and in doing so we develop a less inadequate grasp of what *infinity* is all about.

Many theologians, in attempting to come to terms with these new concepts of emergence and incarnation, look to the past and re-employ the older concepts and language that have become so much a part of their very being they cannot think outside of the framework they provide. But this explodes the framework. 'No one puts new wine into old wineskins.'[97]

> For last year's words belong to last year's language
> And next year's words await another voice.[98]

CHAPTER 7

LIVING AS PART
OF THE WHOLE

> Reflection on experience in the round sharpens awareness of a bottomless mystery, the most appropriate responses to which are awe, gratitude and a heightened sense of ethical imperatives.
>
> RUPERT SHORTT (2016), *GOD IS NO THING*, P. 23

A recurring theme in the old *Lives of the Irish Saints* is the quest to discover the places where God wanted them to establish their monasteries and hermitages. This was never to be just *any* place, so the search is often accompanied by magical or mystical pointers. For example, Ciarán of Saighir will know that he has reached the appointed place when the bell in his satchel (given to him for this purpose by St Patrick in Rome) will sound of its own accord.[1] In an earlier book I talked about the way in which we are made by our evolution to relate intimately to one place, or to one place at a time, for a time sufficient for my relationship with it to unfold and develop in a mutually enhancing way, a place 'with which we are commensurate, of such size that we can get to know and relate to it, and feel we have taken root':

> My life is not lived among the stars or in the realms of the quarks, even though my mind can wander there and be enriched by that exploration. My life is lived in a particular place in a particular corner of the Earth, on a scale that is defined by my biological nature. My ability to travel beyond the horizon merely expands my understanding of the space it defines.
>
> This is the place in which I encounter reality. It is where I come to understand what neighbour and neighbourhood means. It is where I get to experience community. It is where I encounter the other lives that lead me to contemplation of God's creation. It is what nurtures me physically (providing my food and

shelter) as well as emotionally and spiritually – or it used to, before globalisation and modernity began to dissolve the sinews that bound us together and we have found ourselves drifting into our modern placelessness.[2]

Faraway hills are greener only from a distance. 'The elements of true wealth come with the maintenance of a home.' This is not only the place I am meant to settle down in and be satisfied with. It is the place where I can discover myself, in which I can come to see and develop those qualities and abilities within myself that are the most distinctively essential things about me: *here and now*, and not beyond the horizons of space or time, of the parish or of the world, or of my own being, is where I may find eternal life.[3]

This is the place I am *meant* to be. And the chosen spot is often referred to not only in terms of where the monastery itself is to be, but as the place of the saint's *resurrection*. There is another story in the medieval *Lives of the Irish Saints* that tells how when St Fiontan was on his quest for a suitable place to build his church, his journey took him and his companions over Slieve Bloom; and when they paused on top of the mountain to look back southwards, they could see a flock of angels hovering over Clonenagh, which St Colmcille (who was one of the expedition) told Fiontan was a sign that this to be the place of his resurrection. So back he went to found his famous monastery there.

Loss of appreciation

We build the human infrastructure of our world from the raw materials the Earth provides – stone, metal and fibre, and all the sophisticated derivatives thereof – and within that construction we live our lives. We weave it into earlier constructions, retaining much, but often replacing much with our own. But all our human constructions are set into the unconstructed matrix of *creation*.

In earlier times the necessities and luxuries of life were won as a result of a great deal of effort, and this effort counted for much in the way such goods were appreciated: whether food or fuel, clothing or utensils, housing or the infrastructure needed in the functioning of community. The variety of things used was regulated to a large extent by consideration of their usefulness. Only where this was considered appropriate was there extravagance – as it might be in ritual for example. In the beginning all these things had to be produced *directly*, but as society became more complex and roles more specialised, there might be one or more intermediaries between producer and consumer: but they remained *connected*, so that the community as a whole, and each individual within it, continued to appreciate the cost in time and effort and skill. And because people lived close to their crops and herds (even when residing in towns) they were *aware* of this human grounding in the Earth's productivity, and of its limits. The gods they envisioned as the guarantors of nature's bounty might fail to deliver: crops might fail or herd animals sicken; or the violence and selfishness of our animal inheritance – the failure of virtue to triumph – bring about war, famine and destruction.

That appreciation influenced the care with which the things used in everyday life were treated. There was little deliberate waste, and things continued to be used as long as they could do what they were made for.

Today, it is not just that we have more than we need: we are enmeshed in a *superfluity* of having. We don't know where the food on our table, or the clothes and shoes we wear, the tools we use, come from, what environmental costs or what issues of justice are involved in their production. Because our labour, or the labour of people we know, is not involved in their production, our appreciation, our care in their use, are less than they might be.

We know next to nothing about the things we use. In earlier cultures tools were handed on from one generation to the next, and there was an awareness of all the generations of hands that have used them and given thanks for them. We would hardly know where to start even with such simple things as plastic packaging or crisp bags. Take for example the plastic container in which our bottled water comes. Do I know what it is made from, where it is made or by whom, the technology involved, how much energy is required in its manufacture? Regulations now oblige us to give thought to what happens to it when we are finished with it, but it all comes to us so easily, so cheaply, with such a plethora of other goods, that it is difficult for us to fully appreciate all the things we have, too difficult to be properly *grateful* for them.

So much for the crisp bag or chocolate wrapper. More complex goods like cars, television, computers, mobile phones are altogether beyond the understanding and control of all but a tiny few of us, never mind that we have no idea what the hundreds of components of which they are made are or where they come from, what is involved in the shaping of them, or the wonder of the physics and chemistry involved in the way these components work together to perform their functions.

The kingdom is at our door, beyond the threshold and within, but only if we can be present to our experience of the reality about us. There has never been a time when this has been more difficult (and yet, paradoxically, filled with such opportunity): when we are so distracted from the ordinary. But we cannot be extra-ordinary, we cannot experience the extra-ordinary, without appreciating the ordinary in which our life is moulded, through which our personality develops. 'Ordinary' is itself a word that is anything but 'ordinary'. It has its abandoned roots in the Latin *ordo*, order, referring to things that fit together in the right place, that relate to each other as they are meant to. We can discern this attempt to find God in the ordinary in the way Jesus (who is the ultimate example of the extraordinary enmeshed in and born out of the ordinary) struggles in his parables to catch something of it. The 'kingdom' is a farmer in his field; it is a woman baking.

Breaking the bond with place

We have everything we need; most of the time we can get everything we want. We often have too much of every thing that is necessary for life. And so we are led to wonder if it is the case that the virtuous behaviour prescribed for an earlier time when the necessities of life were in short supply made virtue of necessity. We had to be frugal so that there would be enough to go round, our living governed by the cardinal virtues so that there might be enough for all, and the Earth's capacity to provide it not strained or compromised. Of course, that prescription was always more honoured in the breach than by observance: those at the top with the power and the resources always taking the lion's share and a subservient majority at the bottom left with whatever minimum it took to sustain the status quo. And whenever the opportunity presented itself, those who among the majority could do so because they were stronger supplanted those in power. Always and in every society it was like this. Every culture was stratified accordingly: there were kings and nobles at the top, justifying their affluence and extravagance with the argument that such privilege was *due* to those who (by divine edict in the most effective arguments) were chosen to rule. There were soldiers to maintain that right. There was the peasant stratum, the great majority forming the supporting base of this other pyramid of numbers. But there was also a fourth stratum, of those ordained to keep watch and to question, to point it out when the deeper order was offended by those 'ordained' to rule.

We no longer have to order our lives – its daily routine, the planning of the seasons – around the need to procure our daily bread. Our life no longer needs to be anchored to the Earth, or at only one or two removes from it, in the old way. Our growing understanding of how the Earth works has enabled us to move away from the need to maintain this local balance, in the development of which over all the centuries the incomparable diversity of local culture, cuisine, language, craft, belief, blossomed. Down tens of centuries people used their ingenuity to acquire the skills to develop those resources to which they did have access to their fullest potential, in the course of doing so developing the great diversified wealth we find in traditional art and craft. From each of the handful of animal species identified as suited to domestication countless breeds were developed, each adapted to the particular geographical circumstances of their custodians. From each of the species of plants discovered to be especially good to eat tens of thousands of different varieties were developed through selective breeding.

Today our food and drink are increasingly produced in fields that are not our fields, by hands we can never know. Seed is increasingly standardised and globalised, no longer tailored over millennia of adaptation and selection to the particularities of each place. The nutrient bottleneck has been broken, and we no longer need to give careful thought to the maintenance of the Earth's fertility at local level.

The revolutionary changes of our time present us with unforeseen challenges, because they have consequences we failed to take into account at the start: in relation to such issues as climate change, resource depletion, pollution, the loss of biodiversity, overpopulation, etc. But there is also the deeper, deeper challenge of affluence: the superabundance of material wealth: a flood, a torrent of things, more than we can get our heads, hearts, souls, spirit around: not proportionate to our *need*, our ability to use them in order to be and to become the individual selves we are meant to be. Somewhere along the way we reached and passed the point of sufficiency: of having access to what each of us needs to become the person we are capable of being – and 'having access to' does not require us to hold everything we need as personal possessions.

The ideal is community self-sufficiency, each of us living our small life to the full, in proportionate space, even when enclosed by the wall of convent or town, monastery or ghetto. The wall should not be an enclosure, to keep the parish, the community, in, but rather the perimeter of a lens that focuses the attention of those whose lives are centred within on the deepest needs of that community. Light from something more Ultimate illuminates the limited goals of everyday living, like the sun shining through an opaque or frosted glass window. True wealth consists in nurturing and cultivating the resources at our intimate disposal, involving *relationship* with all that such a process of cultivation entails, out of an understanding of all the ways the whole contributes to well-being, our own and that of creation.

For much the greatest part of human existence most people have lived lives characterised by deprivation: of *not having*: of limited access to plenty, to more than merely enough. This is one of the hardest challenges, to be content with enough. It seems that our evolution has conditioned us to always want more, in order to shore up against a future with less. Slowly, slowly, the advance of scientific understanding and the evolution of the art and science of good governance have shown us the possibility of *security*: a possibility realised in most parts of the world to varying extents in our time.

In a very short space of time we have moved from want to sufficiency to surfeit. It is good that we no longer have to worry about whether we will have enough to eat or to wear, but the price we pay for this consumerist lifestyle is increasingly burdensome. The surfeit we enjoy is a surfeit not merely of material things and of energy use, but of things and energy bought. We no longer have to earn them by the sweat of our brow, and indeed the notion that there is virtue in labour willingly undertaken is slipping away from us. We want for few of the things that a generation ago constituted luxury.

But this increase in material well-being (I leave to one side the many questions to do with food and production) has not been paralleled by an increase in understanding and appreciation of the world, or a concern for what might be called things of the spirit. In an earlier time you might say there was more room in our lives for things moral and spiritual, but now that we are *full* we have less need of all this.

It has been a giddying progress, but it has not been a pilgrim's progress. We have left something behind, lost it perhaps. A map? With a destination and a route that takes us there from here. Many of us today see no destination, or therefore a purpose in life that defines itself in terms of that destination, and the more 'educated' we are, the less can we conceive of an adequate redefinition. But 'educate' can also mean to lead away, or to lead astray, as well as to lead out and on. It must lead forward, not round in circles.

The religious edifice into which our lives were woven may have had its shortcomings, but it did provide a foundation on which to ground our personal search for meaning, identity, fulfilment and dignity. Once the material well-being necessary to achieving that goal was reached we lost sight of its other dimensions.

So what is wrong with wanting more? Am I not worth it? Am I not entitled to what my neighbours (or some few of them) have? No, not if I am spiritually disposed; not if I believe that love of neighbour is the flickering ethical flame that defines the very essence of being human; and that may in the course of the eons of future time come to generate such a heat of virtue within us as will lift us above our animal instincts, and enable us to govern in its light.

In this light, what we are *entitled* to is the same share of the Earth's resources as every other human being, provided this does not further impoverish the Earth's diversity or compromise its integrity. And even as things stand, our use of energy and material resources is way beyond what is sustainable, or what it needs to be if we are to avoid catastrophic global warming and its consequences.

Global CO_2 levels are now at their highest for fifteen million years. By 2030 the capacity of the atmosphere to absorb carbon dioxide will have reduced from the current figure of 4 billion tonnes a year to 2.7 billion tonnes. In other words, that is the maximum we can afford to emit if we are to maintain equilibrium (in order to keep temperature rise below 2ºC). Dividing this total 'carbon sink' by the number of people, we find that to achieve stabilisation the weight of carbon emissions per person (the *carbon footprint*) per person should be 0.33 tonnes per year.

If the Antarctic and Greenland ice sheets were to melt in their entirety (which may happen), sea level will rise by 80 m. They are already melting faster than we thought. The Antarctic could lose 60 per cent of its ice by 2100; the fastest glacier in the world, in Greenland, has doubled its rate of movement in the last ten years. There is enough meltwater now to rise sea level by nearly 1 mm a year, three times as much as the IPCC have thought up to now.

The carbon footprint of the average western European is about twelve tonnes. For Americans and Australians it is nearly twice that. The global average is about four tonnes per year, but in Africa and India it is just one tonne. The usual target given for what the average *needs* to be is three tonnes: which is still ten times too much. This figure will ultimately have to drop to below one tonne if we are to reach the level where global emissions are low enough to match nature's ability to absorb them (which is maybe 10-20 per cent of today's emissions). And although developed countries are responsible for only half of today's emissions, they are responsible for 80 per cent of what is already there.

It took one hundred and twenty years (1800 to 1920) for world population to grow from one to two billion, and only forty years to reach three billion; but between 1960 and 2000 it doubled: from three to six billion, added a further billion in the following decade, and is expected to reach at least nine billion by 2030. There are 220,000 more of us every day.

In addition to the burgeoning human population there has been a staggering increase in the numbers of farm animals to met our ever-growing carnivorous appetite. There are now 1.4 billion cattle, one billion pigs and sheep and nineteen billion chickens. Ninety-six per cent of all mammals on Earth today are humans or livestock. Wild animals now account for just 4 per cent. Seven in ten of the world's entire bird populations are chickens and other poultry.

In the last fifty years the economy has grown fourfold: but we are content to think of progress as the ability to increase the human population *without commensurate thought* to ensuring the resources for the individual fulfilment of each.

Thirty to 50 per cent of the Earth's land surface is dominated by humans and our domestic animals and agricultural systems, and we consume half the Earth's accessible freshwater. During the twentieth century our use of water resources increased nine-fold, climate emissions rose seventeen-fold. In 2011, the US mined over a billion tonnes of coal, China three times that. Overfishing has grown by a multiple of thirty-five. In 2010, the UK fishing fleet had to work seventeen times harder to net the same amount of fish. More than half the world's coastal fisheries are over-exploited. Of course, this affluence is concentrated to a large extent on our privileged corner of the Earth, but *it is what everyone else aspires to.* But for everyone to enjoy anything like the lifestyle we have we would need the resources of at least three planet Earths.

Such is the footfall of our species on the Earth, the result of the uncontrolled expansion in our numbers and the heedless determination of so many of us to live far beyond what the Earth supports for us; such is our footfall that the great over-arching rainbow that is the diversity of Life on Earth is becoming ever dimmer and narrower. A stunning overall reduction in vertebrate numbers of 60 per cent has been recorded since 1970. The reduction in Central and South America is 89 per cent. Freshwater fish species have declined by 83 per cent in numbers globally since 1970. German research has found that 76 per cent of flying insects have disappeared in the last twenty-five years, due to intensive agriculture. If habitat destruction continues at present rates, half the species of plants and animals on Earth could be either gone or on their way to extinction by the end of this century.

During the next half century it is thought that a full quarter of all species will drop to this level as a result of climate change alone. By the most conservative estimate the rate at which species are disappearing now is a hundred times what it was before humans appeared on Earth: and over the next few decades is set to become at least a thousand times greater.[4]

The area of natural forest destruction is nearly 150,000 square kilometres a year – an area bigger than Denmark: an area the size of ten football fields every minute, most of it in the last one hundred and fifty years. A straight-line extrapolation of this rate means it would be all gone by 2135. It is much higher in some areas. Madagascar (one of the great hotspots of biological diversity) has lost 93 per cent of its forest cover. The Atlantic forest coast of Brazil is 99 per cent gone. The forests of most of the islands of Polynesia and the Caribbean are gone altogether. The measure of their loss is incalculable: in terms of the materials they provide us with: timber and food and medicine, their contribution to the functioning and integrity of ecological processes or climatic balances, perhaps in terms of their possible genetic contribution to our future well-being.

The conservation argument is based in large measure on our human dependence on nature's instrumental value for us. We depend on it for food; living organisms play key roles in the regulation and maintenance of Earth's life-support systems such as those of the atmosphere, oceans, soil, nutrient cycling, etc. This instrumental value is sometimes discussed in terms of four arguments. There is the *Silo Argument*: we need to look after living organisms because they are useful to us (including organisms whose value in this regard we have not yet discovered but may do so in time). The *Laboratory Argument* is a corollary of this; we need to look after organisms because of their value in experimentation that will yield further insights into how they may better serve our human interest. The *Gymnasium Argument* emphasises the recreational value nature has for us, and the *Cathedral Argument* its aesthetic value.[5]

In the religious tradition of Europe the tendency to see nature as nothing more than the stage on which the human drama is being performed has dominated. In modern times process theology, which is deeply rooted in the evolutionary perspective, is a radical and influential breakthrough, but its influence on mainstream religious instruction or religious education and training at all levels, has been minimal so far.

Our desire to know more about the natural world is to a large extent driven by our wish to dominate the rest of the creation, and traditional interpretations of the Book of Genesis would appear to provide powerful justification for this. But the more deeply the advance of human understanding progresses, the more clearly we begin to see that we have been looking at nature from the back, as it were, or through frosted glass and from a distance. We have traced some of the lines of enquiry that most powerfully influence this deeper way of seeing which is beginning to slowly infuse our entire viewpoint: though a majority of those who raise their voice in both the halls of science and of religion are blinded in a serious way by an astigmatism and colour blindness caused by the way their progress over these many centuries has been accompanied by a fascination with the reductionist viewpoint. But: the infusion is, however slowly, taking place; and we must hope that in the fullness of time it will transform what, with the maturing of both science and religion, will be an outlook in common. This is part of what we mean (in the theological sense) by the cardinal virtue of Hope.

A call to action

We have reached a point in the history of the Earth where two critical developments have come together. On the one hand, our growing scientific understanding has given us an *appreciation* of the utterly marvellous creation that trees embody, the mesmerisingly complex and diverse ecosystems their woods and forests constitute, in ways no people before us could have had: and a deeper *awareness* of the values they represent: utilitarian, psychological, spiritual. And yet, as our understanding has grown, our *appreciation* has diminished, our sense of what their worth is.

However, to date less than 5 per cent of people have made substantial changes to the way they live. Everyone is waiting for everyone else to act. Global warming and over-exploitation of the Earth's resources cannot be reined in unless we persuade the government to force us to change the way we live.

It is extraordinary: we are wrecking the Earth, as burglars will sometimes wantonly wreck a house. It is a strange and terrible moment in history. We who ourselves depend upon it utterly are laying waste to the biosphere, the thin, planet-encircling envelope of life, rushing to degrade the atmosphere above and the ocean below and the soil at the centre and everything it supports; grabbing it, ripping it, scattering it, tearing at it, torching it, slashing at it, shitting on it. Already more than half the rain-forests are gone, pesticide use has decimated wild flowers and the insect populations of farmland and rivers, the beds of the seas are deeply degraded and most of the fish stocks are at danger levels, the acidity of the ocean is steadily rising, coral reefs are under multiple assault, 40 billion tonnes of climate-changing carbon are loading the atmosphere every year, and currently one-fifth, and rising, of all vertebrates – mammals, birds, fish, reptiles, and amphibians – are threatened with extinction. Many are on the brink, if not already gone.[6]

Living in community

The truly ethical life is a life in which you encounter yourself as one person among others, all equally real. This means that the legitimate interests of others, insofar as you can anticipate them, will figure on a par with your own legitimate interests in your practical reasoning – that is, in your reasoning as to what you should do and what you should prefer to happen.

MARK JOHNSTON (2009), *SAVING GOD*, P. 90

We can trace in the history of mankind the gradual development of the realisation that compassion and empathy are the root of morality, and in the broader history of civilisation the awakening and extension of the conditions in society that would foster its growth.[7] The core ethical insight at the heart of all the great religions is that my brother is as important as I am (in the eyes of God). The driving force of the virtuous life is the call to live our lives knowing that every other person values him/herself as much as I value myself.[8]

The deepened grasp of relationship that our understanding of evolution makes possible and necessary provides the scientific underpinning – the rational *ground* – that situates the growth of the empathy in which virtuous practice takes root in the direct line of that evolution. But this awareness needs to take over our lives – to flower as *virtue* – if we are to carry it forward as we are meant to do.[9]

Community sustainability: remaining in control

Technology is the application of the understanding of science to making life easier for ourselves by multiplying the power of physical effort. Early on this consists in making tools – and weapons – of wood, clay and metal (the few metals we could mine and refine): querns and pots, fork and spade, shovel and hoe and plough, ladder and axe, shears and scythe. The invention of the wheelbarrow in the late twelfth century was a breakthrough.

Central to technological progress was the harnessing of the power of animal muscle, and of wind and water. All of this was catapulted onto a different plane with the exploitation of fossil fuels, and onto a different plane again with electronics and the digital manipulation of information in our own day: which depend to a large extent on the parallel, almost un-noticed advance in our understanding of natural materials. But with the wheelbarrow and mill your feet are still on the ground. With multimedia your head is in the clouds and you don't know *where* you are.

In earlier centuries there was *time* for society to accommodate itself to new technologies, to debate and question their use and value, to exercise some control. But while smartphone technology and the internet (including its social media) are inventions of enormous sophistication and value, they have the power to draw us entirely away from encounter with the real world if not used with discernment, and in the hands of most of us they are not used with discernment. We do not appear to possess the wisdom to be able to control this new technology: to integrate it in the service of becoming the mature person I am meant to be, of shaping a society that is the best it can be. But when made to serve in this way not only does it have the capacity to contribute enormously to human progress, but it is perhaps essential to it.

Are not these [technological wizardries] in one sense mere parlor tricks compared with our utter ineptitude in keeping land fit to live upon?[10]

The question of *control*, the possibility that human potential might be distorted or misdirected as a result of this takeover, was never raised when these technologies were first introduced: because what has driven the modern technological revolution is profit. Now, however, the genie is out of the digital bottle. Although we would want to distance ourselves from the Victorian presumption and undertones it contains, there is an inkling of this reservation in something Alfred Wallace wrote in 1864. In the West, he wrote, the 'marvellous developments and vast practical results of science' had been given to societies 'too low morally and intellectually to know how to make the best use of them'. At least on the surface, he thought, natural selection seemed to be advancing the mediocre, if not the 'low': at least if measured in terms of worldly success and increase in numbers. In spite of this, however, he did believe it was responsible for an underlying intellectual and moral advance.[11]

The myth of Lucifer has always been relevant, but never as relevant as it is today. The essential point at the heart of it is that creatures become so aware of their brilliance (how brightly they shine is what the word means: Lucifer's own name means 'carrier of light') that their focus contracts to the sort of navel-gazing that dominates our modern day-to-day encounter with reality, and we can think, in our philosophy as in our shopping, that we're worth it. But this is to *reduce* our true worth: my worth, the worth of those I love, to what can be measured in Euro and fashion: when under different circumstances the *central purpose* of the new technologies might have been to enable me to become the unique person I am capable of becoming.

The virtue of *poverty* does not oblige us to forego the use of useful things, but it does enjoin on us to be discriminating between things that are of use and those that are use-less; and to be appreciative of the beauty and human achievement involved in the making of the things we use, to be always in control of their use, and responsible in relation to all the issues of human and environmental justice and sustainability involved. This is what it means to be poor in spirit. We find ourselves faced with a challenge comparable to that brought about by the application of our understanding of the nature of the atomic nucleus to human ends, except that this new challenge is on an intimate, personal scale that affects the life and direction of everyone at every moment.

We need to be careful when we say we identify with Pope Francis and his Poor Church. The lift out of poverty does not mean setting everybody on lower rings of the same endless Jacob's Ladder of affluence, on the higher rungs of which we are ourselves more comfortably situated (though scarcely content to remain). We have to understand the first Beatitude to mean: blessed *are* the poor in spirit: not because they are now no longer poor, but are poor *in spirit*: content with *enough*, having all they require to live a dignified life but satisfied with that, aware and responsible of the measure Earth can afford each of us – and no more.

The consequences of disproportionate innovation are uncontrollable: in part because they are unforeseeable, and in part because even if foreseen they become uncontrollable beyond a certain tipping point. The attention of younger people is so sucked up by the riches of the cyberworld that they might as well be in prison, so cut off are they from contact with the reality of the real place that is home. They may well be happy in all the ways you can easily measure, but personal contact with the natural and historical environment is fundamental to a richer emotional and intellectual life on all sorts of levels. Natural heritage features in landscape are moorings to which we unconsciously anchor our sense of belonging, being in place, at home: even if that rootedness is something that only matures as we grow older. And the loss or diminution of this is something that has crept up on us, its psychological effects in this regard almost unnoticed although we are increasingly concerned about its effects on fitness and health more generally.

Perhaps the most serious example of this failure to take due account of the consequences of making scientific or technical advance generally available – or even to see them in the first place because the eye is so firmly fixed on the money – is our failure to build into our long-term calculations the disruptive effect on electronic systems of rare, but predictably chronic natural cataclysms. What will happen when we next experience the effects of a major solar storm (or CME: coronal mass ejection)? Solar storms, which are a normal feature of the sun's activity, induce magnetic storms on Earth that can have major disruptive effects on electrical systems. The best known example of such a CME is the Carrington Event that occurred in 1859, which carried an energy surge estimated as the equivalent of two billion 1-megaton H-bombs.[12] It gave rise to spectacular aurorae around the world, even in equatorial latitudes. Another occurred in 1938, causing telegraph systems all over Europe and North America to fail. A similar event occurring today would be incomparably more disruptive, given the degree to which modern life is anchored in advanced technology; it could wipe out power and communications networks worldwide.[13] The cost of such an event occurring today has been estimated at $0.6–2.6 trillion to the United States alone.

CME events of this magnitude occur approximately once every five hundred years, with events at least one-fifth as large occurring several times a century. A CME of comparable magnitude to the Carrington Event occurred in 2012, but it passed Earth's orbit without striking the planet. Less severe storms have occurred in 1921, 1960, and 1989.[14] How well has the advance of science equipped us to withstand such an event or to recover from it? This is an extreme example, but there is a cascade of other reasons tied to a progressively less cataclysmic series of eventualities why we need to maintain at least a measure of agricultural and technological self-sufficiency.

Comparable disruption would be caused by cataclysmic volcanic episodes. According to some estimates, the eruption of Mount Toba in Sumatra seventy-five thousand years ago was three thousand times greater than the

1980 eruption of Mt St Helen's in the United States. The volcanic ash produced reduced average global temperature by 5° Celsius for seven years, triggering a global ice age and (in the view of some) a thousand-year volcanic winter (sulphur dioxide has the opposite effect to a greenhouse gas). Five metres of volcanic ash covered the Indian subcontinent. The human population may have been reduced to ten thousand breeding pairs.[15] This is one of Earth's six supervolcanoes, capable of releasing over one thousand cubic kilometres of material in a single eruption. Some scientists dispute this, claiming much less disruption, but whatever about the detail, eruption of a supervolcano today would wreck the global economy.

Belonging: a deeper level of encounter

In an unpublished essay Aldo Leopold mourned the loss of the vast wilderness areas that had existed in America when the first Europeans arrived, and argued for the preservation in perpetuity of 'the odd bits of wildness which commerce and "development" have regretfully and temporarily left us here and there' as a network of wilderness parks: an argument that would gather momentum and result ultimately in the creation of America's great park network of wilderness places: a 'reaction against the loss of adventure into the unknown which causes the hundreds of thousands to sally forth each year upon little expeditions, afoot, by pack train, or by canoe'.[16] Leopold considered 'the element of Unknown Places' to explore as something essential to the human spirit. Even at the time of writing that essay (1924) there was reason to mourn the way in which this conquest of nature 'has reduced those Unknown Places, one by one, until now there are none left'. Since that time the human population has more than trebled, from two billion to over seven billion today, and wilderness areas have further declined proportionately.

What is it we have lost thereby that is so vital? It is not simply that we need this land to support our ever-growing numbers, or to exploit its resources of timber, minerals or oil for economic gain. It is that the possibility of encounter with the natural world has so diminished as to be well-nigh impossible, at least in the sense of access to areas of large geographical extent; and that this encounter is essentially a spiritual experience. Nowhere else can we encounter the existential reality of the world as it comes from the hand of God: to be opened to what can only come through to us in such places.

How little we know about, or *appreciate*, the lives of the individual species that live together here, interacting to constitute this particular ecosystem. We may know a good deal about the lives of more conspicuous citizens of this wood, this bog, this river – birds or mammals say, or flowering plants – but we still know next to nothing of the lives of the majority of invertebrates, of bryophytes, of fungi. And the more we know the more deeply we are drawn into the wonder of it. In another of his essays Leopold reflected on the limits of our ecological appreciation. He has just been discussing the relationship between bog-birch, deer, grouse, rabbits and white ladyslipper orchids – species of which we know a little – pointing out how much more is going on than our casual inspection reveals.

> The bog-birch is one of hundreds of creatures which the farmer looks at, or steps on, every day ... Disregarding all those species too small or too obscure to be visible to the layman, there are still perhaps five hundred whose lives we might know, but don't. I have translated one little scene out of the life-drama of one species. Each of the five hundred has its own drama. The stage is the farm. The farmer walks among the players in all his daily tasks, but he seldom sees any drama, because he does not understand their language. Neither do I, save for a few lines here and there. Would it add anything to farm life if the farmer learned more of that language? ... There is drama in every bush, if you can see it. When enough men know this, we need fear no indifference to the welfare of bushes, or birds, or soil, or trees. We shall then have no need of the word conservation, for we shall have the thing itself.[17]

How is it then, that in so many of those who are drawn in most deeply, more deeply far than we are it may be, the thrill of the encounter does not flower in the acclaim of worship we call Faith? It is in part because they have not found in religion as they have experienced it (or the theology which purports to be the science of religion) anything that is *commensurate by way of response* to their sensory and intellectual encounter with nature. In this however, they may be closer to the truth than the rest of us, whose immersion in nature's reality may be so much less. Or it may be in part because their personal experience of religion has been superficial. However, we should be careful of taking some comfort in this possibility, because one interpretation of it is that our own conventional spiritual response to the natural world may be profoundly inadequate.

What characterises these 'Unknown Places' is that the species and processes that dominate in them are natural. Here we can encounter the diversity of living things through direct sensory encounter. This sensory encounter evokes a response in us that is initially aesthetic and emotional. That sensory thrill is subsequently magnified by understanding, a progress of augmentation that is well-nigh infinite. It is against the background of encounter with the natural world that the experience of history is to be measured and evaluated, if rules other than those of anthropocentric expediency are to be discovered for the governance of human affairs.

> There can be no doubt that a society rooted in the soil is more stable than one rooted in pavements. Stability seems to vary inversely to the mental distance from fields and woods. The disruptive movements which now threaten the continuity of human culture are born not on the land where the take originates, but in the factories and offices where it is processed and distributed, and in the capitols where the roots of division are written. If courses like this one can decrease our mental distance from the fields and woods, they are worth taking, and worth giving.[18]

Raising community awareness: mapping the parish

> One's native place is the shell of one's soul, and one's church the kernel of that nut.
>
> HILAIRE BELLOC (1902), *THE PATH TO ROME*

The papal encyclical of June 2015 (*Laudato Si'*) marks a turning point in the way the Catholic Church understands the relationship between religion and the environment. It is no longer possible for a 'traditional' Catholic to claim that concern about climate change or environmental degradation, or the New Creation Story are peripheral to Faith, all a bit alternative, like an interest in eastern religions or Celtic spirituality, that it has nothing to do with the life of Jesus. At the stroke of a pen the publication of *Laudato Si'* changes all that:

> The ecological crisis is a summons to profound interior conversion. Living our vocation to be protectors of God's handiwork is essential to a life of virtue; it is not an optional or a secondary aspect of our Christian experience.[19]

Whether or not the encyclical succeeds depends on whether it becomes rooted in the parochial consciousness in a way that facilitates the 'profound interior conversion' for which it calls, and leads to action that is part of an ongoing strategy.

Because this is so much more than a matter of territorial or political definition, it is important for the community of faith to repossess the *place* that is the parish. A valuable and essential first step in the armoury of consciousness-raising in this regard is to cast about it the embrace that is best expressed by the *parish map*. Maps are pictures of the landscape in an international visual language that everyone can read: we all understand them on a basic level because we have, as it were, map-making software in our heads. They have a magnetism to them that is almost magical. We all have maps of strange lands in our brains. Many of the tales of our childhood that enchanted us most had maps. For many of us, the first map we pored over was that of the Holy Land in the book of Bible stories we studied in primary school. For others it might be the map at the front of *Winnie-the-Pooh*, or *Treasure Island*, or the maps of the fascinating make-believe lands of *The Lord of the Rings*.

Where they are available, large-scale Ordnance Survey maps are ideal as base maps for the exercise, but a great advance in recent years is the ready availability for every part of the world of large-scale digital aerial and satellite imagery. The base map is used to identify those areas and land cover types in the parish that are important for biodiversity, the preservation and enhancement of which require action. What exactly is needed, and how can the community facilitate or actively promote this? A particular focus may be placed on parcels of land belonging to or under the influence of the Church. At the same time environmental problems and challenges can be identified and appropriate remedial and enhancement strategies formulated and implemented, keeping in clear sight throughout the need to be alert to the 'preferential option for the poor' so central to *Laudato Si'*. In keeping with Pope Francis' 'appeal to every person living on this planet' and his wish through the encyclical 'to enter into dialogue with all people about our common home', this should be an inter-denominational exercise, involving all the churches and fully open to participation by those with no religious affiliation.[20]

This new map would also show every landscape feature of significance from the perspective of the community's natural, cultural and spiritual heritage. What is available varies enormously from one part of the globe to another, but Ireland is uniquely fortunate in possessing a large-scale map of the entire country on a scale of six inches to a mile that was prepared during the years before the Great Famine (1845-47): a map that is quite simply superb, perhaps the finest map of its kind ever produced.[21] This shows the Irish landscape as it was when the human population was at its peak of eight million: the tide of its impact on the rural landscape was at its greatest, and local resources were used to their fullest extent.[22]

This enables you to identify and locate most of the places which harbour a diverse assemblage of wild plants and animals – the surviving oases of biodiversity that is – and many of the places of special cultural or spiritual meaning: places and things that are part of the legacy we need to hand on to future generations for whom this will be home, and for whose preservation and enhancement therefore we are responsible.

The value of the parish map, whether undertaken as an individual, group or communal exercise, is that it helps to focus attention on the environment for which the believing community is *immediately* responsible: but of course also of necessity that of the rest of the people among whom we live, who are also part of our community, and for whom the exercise is as relevant as it is to us. It is especially valuable where it can be undertaken as an interfaith exercise that is equally open to the involvement of people of no 'faith'. This focusing of attention on place will generate an agenda for action in relation to issues such as biodiversity and conservation, environmental integrity and sufficiency, and infrastructural issues. Many of these are ethical issues ultimately, of concern to the entire concerned community and not just the churches. And it extends beyond this into the realm of aesthetics.

Virtue: the human response

> Dualism, with the harsh asceticism which belongs to it, has given way to a brighter and more hopeful philosophy; men's outlook upon the world is more intelligent, more trustful, more genial; only for those who perversely seek to impose the ethics of selfish individualism upon a world which obeys no such law, science has in reserve a blacker pessimism than ever brooded over the ascetic of the cloister.
>
> WILLIAM RALPH INGE (1899), *CHRISTIAN MYSTICISM*, P. 300

One good reason we hold fast to the faith of our fathers is that it safeguards right behaviour: which is, as it were, sewn into the fabric of faith, and we are afraid that this will leak away if we abandon it. And this, it would appear, is what is happening. For if there is no God watching over us and laying down the rules, why should I behave virtuously? Why should I be hard on myself? Why should I share? Why should I spend my life trying to cultivate virtue? Well, there are good practical reasons of course: because society would collapse otherwise. As long as we have the good fortune to have been born into this age, in a part of the world with Tesco and Walmart, etc., we can be happy in this life; and if we don't have such good fortune, then that's what we must strive for. Isn't it a fair enough deal? Eat and drink, and yes, tomorrow we die, but so what?

Many are discouraged in their faith because they fear it is intellectually compromised, that in fact there can be no God, no afterlife, nothing to call us to account, and so we allow ourselves to be caught up in the things and way of life which the application of science has made possible for us, retreating from the cold, sharp edge where we ask the question: what would You have of me, what is expected of me in light of this creation of which I am part? And virtue gets buried among the ruins.

But, as every creature acclaims, in a metaphorical sense worships, *by its being*, by living the life its evolution has shaped it for: the acclaim to which we are called by virtue of what we are, alone of Earth's creatures not only aware but gifted with the human soul that looks on the world with self-awareness: the acclaim we are called to is the acclaim of virtue. *Virtue* is the disposition and behaviour appropriate to what human being is supposed to be. It is the way through which, as individuals and as a species, we may become what we are meant to be and fulfil our role in the unfolding cosmos. Virtue is what our evolution calls us to, if you like. It is for soldiers, politicians, bricklayers and taxi drivers as much as for nuns, priests, mullahs and atheists. It is, in a wonderful phrase of Thomas Aquinas, *ultimum potentiae*: the absolute best we are capable of as human beings.[23]

This is really important, this grounding of ethical behaviour, of virtue, in the evolutionary process itself: not as an arbitrary set of rules grounded in human society's self-interest. *The trajectory of evolution runs through reason (embodied in mind) and through virtue (as soul)*. Where that further unfolding of the implicate pattern will take us we have no idea. We don't need to know and the level on which we might be able to understand anyway would be as the heat of melting ice to the fire at the heart of suns.

Virtue is practised for its own sake; it has nothing to do with reward. But what the death of that God with his promises and threats has done is burn away the patina that has accumulated over the virtues with the passage of centuries since the magisterial elaboration of Thomas Aquinas in the thirteenth century, building on the earlier insights of Aristotle. Virtue is the multifaceted jewel that illuminates our human life from its core: but a new courage is required of us that it may glow in the dark of the world we have made, courage that burns away the pride, superstition and weakness with which its lustre has become obscured.

There is no room for triumphalism here, for feeling complacent because science vindicates our faith after all: as indeed it does, but at a price. Science takes our hand and guides our steps from myth to truth. More is asked of us: the New Story of Creation calls for new courage in what we believe.

Faith of our fathers?

As I wrestle with these thoughts, I am in a different place. I am in my very, very small way shadowing St Thomas in the writing of *Summa Contra Gentiles*. And I sometimes think of Matteo Ricci in China, and of how it was possible for his critics in Europe to see only the abundant evidence that he had abandoned his culture, wearing those strange clothes and speaking a language never meant for theology. I too speak a different language. But, looking the other way, back, I can see how cultural encrustation has smothered the thing at the heart of it. But is this new way of seeing things not a step too far? Surely this is not the Faith of our fathers?

During the early centuries of Christianity people began to frame the life and teaching of Jesus intellectually: in the philosophical and cosmological context of the times that were in it: of Greece in effect: they began to write theology in other words. The notion of God we grew up with was conceived within the conceptual framework of an outmoded cosmology that is not merely medieval but had not essentially changed for thousands of years. The seventh heaven in which our medieval God dwelt is like the cloud-capped palaces of Shakespeare's *The Tempest*,[24] and has dissolved 'like the baseless fabric of this vision' in the dazzling light of the New Universe astronomy has opened before our eyes, in which there is no heaven for a throne on which a crowned and bearded God may sit, no place for choirs of angels to hide: only for a God who indwells more deeply, remotely, intimately than our comprehension can reach, a God who is not to be conjured up in our image as the Gods of our childhood are, even if in some minutest sense what is best in us echoes what He or She is about.[25]

Surely then a Faith founded on such an outmoded cosmology is outmoded? It would indeed be outmoded if faith *were* indeed *founded* on that cosmology, rather than of necessity simply *overgrown* by it for the time being. If we have to interpret faith we can only do so in terms of how we understand creation at the particular age of history we are born into, which is only one step up the ladder of comprehension from the age that came before us, one step down from what it may be a century hence.

Doctrinal evolution is a part of the broader evolutionary unfolding (and it is as multihued). Truth doesn't change: it is just that our penetration of it deepens over time. But we don't have to deny the doctrine of, say, the Council of Chalcedon to continue to embrace what Jesus was about – we just need the more mature understanding our time permits – requires – of how much a full human being could be in his nature 'god'-like. It's no harm to remind ourselves that the Christianity of Jesus was as far from the doctrinal Christianity of Chalcedon as Chalcedon is from ours! Let me quote Thomas Aquinas again to show that there is nothing new in appreciating that our understanding of these things has to grow in this way. 'Even teachers in matters of faith are not bound to believe everything explicitly in every age,' he wrote. 'For there is a gradual progress in faith for the whole human race just as there is for individual persons.'[26]

Becoming who I am meant to be

At the core of the great ethical systems of formal religion we find the injunction to give up our life if we are to gain eternal life. In the words of Jesus, 'Those who lose their life for my sake will find it' (Mt 10:39) , 'sell your possessions ... follow me' (Mt 19:21). Similarly in Buddhism we are urged to give up all desire. We balk at these calls to 'perfection', which we moderns can hardly see as other than its antithesis. The eye of our timid soul glazes over as we try to focus on these calls to perfection: for how can we give up that which is most precious to us. Is this not *who we are*?

We are called, each one of us, to be the best we can be. Each of us is unique: genetically and on every level that genetics underpins. We are called to make the most of our uniqueness. But we do not progress as a species as individuals, by being on our own. While each of us contributes to the community of which we are a unique part a contribution no other can contribute, it is the totality that constitutes the forward movement that is history. The talent of each is the talent of all. Our sense of this is vitally important to a proper understanding of the call to lose our life in order to find it. The gift of my life is a gift, in both the sense of being given to me and what I give to the whole. The spark that is the life of every other is of equal value to mine in the symphony of the whole, just as mine is to be valued in the same way when viewed from every other's viewpoint. An extension of the commandment to be the best I can is the injunction to help those other sparks of the Creator whom I encounter on my Pilgrim Way to become the best *they* can be.

But still, when we reach the end of our tortuous journeys with the philosophers and theologians we are returned to our individual selves: to what Paul Tillich calls the fragments and riddles of life out of which we have to make a whole.[27] At the centre of the unique embodiment of human personality that I am is that essential core of being for which we have never really been able to find a more adequate word than 'soul'. It may not be particularly accurate in most senses to speak of the eyes as the windows of the soul, but metaphorically it articulates the deep truth that at the very heart of my being (as I look out on the world) is that which is more essential a part of who I am than is the distinguishing attire I put on in the morning.

Animositas is the word the scholastics used for the strength of the soul, its courage to be and to become what I essentially am. And to *become*: because it is not given: it is to be striven for. To act in this way according to my essential being is virtue. The courage to be that Life (God) requires of me is the courage to accept what I am, where I am, and to strive under those limitations and under these circumstances to become all I am capable of becoming, all I am *meant* to be. This is truly possible only in community. In its absence we look to find our identity in the club or gang, where the conformity that defines the club can stifle the experience of growth of the essential self. Another substitute is the more individualistic striving to be different that expresses itself in idiosyncrasy – of behaviour or dress – rather than find my true self through a way of living that calls for the discipline of virtue.

The endeavours and achievements of sport show us what the human body, under the direction of mind, is capable of. Nowhere is this more evident than during the Olympics, where all the different directions of physical endeavour are brought together, and men and women of every nation compete to be the best there is in their particular discipline.

We look on with admiration tinged with envy! Yet theirs is only the perfection of a moment, a high point that recedes from them as life moves on and others ascend behind them. And each is a narrow perfection for all that.[28] How different the synergies of muscle and bone, heart and lung, required of each one! No one perfection constitutes the perfect human being. Nevertheless, each shows the pinnacle of possibility in each area of physical endeavour. There is a spectrum of attainment in each of them. At the moment of supreme achievement the athlete is at the upper end of the spectrum of physical possibility in his/her discipline, drawing forward the leading fringe of violet.

The ancient Greeks sought a better measure of human perfection by evaluating attainment across a variety of disciplines (our decathlon would be a modern derivative). But the *victor ludorum* is not necessarily a better human being ... What is it we actually admire in the Olympian? It is not the person, but his talent, his capacity. It is her speed, not *she*, who runs this fast. What would be left for us to admire when her speed slows, stops?

Who is my family?

The human family to which we belong has been around for something like two hundred thousand generations (five million years).[29] The most widely accepted figure for the time to our common ancestor with chimpanzees is seven to eight million years. The genus to which we belong (*Homo*) evolved from earlier hominids some 2.5 million years ago, and our species (*Homo sapiens*) appeared one hundred and sixty thousand years ago.[30] The common ancestor of all later humans is thought to have been *Homo heidelbergensis*.

The earliest expansion of humans out of Africa began some two million years ago with the migration of *Home erectus*. This was followed by a wave of later migrations, including that of *Homo heidelbergensis* (who is thought to have been the common ancestor of both humans and the people we refer to as Neanderthals). The first modern humans left Africa somewhere between five hundred and two hundred and fifty thousand years ago, journeying up into Ice Age Europe, where their descendants became Neanderthals.

Other migrants headed eastwards across the Middle East, and were in time dispersed throughout the eastern half of Asia. It is thought that in due course – between one hundred thousand and sixty thousand years ago – the range of these Denisovans came to overlap that of the Neanderthals, and that there was some interbreeding between the two. Modern humans migrated out of Africa between seventy thousand and forty thousand years ago and eventually encountered both Neanderthals and Denisovans, with both of which peoples there was a certain amount of interbreeding.[31]

The most recent evidence suggests that our more immediate ancestors left Africa some two hundred thousand years ago, but moved eastwards, ending up in China between eighty thousand and one hundred thousand years ago, where they must have encountered earlier hominins such as *Home erectus*. Europe was in the grip of the Ice Age at this time, and our tropical ancestors were ill-equipped to tolerate such cold conditions: apart from which Neanderthal humans already lived there. There were probably several subsequent migrations out of Africa, one of which took our own immediate ancestors into Europe some thirty-five thousand years ago.[32]

For all but the last three hundred and sixty generations (nine thousand years) we were hunter-gatherers, and our industrial world has been here only for the last six to eight generations. If all human history is condensed into a single week, starting on Monday, this modern world of ours emerges three seconds before midnight on the Sunday. Some two thousand years have elapsed since the time of the Roman Empire in which Christ lived, and most of the history we consider to be of any real importance to us has taken place during those two millennia – a mere eighty generations – with most emphasis on the cultures that could leave a written record.

The process of diversification started when humans began their series of migrations out of Africa. (Indeed, it began much earlier with the migration within Africa itself that resulted in the development of a succession of different humanoid species.) In the course of time humans came to adapt themselves to a greater range of environments than any other animal species, something their increasing technological prowess and the intelligence that made it possible enabled them to do.

Everywhere these early humans went, they encountered a different creation and had to respond to a different set of challenges, though the difference presented itself incrementally, not the way it does when we travel round the world today: the challenge to learn how to use new sorts of plant and animal food, how to deal with new climatic challenges, how to use different materials for making tools: and also how to respond to the new way in which the Great Mystery behind it all, animating everything, manifested itself in each new ecosystem.

The interaction of the human with different ecosystems and climates in different parts of the world produced, slowly and over tens of thousands of years, in each different place a human perspective welded to its resources and constraints. In this way the great richness and diversity of human cultures developed: in agriculture, language, art and craft: and in the nature of spiritual response, which *mirrored* the more material response and *expressed* itself in and through all of them. As humans radiated across the Earth from the ancestral home of our species in Africa there also evolved a diversity of ritual form that reflected the adaptive radiation of humankind: a radiation that resulted in the linguistic and cultural diversity that has been the crowning achievement of humanity.[33]

This is manifestation at a higher level of the driving theme of increasing diversity so familiar in the living world, upon which we have reflected in earlier pages; and just as that is geographically grounded in ecological intimacy with particular places, so too is this. This means that although they have much in common, they are not interchangeable. They are complementary. But while this is true, technological discoveries or genetic developments at any particular place *that are superior in effect* may be adopted by or spread to people in other places and incorporated into their own culture. This is most obvious with things like craft or cuisine or art, but is true also of ways of interpreting and articulating their sense of meaning.

The intimacy with place out of which human culture evolved included an evolving land ethic peculiar to each that is designed to maintain a harmonious relation to land. The result is a civilisation: 'a state of *mutual and interdependent coöperation* between human animals, other animals, plants, and soils, which may be disrupted at any moment by the failure of any of them.'[34]

I am fascinated as my imagination conjures with these early migrations of humans across the Earth. It is especially fascinating to try to imagine the encounters we know took place when these movements of people brought the different kinds of humans in contact with each other: and to reflect that there can be ways of being human so different from each other that they count as distinct species at a biological level. The word 'migration' is rather misleading in the way it speeds up the process, and we are in danger of superimposing images of the seasonal migrations of animals on this very different process, which is so much slower, perhaps no more than a few kilometres a year, but over a span of time that allows a species to spread across and occupy half a continent. But the movement out of Africa of the people who became Neanderthals somewhere between five hundred thousand and two hundred and fifty thousand years ago was spread over perhaps sixteen thousand generations – two hundred times as many as have elapsed since the time of Christ – each a lifetime as definitely rich in all it means to be human as mine is.

The natural world through which people moved and lived their lives during all this time had all of its undimmed natural diversity, richness of experience, opportunity and challenge: the cultures that resulted from that encounter becoming ever more richly varied as humans became part of the ecology in more and more of the Earth, the richness of each culture evolving over time.

The modern revolution in global travel and telecommunications brings the human family together again, presenting us with new opportunities to use our awareness of the deep familial ties that bind us all to exploit our cultural diversity and the variety of our experience of the Earth in new ways, in order to forge a reunification in which science and faith can become one. However, seeing how slowly we progress at interfaith reconciliation and how tenaciously we cling to irrational beliefs, we can easily believe that the timescale required for this will be on an evolutionarily slow scale comparable to that required to produce our human diversity in the first place (in spite of the exponential growth of technology).[35]

The origins of religion

In an earlier page we reflected on the first appearance of self-consciousness – *soul* if you like – within the human family, and tried to get some faint sense of what it must have been like to become aware of that Deeper Something in a way no creature before could be. From that ignition of the human intellect came the interrogation of nature that would in the course of time mature as scientific enquiry. This had two inextricably linked dimensions: an instinctive yearning to touch the Source, and the application of that growing understanding of how things work to the improvement of our own lives.[36]

We have been led to believe that formal religion developed, along with all the other trappings of 'civilisation' – bureaucracy, hierarchy, writing, etc. – as an instrument of political control: because this was the historical scenario conjured up by two learned tomes that have deeply influenced all later commentators: John William Draper's *The History of the Conflict between Religion and Science* (1874) and Andrew Dickson White's *A History of the Warfare of Science and Theology in Christendom* (1896). But as with the popular reading of evolution as 'nature, red in tooth and claw', this is a distortion.[37] We used to think the invention of agriculture provided the womb within which the conditions for organised religion became possible. Now we are beginning to develop a different picture. We are beginning to wonder whether it was *the organised celebration of Wonder at Creation* that made agriculture necessary. Both agriculture and ritual are *essentially products of early intense human encounter with the mystery of the world and our questioning of it.*

It has been argued that *religion* was in its beginnings the communal celebration of this sense of a shared relationship with other creatures, and that it was only with the arrival of farming that a more exploitative attitude to certain animals developed: and that this by degrees altered that primitive sense of a mysterious kinship and led to a new sense of superiority over other animals.[38] It has indeed been suggested that it was the need to feed the much larger groups of people that assembled for these ritual gatherings that initially brought about the need to exploit the more productive possibilities of domestication. 'Hitherto *Homo sapiens* had been just one actor in a cast of thousands. In the new theist drama Sapiens became the central hero around whom the entire universe revolved.'[39]

Gobekli Tepe

Less than fifty years ago an archaeological discovery in south-eastern Turkey transformed our understanding of the origins of religion: indeed, of civilisation. Here at Gobekli Tepe there is an extraordinary complex of archaeological sites. All that is seen at the surface is a series of twenty mounds, but the German archaeologist Klaus Schmidt suspected they were artificial, and so he began to excavate them in 1964. What he found in each of the excavated mounds was a small temple, 10-30 m in diameter, consisting of a cluster of great T-shaped monoliths enclosed by walls.

What is so extraordinary about them is two things especially. First of all their age. They are twelve thousand years old, the oldest structures of this kind in the world: older than agriculture or any civilisation we know of; and secondly in what they depict. There are no human figures; and no weapons, no war or scenes of tribute. The only carvings are wild creatures, from insects, frogs, snakes to lions and boars: no domestic animals, or animals of the chase. Apart from these carvings the monuments are silent as to their purpose, because they long pre-date the origins of writing of any kind. We can only speculate.

It is not long after this in the Annals of Prehistory that these animals disappear from the stone pillars, to be replaced by powerful humans, engaged in scenes of battle and conquest and tribute. The animals that appear are now creatures of the chase and beasts of burden. Religion becomes allied with power, and the natural world moves into the background of a scene primarily concerned with the human story.

It used to be thought that it was the population explosion brought about by the domestication of plants and animals that made possible the organisation of the labour forces that gave rise to civilisation and urbanisation: and that religion grew out of this, evolving in alliance with power. Now we suspect it was the other way round. People were gathering to worship or to celebrate their wonder in ritual *before* they were farming: but these gatherings had to be fed. And this acted as a catalyst to the domestication of plants as food first of all, and then the herding of animals. Now we begin to wonder if it was *the organised celebration of wonder at creation* that made agriculture necessary.

What we glimpse at Gobekli Tepe is how it was before formal religion, priests, a scripture. The only revelation is the primary one, *the one out of which all spoken or written revelation is later born*: the primary revelation that is the encounter between the human mind and spirit and the natural world. And it is only through that encounter that we can touch the purpose behind it all, within it all.

The answer to that Great Question, insofar as it could be read at this early stage would not come from somewhere *outside*. You would not hear it by listening ever more intently for a small voice outside of creation, from somewhere beyond. It could only come from within the creation itself, *through the existential encounter that is the essence of human be-ing in the world*.

The answers human communities began to frame to that question eventually crystallised as thoughts and were articulated in words and sentences and concepts, which in time were woven together into the great stories of gods and men we call myth, out of which in the course of a long journey of cultural evolution religions and philosophies would grow (a treasure trove in which still we can encounter their minds and find the origins of our own in them).

CHAPTER 8

EVOLUTION – LIFE UNFOLDING

Is evolution a theory, a system or a hypothesis? It is much more: it is a general condition to which all theories, all hypotheses, all systems must bow and which they must satisfy henceforward if they are to be thinkable and true. Evolution is a light illuminating all facts, a curve that all lines must follow.

TEILHARD DE CHARDIN, *THE PHENOMENON OF MAN* (1955)

When you look around you, you don't see species change, over a human lifetime or indeed over the lifetime of a culture: any more than you see stars move. And yet our Earth orbits the sun at 30 km/sec, while the sun at the same time orbits the centre of our Milky Way galaxy at 220 km/sec. This movement of our solar system about the galactic centre takes two hundred million years to complete. Meanwhile, our galaxy is wheeling its way towards the centre of our local cluster of galaxies at a speed of 200 km/sec; and this cluster is itself thought to be moving towards the centre of our local 'supercluster' at about the same speed (but in a different direction). And yet we are completely unaware of this movement: it simply does not touch our everyday life and concerns on any level we are aware of.

No more are we aware of evolutionary change in the living world because it happens so slowly (by our watches). Such change is not immediately *apparent* to us in everyday life, any more than is the wheeling of stars. Among the advances of human knowing that have been transformative of how we understand our place in the cosmos is this growing awareness of how limited is our everyday appreciation of the true scales of creation: the timescale over which it unfolds, and the spatial scale in which that unfolding occurs.

But what you can see, as you attempt to make some sense of the great diversity of species on Earth, and of what that means, is a *pattern*. And of course, that quest to make sense of it all is part of a larger quest to understand everything in creation. *Make sense* is a more than apt expression for this, because it is through our senses that we gather the data that we then scrutinise with our mind and soul and which crystallises in understanding.

Searching for harmony and the origins of the world

Scientific method enables us to work out, incrementally and progressively, how creation *works*. It tells us how the framework that embodies being at successive levels of reality is put together and how it operates. It makes these *sensible* things – these successive realisations of being – *intelligible* to us in ever-greater detail as their complexity is progressively elucidated over time. The advance of scientific understanding makes it ever more and more difficult to maintain a position grounded in a belief other than in Ultimate Purpose or Meaning for which, when every attempt to find a better word is found to fail, in our linguistic helplessness we must call God.

The question of the origin of the world has exercised the minds of philosophers and theologians in every culture. These origin stories vary enormously: and it is difficult for us to get our modern heads around the idea that people actually believed them. The sages who framed the tales in the beginning were more conscious of their metaphorical nature, but in transmission they became embalmed as supposed fact, which stymied their capacity to evolve as understanding evolved. But so deeply are these stories rooted in a particular culture that it is difficult to perceive them otherwise when they are viewed from within that culture. Only when one stands back from the individual culture and views the irreconcilable diversity of the stories of origin, it becomes clear they cannot be accounts of what actually, historically, happened. On the other hand, the *explanation* they seek is not the explanation we expect science to provide. The questions to which they sought answers in myth were bigger, older and deeper than the questions science asks. They had to do with *why*, not *how*. They are the ultimate questions that surround existence, the real of experience.

For all their variety, two things they all have in common are a personification (human or animal) of the forces and causes behind everything, and an intimation of intent or purpose, however dimly this is perceived or understood. But in addition we can see the wish to understand phenomena in themselves, independently of the fickle gods, in all cultures: not only in the practical application of a growing understanding of the nature and behaviour of the things around us in craft: but more broadly in the desire to understand, just for the sake of understanding, the workings of the world.

Thus Virgil, several decades before the time of Christ, wrote:

> For my own part, my chiefest prayer would be – May the sweet Muses, whose acolyte I am, smitten with boundless love, accept my service, Teach me to know the paths of the stars in heaven, the eclipses of the sun and the moon's travails, the cause of Earthquakes, what it is that forces deep seas to swell and burst their barriers and then sink back again, why winter suns hasten so fast to plunge themselves in the ocean or what it is that slows the lingering nights.[1]

The famous dissertation of Lucretius on the nature of reality represents an attempt to get away from divinities, and speculate on what actually happened. The debate between Lucretius and his critics presages the continuing debate in our own day between those who see the need for a guiding intelligence behind everything and those who do not. We may say its content is mere speculation, but remember it *is speculation*, holding up what he can make of his experience of reality to the mirror (*speculum*) of the human mind.

Lucretius envisaged the things of the world as having developed from atoms (*semina, principia*), into which they would in the fullness of time dissolve. The prevailing belief was that an intelligent divinity or divinities must be responsible for the order and diversity of nature. Still, it is fascinating to read these early debates as to whether purpose or chance is behind everything. Here is what Marcus Manilius (a first-century AD poet and astrologer) has to say about Lucretius:

> For my part I find no argument so compelling as this to show that the universe moves in obedience to a divine power and is indeed the manifestation of God, and did not come together at the dictation of chance. Yet this is what he [Lucretius] would have us believe who first built the walls of the heavens from minute atoms and into these resolved them again; he held that from these atoms are formed the seas, the lands, and the stars in the sky, and the air by which in its vast space worlds are created and dissolved; and that all matter returns to its first origins and changes the shapes of things. Who could believe that such massive structures have been created from tiny atoms without the operation of a divine will, and that the universe is the creature of a blind compact? If chance gave such a world to us, chance itself would govern it. Then why do we see the stars arise in regular

succession and duly perform as at the word of command their appointed courses, none hurrying ahead, none left behind? Why are the summer nights and the nights of winter ever made beautiful with the selfsame stars? Why does each day of the year bring back to the sky a fixed pattern and a fixed pattern leave at its departure?[2]

The invisible harmony

The invisible harmony is more powerful than the visible, wrote Heraclitus.[3] Its power is seen in the thrill that energised the philosophy and life of those who looked to Pythagoras and the philosophical scaffolding erected around his memory. It is seen in the explanatory schemata elaborated by countless cultures in their attempts *to ground* their experience as individuals and as communities, each a unique constellation of experiences of their encounter with creation over many generations, articulated in the language of myth, the only language adequate in the earlier stages of the human journey to deeper understanding, a *deeper* encounter.

The idea that the universe is harmonious, all its parts and workings elegantly proportioned and governed by laws that can be apprehended by the human mind and expressed mathematically, is an ancient one. It lay at the heart of an influential school of thought that traced its origins back to the sixth-century BC philosopher Pythagoras (c. 570-459 BC). The doctrine was not merely *intuitive*, the rationalisation of an aesthetic sense: it was based partly on observation. The Pythagoreans were particularly intrigued by the way harmony in sound is related to numerical harmony; when the length of the strings on a lute are simple ratios of each other the sound they make together is symphonic; when they are not so proportioned the sound is cacophonous. How could this be explained other than by supposing such harmony is embedded in the very fibre of reality? Similarly, the movements of the stars and planets could be described in mathematical equations, the harmony of which was inaudible to us but could (in later terminology) be heard by the angels.[4] 'There is geometry in the humming of the strings. There is music in the spacing of the spheres' (words attributed to Pythagoras).

This is the most basic premise underlying the scientific enterprise. It is seen particularly clearly in the great natural scientists of the early period. Copernicus, Brahe and Kepler were all ardent (neo) Pythagoreans. Galileo's belief that:

> Philosophy is written in this grand book, the universe, which stands continually open to our gaze. But the book cannot be understood unless one first learns to comprehend the language and read the letters in which it is composed. It is written in the language of mathematics, and its characters are triangles, circles, and geometrical figures without which it is humanly impossible to understand a word of it.

… could be the words of Pythagoras. Newton's Laws of Motion, which spell out in mathematical detail the very laws by which this harmony is achieved, are of the very essence of what Pythagoreanism is all about. So important was the Pythagorean contribution to the thinking of Plato and to the development of early mathematics that Bertrand Russell – as a mathematician able to appreciate this better than the rest of us – considered Pythagoras (as a figurehead for the school of thought he inspired) to be the most influential of all western philosophers. It was in all likelihood from Pythagoras that Plato got the idea that mathematics and abstract thought generally are the foundation of philosophical speculation.

But as striking as *this* intelligible order is the fact that the human mind is tuned to it: that there is this *radical proportionality* between creation and our minds, and this lay at the heart of the other core belief of the Pythagorean school: the eternity of the immaterial soul, which did not simply perish with the body, but took up residence in some newborn other life, the nature of that new body determined by how virtuously you had lived in your human body.

While this harmony could be expressed in number, it was not merely intelligible; it could be *sensed*. It is through the senses it is first apprehended, so that our appreciation of beauty is the ground of our appreciation of the harmony inherent in the universe. This provides us with a link to the very cornerstone of science, right back to Aristotle: *it is from the appearances – the evidence – that we must start in our search for knowledge*: but it reminds us that the first encounter is where reality actually is: not in the numbers we abstract from it.

Plato's great insight was recognition of the essential intelligibility of the world of experience, and of the human intellect as the tool for deciphering it. This he elaborated into as wonderful a philosophical edifice as the linguistic and cultural achievement of his time permitted: but this elaboration belongs more to the history of philosophy than it does in our modern intellectual toolkit, although its profound, pervasive influence on subsequent thinking acted as a brake on the development of a less inadequate theological perspective.

The driving force behind the progress of scientific enquiry was this search for the invisible harmony. It has continued to be so right down to the present time, but as it has progressed and our understanding has deepened, the adequacy of our earlier conceptions of the nature of the source of that invisible harmony has appeared progressively less adequate: a progress recorded in the histories of philosophy, theology and religion.

It is easy to dismiss earlier creation myths as childish fable, but the chronicles of myth were distilled from long human experience. Some parts of this experience arose from actual historical occurrences. It is most insightful to brush lightly against these cross-cultural coincidences of identification of the Ground of Being, but there is little profit in pursuing them further, because the philosophies and theologies – eastern or western – that are now constructed are too intimately enmeshed in cultural conditioning for us to be able to disentangle or identify with them.

Our 'new creation story' of the Unfolding Universe is not to be thought of as a replacement for earlier creation stories – not even in the special sense of its being historically true, or because it makes the earlier stories obsolete. We are likely to miss something essential in the retelling of these tales in a modern cultural setting, because in their original pre-scientific context they had *resonances* the New Story of Creation does not presume to.

The idea of the Great Chain of Being

In the Christian tradition our interpretation of the pattern of life on Earth is not merely coloured, but essentially *moulded* by our early reading of the Book of Genesis: and over the centuries theological speculation has elaborated richly on this. In the Middle Ages the preferred interpretative image was the Great Chain of Being. The concept of the Great Chain of Being was an attempt to explain the orderly progression apparent in creation, from inanimate things of minimal complexity up through things that were alive but insensate, further up through creatures that were sensate but without intellect, and finally to ourselves, creatures that were endowed with intellect as well as all the other qualities of lesser beings. It was, therefore, an attempt to explain the observed order of the world. God, it was thought, out of his infinite goodness had decided to endow creatures with existence, and because God is *infinite* goodness it was thought to be logically necessary that he bring into being as many modes of existence as were necessary to reflect every possible grade of being between nothing and his own infinity. There could be no gaps in this chain of graduated perfection, and no abrupt transitions: every grade of possibility must be represented.

The idea attained its fullest development in the eighteenth century, when the medieval faith in speculative *a priori* metaphysics was waning, and faith in the truthfulness and efficacy of patient empirical enquiry was rapidly growing. The philosophers John Locke (1632-1704) and Gottfried Wilhelm Leibniz (1646-1716) were enthusiastic proponents. According to Leibniz, the maximum differentiation of creation is a manifestation of the rationality of what he called the World-Ground: 'Every monad mirrors the world from its own unique point of view and therefore in its own unique way, and it is by this means that the fullness of diversity which constitutes the perfection of the universe is attained: "the glory of God is multiplied by so many wholly different representations of his world."'[5] It is the function of art to imitate God in this, to strive to display, insofar as this was possible through the most varied human use of sound, shape, colour, the entire spectrum of essences present to the divine mind.

'In all the visible corporeal world we see no chasms or gaps,' wrote Locke.

> When we consider the infinite power and wisdom of the Maker, we have reason to think, that it is suitable to the magnificent harmony of the universe, and the great design and infinite goodness of the architect, that the species of creatures should also, by gentle degrees, ascend upwards from us towards his infinite perfection, as we see they gradually descend from us downwards.[6]

This became known as the Principle of Plenitude. Links of lesser rank or dignity in the Chain were not considered to exist only or primarily in the service of higher links, but each for its own sake and in the service of the completeness of the entire series of forms, 'the realization of which was the chief object of God in creating the world'.[7] 'Though essences were conceived to be unequal in dignity, they all had an equal claim to existence, within the limits of rational possibility and therefore the true *raison d'être* of one species of being was never to be sought in its utility to any other.'[8]

The supreme exponent of this idea was Friedrich von Schiller (1759-1805):

> Every kind of perfection must attain existence in the fullness of the world. ... Every offspring of the brain, everything that wit can fashion, has an unchallengeable right to citizenship in this larger understanding of the creation. In the infinite

chasm of nature no activity could be omitted, no grade of enjoyment be wanting in the universal happiness.[9]

But interwoven with this was the widespread belief, firmly rooted in a literal reading of the Book of Genesis, that everything had been created specifically to serve mankind. As Francis Bacon summed it up:

Man, if we look to final causes, may be regarded as the centre of the world; insomuch that if man were taken away from the world, the rest would seem to be all astray, without aim or purpose ... and leading to nothing. For the whole world works together in the service of man and there is nothing from which he does not derive use and fruit ... insomuch that all things seem to be going about man's business and not their own.[10]

This however is not at all implied by the logic or philosophy of the Great Chain, which indeed suggests something very different:

We are not to be scandalised ... that there is such careful provision made for such contemptible vermine as we conceive them [the lower animals] to be. For this only comes out of Pride and Ignorance, or a haughty Presumption, that because we are encouraged to believe that in some Sense all things are made for Man, therefore they are not at all made for themselves. But he that pronounces this is ignorant of the Nature of God, and the Knowledge of things.[11]

Between ourselves – the embodied creature endowed with reason and soul – and God there must therefore be an uncountable number of graded intelligences (an idea with which speculative metaphysics could run riot – and did, especially in earlier medieval discussion of the topic). Even John Locke believed that 'we have reason to be persuaded that there are far more species of creatures above us, than there are beneath; we being in degrees of perfection much more remote from the infinite Being of God, than we are from the lowest state of being, and that which approaches nearest to nothing.'[12]

The advance of astronomy made it necessary to extend the concept far beyond the Earth, no longer considered to be the centre of the universe. Life and intelligence could not be confined to one small planet. It became necessary to extend its embrace to the idea that there must also be an uncountable number of other worlds, each inhabited by its own sequence of possible beings. The theologian Soame Jenyns (1790) was one among the many who argued that the appropriate human response to all of this was humility:

> The superiority of man to other terrestrial animals is as inconsiderable, in proportion to the immense plan of universal existence, as the difference of climate between the north and south end of the paper I now write upon, with regard to the heat and distance of the sun.[13]

Another conclusion drawn by Soame Jenyns was how limited our capacity to understand might be – especially in relation to our understanding of God – given our modest station somewhere in the middle of the Great Chain, the embodied lowest level in a sequence of intelligences that extended away beyond our comprehension:

> God cannot impart knowledge to creatures, of which he himself has made them incapable by their nature and formation: he cannot instruct a mole in astronomy or an oyster in music, because he has not given them members or faculties necessary for the acquisition of those sciences ... a religion therefore from God can never be such as we might expect from infinite Power, Wisdom and Goodness, but must condescend to the ignorance and infirmities of man: as the wisest legislator in the world to compose laws for a nursery they must be childish laws: so was God to reveal a religion to mankind, tho' the Revealer was divine the Religion must be human ... and therefore liable to numberless imperfections.[14]

It is important to notice that the Great Chain of Being was based in the first instance on what we observe in nature: it is empirical in the sense insisted upon by Locke: 'All knowledge is founded on and ultimately derives from sense ... or sensation' (echoing the long tradition that goes back as far as Aristotle and which became the bedrock of science: but amplified by shaky speculation and shot through and through with *a priori* assumptions about the nature of God). What we observe in nature of course grows with the progress of biology and of scientific enquiry in general, from the seventeenth century on in particular, with the development of improved microscopes, and this made it necessary to review and refine the concept. The search for creatures to fill the gaps proved a tremendous stimulus to the growth of biological knowledge; the rediscovery of the freshwater coelenterate *Hydra* by Abraham Trembley (1710-1784) in 1739 for instance caused tremendous excitement, because it was thought to bridge the gap between plants and animals.[15]

It was that very advance in what we see and know that made it necessary to dismantle the paradigm; but it was a *metamorphosis*, a process of radical transformation rather than simply the abandonment of the old idea and its *replacement*. Those who formulated the modern concept of evolution all started out with the ideas of the Great Chain, and vestiges of the latter clung to the branches of the new image, which is still that of a graded upwards progression, but now it is represented as a tree, not a ladder. But what stands at the centre is an *ascent* of man (and of course everything else) rather than a *descent*. And in the intellectual exhilaration of seeing the truth of evolution snap into focus, and the discovery of an apparently adequate mechanism to explain its operation, the calling into existence of graded living essences from above no longer appeared to be necessary. But as further *evidence* accumulated, and continues to mount at an exponentially accelerated rate in our own day, this explanation begins to appear ever more naive and inadequate to experience and understanding.

Early intimations of cosmic and organic evolution

The paradigm shift that concerns us most in these pages is that which took place in the latter part of the nineteenth century: the idea that all of the species of living creatures alive on Earth today have evolved from earlier forms, rather than having been individually created, and ever after immutable. What we must consider the great breakthrough in our understanding of how organic evolution might work came in the second half of the nineteenth century with the brilliant insights of Charles Darwin and Alfred Russel Wallace, though (as we will see shortly) evolutionary thinking had been very much in the air for millennia before this. The great advance of Darwin and Wallace's epoch-making volume is that it proposed a convincing *mechanism* for how organic evolution had come about: the theory of natural selection of chance genetic changes (mutations). *Imaginative speculation* that everything that was to unfold later was contained in the atoms of the Beginning was widespread long before there was *proof* of any kind: speculation it must be stressed that was supported by little in the way of *evidence* of the sort discussed earlier.

We cannot look to the ideas and writings of earlier philosophers for confirmation of new concepts that have crystallised out of the progressive, step by step, accumulation of scientific knowledge. Sometimes however we find a striking congruence of ideas. Intimations of evolutionary development are to be found even in the speculations of the pre-Socratic philosophers of Greece, though the underpinning of these speculations with *evidence* was very tenuous. Anaximander (610-546 BC) speculated that the Earth had undergone a process of metamorphosis from uncreated primordial matter that condensed to a fluid state, and as the sun dried out the watery planet all life forms emerged from it. His pupil Anaximenes (588-524 BC) took these ideas further and envisaged a primordial slime from which all life originated. Xenophanes (576-480 BC) expounded further the notion of spontaneous generation (and was the first to recognise fossils for what they were). The contribution of Heraclitus (d. 460 BC) is often considered to be of great importance even though nothing of his survives except occasional snippets quoted by later philosophers. His idea that the most fundamental aspect of reality is *change* clearly sets the tone for later thinking along these lines, and his model of reality is the starting point for all later western speculation on nature and the universe. Equally influential is his notion that there is an underlying ordering principle behind this all-pervading change which he called *logos*: reason.

In Stoic cosmology God is immanent in the whole of creation, directing its development down to the smallest detail, and the story of the world is a cycle of endless recurrence in the course of which all the possibilities of being that would subsequently unfold are contained in an initial seed or creative force, the *logos spermatikos*: 'as it were a seed, possessing the *logoi* of all things and the causes of events, past, present, and future.'[16] In their view the world does not evolve under the directing influence of a God who crafts the world in accordance with his (or its) plan from the outside (as the demiurge in Plato's *Timaeus* is described as doing). Instead, the history of the universe is determined by God's immanent activity, directing a process of progressive differentiation.

In the European Christian world we can trace this intimation of an ineffable 'Something' at the core of all experienced reality in a tradition frowned upon by the Church and eventually banned and persecuted: the Hermetic tradition so influential in the thinking of many early thinkers, including Giordano Bruno, Copernicus and Newton. At the core of their world view was the belief that the universe is an emanation of God, 'in some majestically transcendent, but also ultimately practical manner' the *thought* of God: indeed, the very realisation of godself.[17]

> The essential elements of the Hermeticist conception of reality is that the world emanates from the divine intelligence, and, as a *whole* in which *each* part is an essential component member, expresses that great Mind.[18]

This is another example of how speculative thought can anticipate scientific corroboration. The Hermetic tradition claimed that its own roots lay in the Pure Religion of ancient Egypt, which it believed had been tainted and smothered by the rise of Christianity and Judaism.

We can also find what we may call intimations of how this unfolding universe of ours began in the speculations of early scientists and philosophers. Robert Grosseteste had the idea that what is meant by the first words God speaks in Genesis ('Let there be light.') is that God brought into Being a single point of light that subsequently expanded and filled out to become all that is.[19] Giordano Bruno (1548-1600) seems to have envisaged each grade in the scale of being as a starting point for the next (a sort of temporalised version of Aristotle's hierarchy of Being). Bruno envisaged God as animating the whole of creation as 'world soul'.[20]

As science began its modern advance in Europe in the early eighteenth century, increasingly confident in itself as the discoveries of this new Enlightenment were harnessed to human improvement in agriculture, medicine and manufactures, the idea of God as the great artificer who had imagined, designed and manufactured this supremely intricate machine that is the universe (with all its complexes of cogs, wheels and levers at all the interconnected levels of existence: mechanical, chemical, biological and psychological) came into clearer focus: an idea modelled on this new image of Man at his supreme best. This is *deism*: the confident belief in a God who in the beginning set all of creation in motion, endowed from the very start with all the laws and properties to enable its self-regulation and continuance. The outlines of this new deism were clearly and firmly sketched by Newton, and further elaborated by a host of the new philosophers through the eighteenth and nineteenth centuries.[21] The American Cotton Mather (1663-1728) saw in this new 'philosophical religion' a creed that could be accepted by everyone, Christian or pagan.[22]

The new deism came to be seen as the Primordial Faith out of which the biblical faith had been born, and scientific knowledge and education the language in which this new religion would be articulated, in the face of which ignorance and superstition would evaporate like mists in the light and heat of the rising sun. Matthew Tindal's *Christianity as Old as Creation* (1730) became something of a bible for these eighteenth century deists. Among its more prominent and familiar exponents on the continent was Voltaire (1694-1778) and in America Benjamin Franklin (1706-1790).

The Great Chain concept was hamstrung by several blocks: first of all by the limits to our ability to see and appreciate the complexity of living things without the microscope; and secondly the literal interpretation of the Bible. To take one example of the latter, as the tally of plant and animal species grew, and we began to realise that most species are small, the problem of space in the Ark becomes more acute. Or, if species were all made for our benefit, how do we explain that the majority of living species have never been seen or described (not to mention – if we jump forward a bit – fossil species: or rather the 19,999 out of every twenty thousand that were never preserved as fossils!).

The idea that species were fixed: that they are the same today as when God created them, was deeply embedded in Christian thought. But as time went by, in the Christian world where science (in our modern sense) was born and developing rapidly, reflective individuals looking at the growing evidence began to consider the possibility that species were not immutable: that species could change over time. From very early times inquisitive eyes have noted the presence of shapes clearly resembling shells, bones, plants and other organic forms in rocks; and the enquiring mind, seeking an explanation, attributed these to the Great Flood that had swept the Earth in Noah's time. But sometimes these fossils occurred in rocks at the tops of mountains. Surely a flood, no matter how great, could not account for these?[23] And so, in time various naturalists began to wonder if species were fixed after all, or whether with the new perspective on time now becoming available they might have changed. By the time of Linnaeus devout naturalists were troubled by the production of hybrids: apparently new forms of life produced by cross-breeding different species.

In the earlier part of the nineteenth century there were many philosophers and naturalists – and theologians indeed – who had speculated that some sort of continuing, progressive developmental process was involved in creation. As we will see later, the debt of Darwin to these earlier thinkers is greater than is generally recognised. The most important of these earlier great minds include Francis Bacon (1561-1626), Gottfried Leibniz (1646-1716), Immanuel

Kant (1724-1804), Erasmus Darwin (1731-1802), Jean Baptiste Lamarck (1744-1829), Georges-Louis Leclerc, Comte de Buffon (1707-1788), Robert Chambers (1802-1871) and Harlow Shapley (1885-1972).

The first naturalist to speculate that all living species had evolved from a common ancestor, and that the Earth was much older than was generally supposed, was Benoît de Maillet (1656-1738), whose *Telliamed* appeared in 1748. It is easy to see many of his ideas as absurd from today's perspective, but some of his insights are remarkably suggestive. His most important observation was that the animals and plants found as fossils in the lower sedimentary strata are different from those we see today, and some of them are not represented at all in today's world. His conclusion that it must have taken two billion years for the sedimentary record to form was shockingly at variance with received opinion at the time. The following year saw the publication of the first volume of the Comte de Buffon's magisterial *Histoire Naturelle*, in which the idea of evolution echoes like the approach of distant thunder.

Although not an evolutionary biologist in the modern sense, Comte de Buffon is regarded as the father of evolutionism, because he brought the question to the forefront of scientific debate. His thirty-seven volume *Histoire Naturelle* was read by every educated person in Europe, and was enormously influential: in part because of its brilliant style and encyclopedic scope, but in part also because his writing showed an ability to think outside the confines of the box of Genesis.[24] He argued that animal species had changed since their creation, some 'improving' while others degenerated; and that all the world's quadrupeds had descended from an original set of thirty-eight ancestors. In spite of this he somehow managed to maintain a belief in the immutability of species. His argument that the world was all of seventy-five thousand years old exerted a loosening effect on the vice-grip estimate of 4004 BC computed by Archbishop Ussher.[25]

Jean-Baptiste Lamarck (1744-1829) is an important link between de Maillet, Buffon and Erasmus Darwin on the one hand, and Charles Darwin and Alfred Wallace on the other. His masterly *Philosophie Zoologique*, in which he discussed the change in fossil forms through geological time, appeared in 1809. 'In considering the natural order of animals', he wrote, 'the very positive gradation which exists in their structure, organisation, and in the number as well as in the perfection of their faculties, is very far removed from being a new truth, because the Greeks themselves fully perceived it; but they were unable to expose the principles and the proofs of this evolution, because they lacked the knowledge necessary to establish it.'

In his *Vestiges of the Natural History of Creation* (1844), Robert Chambers propounded an evolutionary development for the universe as a whole. 'The whole of our firmament', he wrote, 'was at one time a diffused mass of nebulous matter.' Eric Chaisson described this masterpiece as, 'a marvellous attempt at a grand synthesis from nebula to human, employing astronomy, biology, geology, and anthropology. In short, a genuine piece of heresy, given the stuffy Victorian environment in which it was penned.'[26] Chambers envisaged life as the result of an initial impulse imparted by God, after which a form of evolution kicks in to adapt organic structures in response to their environment. He then takes up and elaborates on Buffon's idea of the influence of *environmental change*: something Leibniz had alluded to a century and a half earlier. 'Indeed', he wrote (with reference to the relationship of the living Nautilus to fossil ammonites), 'it is credible that by means of such great changes [of habitat] even the species of animals have been many times transformed.'

The pantheist Harlow Shapley is often regarded as the father of the modern concept of cosmic evolution. This is the idea that all of creation's potential to flower into the diversity of the living world was somehow enfolded in a single grain of all-possibility at the moment of Creation. However, it had been in the background of human thought for a long time: not only in earlier speculative philosophy, but more recently in the mind of scientists. Thomas Huxley had appreciated the cosmic context of evolution as far back as 1873: 'The whole world, living and not living, is the result of the mutual interaction, according to definite laws, of the forces possessed by the molecules of which the primitive nebulosity of the universe was composed.'[27]

Long before this, in his *Exposition du système du monde* (1796) Pierre Simon Laplace advanced the hypothesis that the cosmos began as a vast cloud of nebular gas that became concentrated and condensed under the influence of gravity. Everything is there in embryo from the beginning:

> An intellect which at a given instant knew all the forces with which nature is animated, and the respective situations of the beings that compose nature – supposing the said intellect were vast enough to subject these data to analysis – would embrace in the same formula the motions of the greatest bodies in the universe and those of the slightest atom; nothing would be uncertain for it, and the future, like the past, would be present to its eyes.[28]

We now know, it is not the 'atoms', but the much more fundamental 'entities' of the first instant that possess those 'forces'. Indeed it must be so enfolded, *but it is only enfolded as possibility*. But even if we could reduce everything to the unattainable formula it would not a whit diminish the sheer wonder of it, or the question it puts to the intellect capable of arriving at that formula! How incommensurate our intellectual groping with *the sheer achievement of its actual being.*[29]

Evolutionary ideas become more explicit in the writings of Erasmus Darwin, whose *Zoonomia, or the Laws of Organic Life* (1794) put forward the bold hypothesis that all warm-blooded animals had originated from 'one living filament … endued with animality, with the power of acquiring new parts … possessing the faculty of continuing to improve by its own inherent activity': and that these acquisitions can be passed on from one generation to the next. He put forward the idea of an eternal universe, with endless creations succeeding one another, each emerging from the ashes of the one before, evolving, and disappearing before the next was born.

More evidence-based was the work of James Hutton, best remembered today for his ground-breaking contribution to geology (he is often referred to as the Father of Geology), but who in 1794 (sixty-five years before Darwin and Wallace) also clearly spelled out the basic idea that natural selection is at work in nature:

> In conceiving an indefinite variety among the individuals of [a] species, we must be assured, that, on the one hand, those which depart most from the best adapted constitution, will be most liable to perish, while, on the other hand, those organised bodies, which most approach to the best constitution for the present circumstances, will be best adapted to continue, in preserving themselves and multiplying the individuals of their race.[30]

The growth of a new paradigm

In bigger dictionaries you will find a word that was hardly ever used before the philosopher of science Thomas Kühn elevated it from obscurity. The word is 'paradigm', which was originally a Greek word meaning 'image'. But in rescuing the word from lexicographic obscurity, Kühn invested it with a whole new meaning. 'Paradigm' became the conceptual image we have of reality in its entirety: our explanatory framework for everything that is going on in the world around us. When you encounter the word today it is almost always coupled with the word 'shift', because what Thomas Kühn was interested in was showing that at any given time there is a dominant paradigm that resists the sort of changes that would necessitate its deconstruction and replacement by a new paradigm that more adequately conforms to the evidence of reality.[31]

Among the most familiar examples of a paradigm shift is the transition from the Ptolemaic view of the cosmos, with the Earth at its centre, to the Copernican, which placed the sun at the centre, and dethroned the Earth to a planetary orbit. Another is the displacement of our solar system from a comparable central position as hub of the universe, and the explosive replacement of that image by our modern comprehension of a universe of a trillion galaxies – of which our Milky Way is *one* – each made up of hundreds of billions of stars, of which our sun is *one*.[32] An outstanding example in chemistry is the overthrow of the phlogiston theory by Lavoisier's theory of combustion in the late eighteenth century, and in geology the way the theory of plate tectonics began to revolutionise that science only fifty years ago. Perhaps the most dramatic examples however are in physics. In 1900 Lord Kelvin famously announced, 'There is nothing new to be discovered in physics now. All that remains is more and more precise measurement,' only five years before Einstein published his paper on special relativity, ushering in a new era that reduced Newtonian physics to a special case.

But whether growth in our cosmic comprehension is punctuated or gradual, stuttering or smooth, there can be no doubt of the *progression*. The incontrovertible essence of the whole thing is that our understanding of how the world works and of what it is all about *does evolve*: is itself a part of the unfolding that is at the heart of the cosmic process, and that cognitive evolution is the progressive growth of a deeper, richer and more mature grasp of what the universe is about.

What remains essentially unchanged through the course of this evolutionary progression are the two poles of the encounter to which the paradigm is a response: the human mind that seeks understanding, and the world around us, the creation. Our intellectual *capacity* has not changed essentially since the dawn of human awareness. But while capacity has not changed, what *has* changed by a process of gradual development is our ability to comprehend, to put together an explanatory conceptual framework. And the only tools we have at our disposal to do this are our senses, and the central nervous system that has evolved to interpret what our senses can tell us about the world.

Kühn restricted the concept to the natural sciences, but it was subsequently used in other fields such as philosophy and the social sciences, which he considered inappropriate. With the passage of time it has come to be used much more loosely and the idea should now be used with some caution. Kühn himself eventually developed a modified version that allowed a more significant role for *graduated* development in the formulation of a new paradigm. In the 1980s however, Hans Küng applied the concept to the development of Christian theology to good effect. In doing so, he noted five analogies between natural science and theology, identifying a succession of six theological 'macromodels' that followed one after the other over time.[33]

In the beginning, and for most of the time the human mind has queried creation, we had to rely on our unaided senses and a capacity to harness energy at first limited to manpower and the strength of domesticated animals. This gradually changed with the advance of technology, itself a facet of growing scientific understanding and an utterly fascinating story in its own right.[34] Until the time of Galileo we had only our unaided eyes to study the heavens. Tycho Brahe mapped the stars from the rooftop of his observatory home in Copenhagen *by eye*, a work of sustained dedication difficult to imagine today, because in those days there were no glasses; your days of observing the stars were over when your eyes began to fail. Without the maps produced by Brahe and his assistants it would not have been possible for Johannes Kepler to compute the revolutions of the planets (the next great step in understanding after Copernicus' outline of a heliocentric universe in which the sun replaced the Earth as the hub of the cosmos).

————

Charles Darwin (1808–1882) and Darwinism

When Charles Darwin left England on HMS *Beagle* as it set off on its five-year voyage of the world in 1831, his views were those of a devout member of the Church of England who was thinking of becoming a parson in that church. Among the books he brought with him for the long voyage was a copy of William Paley's *Natural Theology*. But he also brought a copy of the first volume of Sir Charles Lyell's magisterial *Principles of Geology* (1830), which had a hugely formative influence on him, as it did on the entire scientific world of the day: and he had arranged for the second volume to be waiting for him in South America. The *Beagle's* captain was Robert Fitzroy, and its assignment was to chart coastal waters; but – ironically – Fitzroy passionately believed in the literal interpretation of the Bible's creation account and saw it as his mission to seek out evidence that would bolster this.[35]

The voyage was a transformative experience, and raised many questions in Darwin's mind about the 'fixity of species', but he had not formulated any clear conclusions by the time he returned to England in 1836, and never again left it. The evolutionary penny had not dropped for him, as is sometimes mistakenly thought, on the Galapagos Islands, whose giant tortoises and finches provided such convincing evidence of natural selection. Darwin's account of his *Beagle* voyage (1839), was published to considerable critical acclaim. In the years between 1842 and 1846 he wrote several volumes dealing with coral reefs, volcanic islands and the geology of South America, but nothing on 'evolution', although he had now become convinced that species were not immutable. Many other naturalists before him had already reached the same conclusion however. The question was: *how* could it happen?

By 1842 Darwin had become clear in his mind that evolution came about through natural selection. He began to sketch out his ideas on paper, and in 1844 prepared a summary essay which he had printed at his own expense and distributed to a few carefully selected friends and colleagues that included Charles Lyell, Joseph Hooker and Asa Gray, with the intention of producing an irrefutably detailed book in due course.[36] But he then put his sketch to one side and – reluctant to publish because he knew how the idea of evolution would be received – went to look at other things that interested him. It is probably no coincidence that 1844 was also the year Robert Chambers' highly controversial *Vestiges of the Natural History of Creation* was published.

The main ideas behind 'Darwin's theory' appear very simple. Variations are observed to occur between the individuals in a species. Sometimes these are unfavourable or harmful, making it unlikely such individuals will survive to reproduce. In many cases the variations may be neutral in their effects, but in some they are favourable, and assist the individuals possessing them in the struggle for survival that is inevitable where a population increases to a level above what the environment can support. His discovery in 1838 of *Essay on the Principle of Population* by Thomas Malthus (1766-1834) gave him an important clue here. Malthus' essay persuasively argued that population has a natural tendency to increase faster than the means of subsistence, and that accordingly there must be a struggle between individuals for survival: 'Population, when unchecked, increases in a geometrical ratio. Subsistence only increases in an arithmetical ratio.' There must therefore be 'a perpetual struggle for room and food'. Darwin postulated (relying largely on his extensive knowledge of what happens in animal and plant breeding) that favourable variations are inherited in some mysterious way, and that such changes, accumulating over time, would result in new species. He had no idea what the cause of these random variations might be. But the fossil record, incomplete and broken though it is, provided convincing proof that plants and animals *had* changed over the long ages of geological time.

Then, like a bolt from the blue, Darwin got the shock of his life in the early summer of 1858 when a package arrived in the post containing an essay written by a virtually unknown collector of exotic plant and animal specimens in the Malay Archipelago named Alfred Wallace: an essay that was essentially an independent summary of his own ideas on evolution. Dismayed, he turned to his closest confidantes, Charles Lyell and Joseph Hooker, for advice. Their solution was a joint paper to be presented on behalf of Darwin and Wallace to the Linnean Society, consisting of extracts from Darwin's 1844 sketch along with part of a letter he had written to Asa Gray in 1857, followed by Wallace's twenty-page essay.[37] The paper was duly presented on 1 July 1858. Darwin now returned to his book; *The Origin of Species* – a much slimmer tome than the volume he had originally planned – appeared the following year.[38]

The reception of Darwinism

The Origin of Species was an immediate commercial success: but it had a rather more cautious reception among those best qualified to judge. Biologists of the late nineteenth century were well aware of how threadbare the evidence for 'the origin of species through the natural selection of small variations' actually was. There was no evidence in the fossil record of one species actually being transformed into a different species. What you saw was a pattern of jumps between species. Darwin explained the absence of intermediate forms – 'missing links' – by arguing that the fossil record of its nature only allows us glimpses into the narrative. It is as though the story of evolution is a long film of which only individual widely spaced frames have survived. Besides: how could evolution have taken place on the scale it did? – Earth history simply doesn't allow enough time (or so it was thought at the time).

Gregor Mendel (1822–1884) and Mendelism

Gregor Mendel was an Augustinian monk born near Udrau in Austria and ordained in 1847. He became fascinated by the conundrum of heredity during his time at the University of Vienna (1851-1853), after which he began a series of experiments into the inheritance of specific traits in garden peas that lasted several years (between 1856 and 1864) in the experimental garden of his monastery of Brünn (in what is now the Czech Republic). He bred seven varieties of peas for many generations, starting with plants that bred true for the particular traits he wanted to study. What he found was that there were two variants of each trait, one of which was 'dominant' and the other 'recessive'. Every individual had two copies of each trait, but only one copy was passed on to each of its offspring by each parent; if just one of these was dominant it determined the appearance of the plant. For example, the first trait he studied was seed shape. Plants either had round seeds or angular seeds; there were no in-between-shaped peas. He crossed plants with round seeds with plants that had angular seeds. Round is dominant over angular, and so, the first generation of hybrid plants (F1) *all* had round seeds. But then, if these F1 plants were allowed to self-fertilise among themselves the recessive trait reappeared in the next (F2) generation, but only in those plants that had two copies of the recessive trait. Out of every four plants in this F2 generation three had round seeds and one had angular seeds, but even though all three *looked* the same, two of them had inherited a copy of the dominant trait from both parents whereas the third had inherited a dominant copy from one and a recessive copy from the other. In other words, you could not tell the genetic makeup from the appearance, a distinction between what we now call 'phenotype' and 'genotype'. This pattern was maintained through all subsequent generations, and when later generations were back-crossed with earlier ones.

What was so special about Mendel's work was the care with which he followed the transmission of particular traits over several generations; what he found was that particular features of the species he studied – garden peas – were *conserved rather than blended* when individuals with different features were crossed – which is what everybody else thought.

What this suggests is that there was something *particulate* about whatever transmitted these features. That is as far as he could go, because at that time very little was known about the detailed structure and workings of the cell. In our day we talk confidently about chromosomes and genes, but in Mendel's day nothing was known about chromosomes. By the time he had finished his research on peas Mendel must have examined the progeny of more than forty thousand flowers on ten thousand plants: a total of something like three hundred thousand peas.[39]

Mendel presented his findings in two lectures to the Brünn Society for the Study of Natural Sciences in 1865 and published them in the Society's Proceedings the following year. They aroused no response in his audience, and of the many scientists to whom he sent copies only one replied, and that dismissively. For the rest of the century Mendel's forgotten paper, the importance of which nobody appreciated at the time of its publication, gathered dust in the few libraries that had copies. It resurfaced in 1900 as its significance began to dawn more or less simultaneously on several of the scientists studying heredity at that time; but it was the English biologist William Bateson (1861-1926) who became its main evangelist. Bateson described his discovery of Mendel as something in the nature of a conversion, and he effectively set about the scientific canonisation of the monk: which is delightfully ironic considering that it would be difficult to imagine two more different personalities! His halo has also had the unfortunate effect of somewhat distorting and in a sense diminishing Mendel's achievement.

By the 1920s Mendel's discoveries had become the foundation of the new science of genetics. (Bateson coined the term in 1905; up to this the subject had been known as 'the study of heredity and variation'; the word 'gene' was coined by Wilhelm Johannsen, a professor of plant physiology at Copenhagen Agricultural College).

Robin Henig summarises Mendel's achievement well:

> He might not have known, prior to the twentieth-century understanding of the gene, exactly what his findings meant, but he arrived at them in a logical and sophisticated way, making him decidedly the first in a long line of modern genetic investigators. Using methods quite different from those of his hybridizing peers – but true to his own life story with time, patience, brilliance, and perseverance – Mendel turned a few good insights into scientific gold. He had the modern sensibility required to carry out his experiments over several generations; to regard each characterisic separately from every other; and to count his results and look for mathematical relationships between them.[40]

With the rediscovery in 1900 of Mendel's extraordinarily painstaking research on inheritance in plants natural selection could be seen in a whole new light.

Mendel's work established that the inheritance of traits was *particulate*, and that particular traits *are* in fact transmitted between successive generations without 'dilution', even if their expression is muted in some generations by more dominant factors for the same character.

With the incorporation of Mendel's discoveries – and the subsequent development of population genetics – the new and convincing synthesis known as neo-Darwinism was formulated, which by the 1930s and 1940s had gained widespread acceptance by most scientists. One of its defining features was mathematical demonstration of how the natural selection of small variations could over time bring about major changes in form and function. The discovery that the basic units of heredity – the genes – are arranged in linear fashion in the cell's chromosomes was made in 1914 by T.H. Morgan. It came to be widely accepted that the principal cause of the variation in particular characters within a species was spontaneous and permanent changes in the genes: genetic mutations. Step by step the chemical identity of the genes came into focus. In 1943 Erwin Schrödinger speculated that the genetic information is carried in the form of a code in the genes. By the early 1950s it had become clear that deoxyribonucleic acid (DNA) was the likely candidate for the bearer of the code, and in 1953 the structure of DNA was deduced by James Watson, Francis Crick, and others in England.[41] 'Working out the detailed mechanisms, and providing experimental proof, of Watson and Crick's insight into the physico-biochemical nature of genes dominated biology for the next twenty-five years.'[42]

This new paradigm, to which the great majority of biologists now subscribe, can be stated under the following six headings.[43]

1. Species living today have all descended from species that lived in the past.
2. New forms of life arise from the splitting of a single lineage into two. This process is known as speciation, and is characterised by an inability of the daughter lineages to breed together. Over time this process results in a nested genealogy of species, a 'tree of life', whose root is the first species to arise, and the live twigs of which are the vast number of species on Earth today. If pairs of twigs are traced back to where they split, and branches are similarly and successively traced back towards the trunk, we arrive at a common ancestor.[44]
3. New species evolve through the gradual genetic transformation of populations of individual species members over thousands or more generations.

4. This transformation is brought about through the accumulation of random genetic mutations in individuals, the mixing of genes from each parent during sexual reproduction leading to offspring having different combinations of genes from either parent, and the consequent spreading of such genetic mutations over successive generations throughout the population's gene pool.

5. Mutations for characteristics that enable individuals to compete for resources more successfully, and to survive longer and produce more offspring are naturally selected by being inherited in greater numbers.

6. Information is a one-way flow from genes to proteins in a cell, never the other way round: the environment is not an influence here.

The extraordinary advance in genetic understanding initiated by the breakthrough in our understanding of the genetic code strengthened the belief that genes explained everything. It was supposed that the genome consisted of neatly linked genes the length of the DNA double helix, each one the code for a particular protein.[45] So firm was belief in this simple and elegant picture that when it was discovered in the 1970s that 98 per cent of the human genome does *not* consist of genes, this 98 per cent was described as 'junk DNA'.

Darwin's achievement

When Darwin left England for his voyage aboard HMS *Beagle* he was familiar with Lamarck's *transformisme* from Robert Grant's lectures at Edinburgh, and with James Hutton's New Geology through his friendship with Sir Charles Lyell, who was an immensely influential promoter of his ideas. It is widely held today that Darwin was somewhat 'backward in coming forward' in respect of the influence on his own ideas of these earlier proponents of 'descent with modification' and 'natural selection': which is not to denigrate his own supremely important contribution. And it is surely more than coincidence that when he began his private evolution notebook in July 1837 it opens with some phrases from his grandfather's *Zoonomia*.

Darwin and his followers were dismissive of Lamarck: but several of the key lines of evidence brought forward by Lamarck in support of his hypothesis that species had changed over the course of geological time are suspiciously similar to those of Darwin and his followers: the fossil record, the great variation in the forms of plants and animals under domestication, the significance of no longer functional organs (vestigial organs) in many animals, and of the presence in embryos of structures that are not functionally present in adults.

Lamarck believed that changes come about as a response to change in the environment in which the animal lives: and that these changes can be inherited. (It is to Lamarck's great supporter Étienne Geoffroy Saint-Hilaire that we owe the term 'evolution' in the sense we use it today.[46]) The idea most closely at the centre to Lamarck's evolutionary theory – the inheritance by the offspring of features acquired by parents during their lifetime – was also central to Darwin's theory. In the first edition of the *Origin* he wrote:

> I think there can be little doubt that use in our domestic animals strengthens and enlarges certain parts, and disuse diminishes them; and that such modifications are inherited. Under free nature … many animals have structures which can be explained by the effects of disuse.[47]

And in his later work on human evolution:

> I may take the opportunity of remarking that my critics frequently assume that I attribute all changes of corporeal structure and mental power exclusively to the natural selection … whereas, even in the first edition of the 'Origin of Species,' I distinctly stated that great weight must be attributed to the inherited effects of use and disuse.[48]

Which explains the anger and frustration in a letter written to Darwin by John Grey, who was keeper of the British Museum's Zoological Collection:

> You have just reproduced Lamarck's doctrine, and nothing else, and here Lyell and others have been attacking him for twenty years, and because you (with a sneer and a laugh) say the same thing, they are all coming round; it is the most ridiculous inconsistency.[49]

There was initially some reluctance to accept the idea that evolution occurred in small steps, because this is not evident from the fossil record, where it appears to take place in *leaps* (*saltation* as against *gradualism*). Indeed, Darwin's most articulate disciple, the eminent zoologist Thomas Huxley – who was as familiar as anybody alive with the fossil record of animals – was himself a saltationist; he thought the fossil record supported the idea that evolution occurred suddenly rather than in tiny steps; that it was surely impossible to account in this way for the immensely complex structures and behaviours that characterise animal life (the complexity and intricacy of which become ever more evident the more we know about them). The most familiar, and most frequently discussed example at that time, was the eye. Secretly, Darwin himself had moments of doubt; 'The eye to this day gives me a cold shudder,' he wrote in a letter. In spite of its title, *The Origin of Species* never actually addresses the question of the actual *origin* of new species. The examples Darwin presented in his book are variations *within* species as a result of selective breeding rather than new species originating in this way.

Another great difficulty was that nobody had any idea how variation could be inherited – especially variations that an individual plant or animal acquired during its own life. The general assumption was that blending of parental characteristics took place in the offspring. In fact, unknown to Darwin (and virtually everyone else in the scientific world) the breakthrough in understanding that would lead to the genetic revolution of the twentieth century was made during Darwin's own lifetime, but went unnoticed for some thirty-five years.

Darwinism argued that evolution proceeds by the natural selection of small variations that arise by chance, and the inheritance of these by offspring. Opposing this is the notion that there is a predetermined direction to evolution. Such *orthogenesis* was important in the thinking of Erasmus Darwin and of Lamarck, who believed that evolution occurred because there is an increasing *tendency* to increase in complexity.[50] On orthogenesis, it is worth noting that of the four architects of neo-Darwinism in the late 1930s and early 1940s, one (Julian Huxley) wrote the introduction to the 1959 edition of Teilhard de Chardin's *The Phenomenon of Man* (endorsing most of its ideas), and another – Theodosius Dobzhansky – was a founder-member and President (1968-1971) of the American Teilhard de Chardin Association.[51] What was so exciting about Teilhard for those of us who encountered him in the 1960s was the bold and imaginative way he took the Standard Theory as a starting point and opened wide its spiritual implications. Where he laid himself open to blistering attack from some neo-Darwinists was that he had to invent a new language for his ideas, and it was easy to attack this as not 'scientific' in the accepted sense. *The Phenomenon of Man* is somewhat dated now, but it remains an imaginative spiritual classic in the way *The City of God* is a spiritual classic even if it is one that no one reads today.

Collaboration and sociability in evolution

Although Darwin had conceded that sociability and cooperation had a role to play in evolution, others came to believe that it was *central*. A key figure here was Peter Kropotkin (1842-1921). In an important contribution first published in 1902 he argued that Darwinism lacked adequate proof that 'the struggle for existence' and 'survival of the fittest' were the key controlling factors in evolution. He claimed that 'those animals which acquire habits of mutual aid are undoubtedly the fittest' (i.e. have the best chance of passing on their genes).[52] Kropotkin concluded that the species most favoured by evolution were those that had adopted strategies to avoid competition (in the widest sense).

Contrast Darwin's own summing-up of his theory in *The Variation of Plants and Animals under Domestication* (1868) with Kropotkin in *Mutual Aid: A Factor in Evolution* (1914):

> It has been truly said that all nature is at war; the strongest ultimately prevail, the weaker fail … the severe and often-recurrent struggle for existence will determine that those variations, however slight, which are favourable shall be preserved or selected, and those which are unfavourable shall be destroyed. (Darwin)

> Those species which willingly or unwillingly abandon [sociability] are doomed to decay; while those animals which know how best to combine, have the greatest chances of survival and evolution … The fittest are thus the most sociable animals, and sociability appears as the chief factor of evolution. (Kropotkin)

Darwin came to reject Christianity for various reasons, two of which were particularly influential for him. The first was his inability to reconcile the pain and suffering he saw in the natural world (and in his own life) with a supremely good and omnipotent creator. The second was his belief that the Old Testament could not be reconciled with what geology tells us about the origins of the world:

> I had gradually come, by [1839] to see that the Old Testament from its manifestly false history of the world … was no more to be trusted than the sacred books of the Hindoos, or the beliefs of any barbarian.[53]

On this second point, however, most biblical scholars of today would (with some qualifications!) agree.

For all that, even Darwin himself could not believe that blind chance is sufficient to account for evolution's outcomes:

> I cannot anyhow be contented to view this wonderful universe, and especially the nature of man, and to conclude that everything is the result of brute force. I am inclined to look at everything as resulting from designed laws, with the details, whether good or bad, left to the working out of what we may call chance. Not that this notion at all satisfies me ... But the more I think the more bewildered I become.[54]

Conclusions

It is critically important to be clear that there can be no doubt about the *fact* of cosmic and organic evolution (any more than that the Earth revolves around the sun): but it is equally important to make a very clear distinction between the *fact* of evolution and our explanation of what it is all about: not just the *why* of it, but even the nature of the mechanisms at work in bringing it about. There is no denying the fact, but questions that relate to *how* and *why* are of a different order.

Darwin himself clearly recognised this. In one of his letters he wrote:

> Whether the naturalist believes in the views given by Lamarck, by Geoffrey St-Hilaire, by the author of the *Vestiges*, by Mr Wallace and myself, or in any other such view, signifies extremely little in comparison with the admission that species have descended from other species and have not been created immutable.[55]

For neo-Darwinists the mechanism is natural selection and nothing else. Evolution is brought about through the selection by environmental conditions of favourable mutations that are random. From this point of view what *meaning* we may see in creation is incidental.

The most familiar advocates of neo-Darwinism are as strident in its defence as their opponents at the far end of the spectrum of 'faith' are in attacking it. But the more we learn, the more we come to suspect that there is more to it than natural selection. Although the high priests of Darwinism take great pains to demonstrate that organs of apparently 'irreducible complexity' can always be described in terms of changes in a stepwise fashion, this does not *account* for it. While (for example) biochemical complexity can be described and explained as a step-by-step development, this is not a *sufficient* explanation; the ground of our amazement is WHAT is achieved thereby: not THAT it can come about or does come about by entirely 'natural' processes.[56]

This is not to deny that natural selection takes place, but to say that *there is something else going on*. Natural selection is neither the only nor the principal mechanism at work in evolution.

Neo-Darwinists (and scientism in general) hold that natural selection explains everything, but the more we see of what evolution has achieved, the WHATNESS of things (as well as the THATNESS of things), the more inadequately rational such a simplistic position appears: particularly when you factor in cosmic evolution: the fact that all this was enfolded in the seed of the beginning, and of the unbelievably precise series of conditions necessary, each and every one of them, to bring it all about. A so-called 'multiverse' hypothesis is invoked to account for this, but it is purely speculative, and more an excuse to evade an acknowledgement that this is MEANT, that what is happening in organic, and more broadly in cosmic, evolution is the unfolding of a *plan*.

Many people of faith insist that the hand of God must be directly involved at particular stages in order to steer the plan in the right direction or to correct its course (Creationism) (as if God needed to stick a hand IN!). This is strenuously denied by most biologists. And while I would on the whole agree with those who argue against the need for divine interference in order to describe irreducible complexity, I am not sure that the arguments are themselves not unduly facile; and in any case of course *design* in some ultimate sense heavens removed from our ability to see or grasp its nature, is at work from the beginning: in the sense that the possibility for all this to happen is built into the 'impossible' seed of the beginning.

The evolution story is of central importance for the people of God, because it is *the* Book of Revelation, profoundly and repeatedly to be dipped into, experienced and contemplated. It is *essential* to a mature faith position, not just acceptable. It is in many circles of course presumed that it is antagonistic. Yet for all that, such an immature faith is the faith of a majority of humanity, many of whom see evolution as a threat rather than a call to a deeper and purer spirituality.[57]

The evolution of a new spiritual understanding

Our grasp of the profound truth that evolution is the way everything in the universe works is *itself* a process of evolution: of progressive development to a better comprehension of *how* certainly, and perhaps also in a slightly less inadequate way than before, of *why*. Our questioning of creation is, and continues to be, a *process*, the process that defines being human: in the unfolding of which our understanding becomes progressively deeper, clearer, more accurate in the sense of being closer to the truth of what is really going on, and at the same time increasingly aware of the extent to which our knowledge is immeasurably outstripped by our ignorance.

As our appropriation of reality through science advances, we come to realise ever more clearly the primitive nature of our earlier understanding: 'primitive' not in the sense of something to be rejected, but as *primus*, an earlier understanding from which we must progress to one more mature. In rejecting the idolatrous god of our childhood – as individuals and culturally, all together in society – we can move in either of two directions. We can, as part of that growing-up, reject the intuition at the heart of it as unscientific, or we can nurture that intuition, stripped now of the elaborate ornamental panoply bestowed upon it by formal religion: clothing that so often and easily smothers the kernel at its core, and seek new conceptual clothing in which to articulate it in ways that are in harmony with modern scientific understanding.

Given the nature of our human being, it is inevitable that we must erect an elaborate intellectual scaffolding to support our insights. But the maturing of that insight over time requires us to let that earlier scaffolding fall away so that we may ascend further. Dean Inge expressed the form of this essential pilgrim's progress most elegantly in his review of Christian mysticism – though not foreseeing how much of his own elegant theology would become part of that discarded scaffolding a century in the future:

> We must die to our first superficial views of the world around us, nay, even to our first views of God and religion, unless the childlike in our faith is by arrest of growth to become the childish.[58]

A new creation spirituality is taking shape in our time as a result of the enhanced comprehension the advance of science enables in us – and nourished by that enhanced comprehension – but which is directed by what lies at the heart of older spiritualities. This will have a paradigm-altering effect on theology comparable to that of plate tectonics on geology sixty years ago and evolution on biology a century earlier: not only as a science, but *existentially*, on our experience of that which theology studies and our comprehension of that experience. It may take centuries, and see the falling away of structures and notions we thought indispensable to the intellectual framework within which our earlier comprehension hung its net over the groping progress of our god-talk.

That is how the great Catholic theologian Karl Rahner saw it, writing sixty years or so ago, I think without realising how true or imminent it was, when he compared the Christian church of the future to embers buried in the ashes. The fire may seem to have gone out, but under that pile of ash are the gently glowing embers. If they cannot get oxygen they too will go out. But it can feel uncomfortable to be lifted out of the gentle, warm comfort of the enclosing ash pile in order to be kindled into flame.

It is not a question of picking and choosing the bits we think relevant and welding them into a new structure, the intellectual architecture of which would be incoherent and unstable. But neither is it a question of casting aside what we have grown up with. It is a question of allowing ourselves to *grow out of and beyond*: rather than away from. Nevertheless, the change that is required of us is a radical change. The most apt metaphor is that of insect metamorphosis: where the body dissolves to nourish the seeds of new being embedded within. But metamorphosis builds entirely on what has come before. It is what fulfils the earlier process of growth. It is not a rejection but an affirmation of everything that led up to it.

The transformation is not easy nor is it automatic. It is not just a question of reading the right books and getting good marks for essays. You will not be taken by the hand and stood in front of a doorway that leads through to a more mature spiritual perspective. But you will be given the planks, and a hammer and nails, and you make the door yourself. This is an ongoing process of conversion that is always challenging and at times painful – emotionally, intellectually and spiritually – but exhilarating and at times thrilling also. And even when you go through the doorway, a new vision doesn't automatically present itself, as though you had stepped through a wardrobe into C.S. Lewis' Narnia. You need to attend to the world always about you with disciplined attention rather than drifting forward in the fog of distraction that saturates our entire life, because it is through that attention only that Ultimate Purpose reveals itself.

What does it all mean?

This is not just another chapter. It changes everything: but not by abandoning the core of what directs our Christian lives. A transformation is called for: part of the 'conversion' Pope Francis calls for no fewer than thirteen times in *Laudato Si'*.[59] Paul Tillich writes of religion as the dimension of depth in all the functions of human culture.[60] This conversion breathes new life into that dimension. It requires us to bring a new awareness into every moment of our living.

The truths of evolution are matters of fact. These truths are not mysteries in the sense that we usually mean when we speak of mysteries of faith. But they are mysterious in the sense that they open up awesome depths of wonder and complexity that the sensory and intellectual ropes and grapnels of enquiry enable us to descend to. But there is no bottom to this descent, because ultimately it takes us to places our intellect cannot go: not into irrational depths, but depths beyond human reason: depths in which our intellectual toes cannot find bottom.

The question of evolution poses three questions: if, how and why. Of the first there can be no doubt. It is as certain as anything we can know. The message of atheistic scientism is that if evolution is true, we have no need of God by way of explanation. But all that science can teach us is something profoundly important about the *how* of it. It tells us nothing about *the reality that exists*, about what we are confronted with in experience, what we encounter.

Scientists like Richard Dawkins write as though they were the first to discover that natural selection seems to make nonsense of the idea of a just, good God, whereas theologians – and so, people of Faith – have faced up to and struggled with this dilemma for millennia. It didn't need Darwin to point out that experience suggests a cruel God. What our understanding of evolution does is reinforce our apprehension of the truth that the God behind All cannot be the God our human imagination is able to construct. Only shafts and glimmers of that mystery can come through to us.

Much is made of the fact that, given enough time, even the most statistically improbable of possible events can, indeed must, occur. This is taken as a sufficient explanation of the most 'impossibly amazing' developments in evolution, whereas all that explanation does is partly explain that it is possible for such developments to happen in the course of an evolutionary unfolding into which these possibilities are built as possibilities. It is the *what* of the result that is the greater miracle.

CHAPTER 9

DEEP ECUMENISM: ACTIONS AND DIRECTIONS

Varieties of Faith

> Self-regarding hopes and schemes may be schoolmasters to bring us to Christ; it seems, indeed, to be part of our education to form them, and then see them shattered one after another, that better and deeper hopes may be constructed out of the fragments; but a selfish Christianity is a contradiction in terms.
>
> WILLIAM RALPH INGE (1899), *CHRISTIAN MYSTICISM*, P. 241

The different religious systems are cultural correlatives. But no one of them is adequate beyond the cultural limits within which they originated and proliferated. Their limitation is demonstrated not merely by geographical comparison that exhibits their kaleidoscopic nature. It also highlights the differences between them: and in every case subsequent advance of understanding of *what really is*, of how the world actually works, exposes this limitation is. The advance required of each system tends in a common direction towards a common goal, a story that is cross-cultural, uniting them all. We do not need to jettison our religious heritage, but we do need to build upon it, grow beyond it. We need the psychological anchor of the tradition into which we were born so that we can *ground ourselves* in order to grow beyond. Religion is a resting place, an oasis along the way. We are not meant to rest too long here, nor build an eternal city in the desert across which our journey is taking us.

> We should be aware that we always speak from within a given context, and that we must stand somewhere in order to 'under-stand' ... *Our context is the overall situation of contemporary Man in our world.*[1]

If your house is structurally unsound and in danger of falling, I don't come along with a ball and chain and knock it down. I tell you what the problem is and you deal with it yourself. You know your house better than I do, and you will know best what needs to change. Awareness of the structural deficiency may make my engineer's mind blind to the beauty, comfort and functional efficiency of the house; on the other hand, awareness of these latter qualities will certainly encourage you to resist change. Truth is more *efficient* when it can be grafted onto an existing body of knowledge and experience.

Charles Darwin's son George wrote to his father on one occasion asking his advice about how best to compose an attack on the subject of 'future rewards and punishments' he was writing for publication in *The Canterbury Review*. In reply Darwin reminded his son of Voltaire's words: 'Direct attacks on Christianity ... produce little permanent effect' and 'good seems only to follow from slow and silent side attacks ... It appears to me (whether rightly or wrongly) that direct attacks against Christianity and theism produce hardly any effect on the public; and freedom of thought is best promoted by the gradual illumination of men's minds, which follows from the advance of science. It has, therefore, been always my object to avoid writing on religion, and I have confined myself to science.'[2]

What happens in the natural world is a useful metaphor for the progress of theological understanding: as in evolution generally, there must always be an interplay between *tradition* (what is handed down to us: in biology, our genetic inheritance, ecological stability) and *innovation*: but this must be mediated by our contemporary experience of a changing environment, by the evolving circumstances of this time in history.

While that progression is clear, its achievement is as incremental as the accumulation of random favourable mutations in the genome. Its achievement is the work of centuries, of millennia, to which the contribution of any one individual, of any one generation, is no more than incremental: even with the perhaps more appropriate metaphor of punctuated equilibrium.[3]

Believers of particular faiths can of course be recognised by behaviours prescribed by their particular brand of faith. This has nothing to do with being bad or good, and the taxonomy of the gods in whose honour they are practised is as varied as the practices themselves. But while the cultural richness that envelopes this practice will always remain a valued and indispensable part of a tradition's spiritual heritage, the progress of science enables the transmutation, maturation, of the embryonic understandings embodied in them: and enables a convergence towards a core understanding that is, like science itself, common to every culture. That core understanding is enriched by the kaleidoscope of story, imagery, artistic and technological achievement of evolving religion, much as our appreciation of life on Earth today is enriched by understanding of its evolution.

Even in traditional religion there is some acknowledgement that all our formulations stop short. For each of the thirty-three beads on Muslim prayer beads, the devout Muslim recites one of the names of Allah recorded in the Quran: three times round, stopping short of one hundred as a reminder that there are thousands of names of Allah, each one an expression of a different attribute. There are thousands of gods in the Hindu pantheon, each understood to be a different manifestation of the Ultimate, Transcendent Reality.

It often comes as a great surprise for Christians to discover that Islam, Taoism, Buddhism and Hinduism all have compendia of philosophy and theology as elaborate and voluminous as those of Christianity, all independently worked out, splendidly imaginative and thought-provoking, all equally founded on axioms as outmoded as the elephant upon whose back Hindu cosmology balanced the Earth is outmoded. But as long as they remain radically open to reason, the seed of their own revision is contained within each of them: but that revision must begin at the level of basic concepts and terms.

Vive la différence! It is in that word *différence* that the light glimmering at the end of this twisting pathway through dark woods twinkles to beckon us on. One of the most memorable things Raimon Panikkar wrote is that when I encounter the religion of another – or rather, when I encounter the other in his life, of which religion is part of the framework – I should not be concerned to correct or convert him, but to understand what it is in the difference of his approach and his understanding that holds, drives and directs him, and to the extent that I succeed use that insight to improve my own.[4] True dialogue occurs when the effort is mutual.

But how do we reconcile these conflicting 'metanarratives'? We must recognise that the endlessly rich and varied cultural and religious traditions within which others conduct their lives are the product of tens of centuries of encounter with Creation in a particular part of the world, just as ours is. Gianni Vattimo writes:

The third option is that all religions are partly true, depending on how they are interpreted. The truths of these diverse traditions are shaped by specific historical and cultural factors, embedded in profound mythologies, rich symbol systems, and metaphysical intuitions winnowed through centuries of human experimentation and experience.[5]

The other two options to which he refers are that there is only one true religion and that all religions are false. 'When someone wants to tell me the absolute truth', wrote Gianni Vattimo, 'it is because he wants to put me under his control.'[6] That's the way it is with religious certainty: it is something we wear as a protective carapace to shelter us from the dark. Each account of religious certainty contradicts the others, and emphasises the differences. It follows that most of them have to be in error; it is in the nature of such certainty that there is only one true version, and that is always mine.

Our Christian story may be privileged in the sense that it provided the context in which scientific understanding eventually developed: and it is through the fertilisation of other metanarratives with this understanding that their unification becomes possible. That context might have evolved within other cultures had their evolutionary and historical circumstances been different. In this sense it was accidental, contingent upon the development of those circumstances. The birth of Jesus represented a paradigm shift in human behaviour and understanding that might have occurred in an entirely different culture in some other part of the world; but for a complex concatenation of reasons and circumstances burst into flame in a remote corner of the Roman Empire, though it had flared brightly in human thought in several other cultures in the centuries leading up to this.[7] In its early years Christianity thought of itself as a uniquely Jewish sect, and after assuming imperial power began, albeit unconsciously, to clothe itself in the trappings of European culture. With the rejection of western Christianity that characterises 'the developed world' in our time, the essence of that core belief is in danger of being lost, even though it is Christianity that has bequeathed to the world the ethical norms we have come to believe constitutive of human behaviour.

This is nothing new. Over and over again in the course of human evolution innovations that originated in a particular culture subsequently spread to other cultures, on which they had a transformative effect. Such diffusion in earlier times was very slow, so that there was time for the innovation to be incorporated within the culture organically – without catalysing its disintegration – so that it could energise its development in new and richer directions. This is the way in which (to use William Grassie's words), 'God may well enough choose one particular historical moment and one particular revelation to be the definitive text.'[8] Perhaps it is even possible to extend this further, and express it as a theological interpretation of emergent probability at work in all evolution.

> Even in Europe — a continent with churches far emptier than in the United States — the trace elements of Christianity continued to infuse people's morals and presumptions so utterly that many failed to detect their presence. Like dust particles so fine as to be invisible to the naked eye, they were breathed in equally by everyone: believers, atheists, and those who never paused so much as to think about religion.
>   Had it been otherwise, then no one would ever have got woke.
>
> Tom Holland (2019), *Dominion*, p. 517
>
> Today, as the flood-tide of Western power and influence ebbs, the illusions of European and Western liberals risk being left stranded. Much that they have sought to cast as universal stand exposed as never having been anything of the kind.
>
> Tom Holland (2019), *Dominion*, p. 523
>
> It is manifest in the great surge of conversions that has swept Africa and Asia over the past century; in the conviction of millions upon millions that the breath of the Spirit, like a living fire, still blows upon the world; and, in Europe and North America, in the assumptions of many more millions who would never think to describe themselves as Christian. All are heirs to the same revolution: a revolution that has, at its molten heart, the image of a god dead on a cross.
>
> Tom Holland (2019), *Dominion*, pp. 524–525

Around the time that science was beginning to assume its modern professional dominance, the eminent geologist Adam Sedgwick wrote of science as 'the consideration of all subjects, whether of a mixed or pure nature, capable of being reduced to measurement or calculation', i.e. reduced to those physical aspects that are susceptible of *measurement*.[9] We were entering what the French philosopher Comte saw as the Third Age of man's intellectual history, when meaning and progress would condense out of experienced reality as simple measurement. In the earlier stages the ultimate explanation of things was in terms of gods or metaphysical abstractions. The mind would now think no longer in terms of an 'inner essence' of things.

Abandonment of religious faith came to be seen as a progression from childhood to maturity. A new modern myth began to take shape: of science and religion locked in mortal combat: of science as enlightened and good, religion as dark and evil. For Thomas Huxley you had to choose between the myth of religion and the truth of science. There could be no compromise: 'One or the other would have to succumb after a struggle of unknown duration.'[10] Although there is little aggression in Huxley's outlook towards religion, there were many passionate and vitriolic anti-religious scientists in the late nineteenth and early twentieth centuries (see chapter eight).

The overwhelmingly predominant view among social scientists during the twentieth century (the origins of which can be traced back to Max Weber's antipathy towards religion) was that religion would fade away with progress: its decline chronicled by such milestones as better education, the rise of capitalism, progress in science and technology, the development of mature and responsible capitalism, and increased well-being all round. This has not happened. The sociologist Peter Berger predicts that, far from being the century in which we cast off the last vestiges of religion – appropriate and useful in the earlier stages of our evolutionary progress – the twenty-first century will be the most religious century in five hundred years.[11]

The problem is that this growth is dominated by varieties of religion that are a response to scientism, materialism and a fear of a type of globalisation in which cultural identity may be diluted, neglected, even lost. Two forms are more particularly familiar to us: fundamentalist Christianity and militant Islam; whereas what we need is an *essential* religion which is fired by the spark that lies at the core of faith, but does not cause the cultural frameworks in which it variously catches flame to disintegrate.

> Instead of religion's being something that divides us, more and better religion can be something that unites us, here in our increasingly diverse communities and throughout our increasingly globalized world.[12]

At the same time, the reality we call God is so ineffable that the best verbal explanations of it are capable of being interpreted as heresy from various other orthodox viewpoints.

I find the multiplicity of religions to be grounded in the nature of religion … This multiplicity is necessary for the complete manifestation of religion. It must seek for distinctive character, not only in the individual but in society.[13]

You must abandon the vain and foolish wish that there should be only one religion; you must lay aside all repugnance to its multiplicity; as candidly as possible, you must approach everything that has ever, in the changing forms of humanity, been developed in its advancing career from the ever fruitful bosom of spiritual life … You are wrong, therefore, with your universal religion that is supposed to be natural to all; for no one will have his own true and right religion if it is the same for all. As long as we each of us occupy a separate place, there must be in these relations of man to the universe a nearer and a farther, which will determine such feeling differently in every life … *Nur in der Totalität aller solcher möglichen Formen kann die ganze Religion wirklich gegeben werden.*[14]

Ecumenism: 'There is a greater book'

Most of us can accept the idea of two books of revelation on some level. But I think few of us draw a startling but necessary conclusion. Because this is the *greater* book, the *primary* revelation, the lesser, secondary books of scripture are to be read in its light, informed by the understandings of that primary revelation of creation that the advance of human understanding makes possible. Scriptural revelation is distilled from that greater book of creation, grows out of it, in a rainbow of different ways by all our cultures over all the human ages. We cannot read scripture as though the understanding that our immediate encounter with creation gives can somehow be derived from it. On the contrary, we can only achieve our deepest appreciation of scripture in the light of a growing understanding of creation. When he declares that 'the pluralism and the diversity of religions, colour, sex, race and language are willed by God in His Wisdom, through which He created human beings' Pope Francis is opening (if by no more than a hair's breath) a door to the implications of this realisation.[15]

But what about 'outside the church there is no salvation'? The Pope's declaration also opens a door by that same hair's breadth to a dissenting orthodox gale, flapping into indignant fury banners bearing the apparently contradictory words of the Second Vatican Council's Decree on Ecumenism, which states that 'it is through Christ's Catholic Church alone, which is the universal help toward salvation, that the fullness of the means of salvation can be obtained'. In spite of this opposition, the Vatican's office for promoting interreligious dialogue followed up on the declaration by asking Catholic university professors to give the 'widest possible dissemination' to the joint statement. All of this is part of the Pope's broader agenda to open the doors of the Church so that young people don't have to 'accept fully all the teachings of the Church to take part' (*Christus Vivit*, 234).

This new agenda inches one step further forward in the documents prepared for the Synod on the Amazon held in Rome in October 2019.

> The creative Spirit who fills the universe (cf. Wisdom 1:7) has for centuries nourished the spirituality of these peoples even before the proclamation of the Gospel and moves them to accept in their own cultures and traditions ... This implies listening respectfully and not imposing expressions of the faith in terms of other cultural references that do not speak to the context of their lives ... We have to grasp what the Spirit of the Lord has been teaching these people for centuries: faith in God who is Father-Mother-Creator, the sense of communion and harmony with the Earth, the sense of solidarity with their Fellows, the idea of 'living well.'[16]

The progress of science increases by progressive increments the distance between ourselves and a God or gods *imagined in our image* – or in any image we can conceive or construct. Human history has now reached the point where we can see that using words like 'God' or 'Brahmin' to stand for 'That Yonder' is an anchor that holds us back from any further reach. But if we are to communicate, we cannot do without *words as pointers*. Somewhere in a distant future we may hope to reach that common language which is the Grail of Deep Ecumenism, in John Cobb's sense, 'beyond dialogue'.

Those of us whose tradition or faith enables us to experience and understand creation as the material expression of Godself in the panentheistic sense explored in earlier pages; those of us for whom the natural world is this and more, can make common cause with those for whom, for whatever combination of reasons, whose tradition, calling, faith do not find they are at home with this mode of response, but in whom the primary encounter and wordless, deepest response is the same as ours. We experience the same wonder. We are in the presence of the same God, however inadequate we may have come to feel that word to be. We can therefore share our wonder, and for much of our sharing we have a common language. We can also share the same anger and bewilderment, bordering on despair, at what is happening; and we can engage in action together on each of the three battlefronts on which action is so urgently needed: local community (parish), national (political), international. As Donal Dorr reminds us, 'Some of the people who are reluctant to call themselves believers may in fact be far more profoundly and authentically immersed in the mystery than those who imagine they are close to God and who have substituted the word "God" for the actual experience of mystery.'[17] (He grounds his understanding of the word 'mystery' in Otto's *mysterium tremendum et fascinans*.)

However different the depth of understanding the advance of reason allows in a particular culture, whatever the degree of educational capacity or attainment of individuals within it, the nature of the fundamental encounter upon which it is founded and from which it rises is the same for all. This we all share, however different our attempts to find words for it, ideas in which to embody it.

This is therefore the source to which we need to return in our attempt to find the common ground of a new ecumenism in which we may engage with others: within the family of Christians first of all, and beyond that both with those within our own culture who reject or ignore religion, and in the extended human family beyond. It is not that, as we set about the task before us, we simply agree to disagree, but we set about the task of developing a common responsibility that binds rather than separates us, because it is based on something more essential to who we are as humans, and to what we are called to become.

Many of the issues we face cannot be addressed adequately at local level: at what we may wish to call parish level. If we are to engage for example in challenges that relate to water quality, we may have to act at the level of the river catchment. And on all levels we can call on secular help: in this case for example the organisations charged with implementing the Water Framework Directive.

Topics discussed or issues focused on at these three levels are not mutually exclusive, but they have a different focus at the different levels. So, for example, where climate change is the issue, at national or international level the focus is likely to be on devising policy, legislation or incentives, whereas at local level the focus will be on community or personal implementation of these. Where conservation of habitats is the issue, measures at local level are likely to be more specific to place.

The more pious among us may need to beware of thinking of the 'secular' as somehow less 'religious'. Yet even the word carries a hint of warning. *Saeculum* is the Latin word for the material Earth, the world under heaven. Perhaps it is as good a verbal umbrella as our word 'religious', which echoes the binding together of all things through which we catch a glimpse, an echo, of the Maker. Our religious initiatives under the heading of 'Care for the Earth' often evoke limited response beyond the parochial umbrella because – and albeit unconsciously – we are seen to be preaching from the same 'book of revelation' that the post-religious world has rejected. Breaking through that barrier is a real challenge. We must not be seen as somehow out to convert. Conversion is not needed; any perception that it is part of our agenda is an impediment. In the fullness of time (God's own time) the deep consilience we desire may be achieved, but it is round a distant corner.

Most of the attempts to date at a deeper ecumenism have taken the form of debates between academic theologians (I mean now not primarily between different denominations of Christians). If the debating parties ever reach the other side of this endeavour they will look back with astonishment at the difference in construction in the different ladders they have used to get where they are, wondering why they didn't collapse at some point, and see that in fact they should have gone in the opposite direction, in search of the common starting point of all religions. In fact, they will never get to the other side, because each side has to use the language and conceptual framework of its starting point, whereas while moving in the other direction they will be endeavouring to shed this step by step.

Teilhard de Chardin and a deeper ecumenism

The cultural efflorescence brought about in the course of human development is comparable to the biological diversity achieved in the course of organic evolution and the supreme achievement of human history. One of the reasons Teilhard de Chardin had reservations about the ethos of UNESCO at the outset was its emphasis on 'equality' of the different traditions, where what he emphasised was the complementarity of diverse cultures of equal dignity, all of equal worth: 'complementary and capable of synthesis in a world of sympathetic collaboration.'[18]

Teilhard saw the unification of mankind which he saw as the future, achieved not through some process in which difference was levelled, but in a mutually enriching recognition of commonality in difference where the binding element was the 'Christification' of humanity: but in an understanding of the significance of Christ purified and shorn of its western cultural trappings. And while he would perhaps be astonished by the speed at which the capacity for unification has been accelerated by the digital revolution over the half century since his death, he would have been as troubled by the waste of human potential evident in the materialist levelling which characterises its current state of development as he was by the waste of two world wars during his lifetime (which compelled him to his Appeal of 1940 in *Sauvons l'humanité*).

In spite of the centrality of Catholicism to his thought and way of life, Teilhard was better placed in terms of his experience of the world to appreciate the achievement of other cultures than most. He only visited Rome during his final years (to argue in vain for ratification of his appointment to a professorship at the Collège de France, and to try to get the approval of the Holy Office for the final version of *Le phénomène humain*): 'Rome has given and will give me no shock either aesthetic or spiritual: I am immunised against the past; and as for the picturesque there is nothing to compare with the grandeur of the East. It represents the extremity of an arch that leads from man to what is above man.'[19]

He had profound misgivings about the disengagement with the world that characterised much eastern religion, but the smile on the face of the Jade Buddha, 'radiant with quiet joy, the calm of happiness, with a trace of a smile, the dawning of a smile' (as Abbé Breuil described it) led him to say: 'If Buddhism can produce this smile, then we cannot set it outside the socialisation and unity of the future.'[20]

The Word and the Way[21]

It is at the very sources that one extracts pure doctrine.

ERASMUS OF ROTTERDAM[22]

> My hope is that 'all rational souls not only shall come into harmony in the one mind which is above all minds but shall in some ineffable way become altogether one.'
> GIOVANNI PICO DELLA MIRANDOLA[23]

Among the less polemical works of Richard Dawkins is *The Ancestor's Tale*, in which he moves backward through geological time in order to trace our human family tree, encountering along the way the common ancestors we share successively: with other primates, with all vertebrates, and ultimately, way way back, with LUCA: the Last Universal Common Ancestor of all that lives.[24]

It is instructive to do something similar, in a metaphorical sense at least, for our human *outlook* upon the world in which we find ourselves, and for our response to what we *intuit* at its heart. And I use the word 'intuit' now, not in the sense of unfounded guesswork, but to signify the natural response that arises from our unmediated, direct encounter with the reality of the world.[25] Such encounter is grounded in our sensory awareness, supported by aesthetic appreciation and intellectual understanding; and it presents an ethical and moral demand and challenge for human behaviour.

The progressive and successive genetic deviations from a common ancestor that underpin the elaboration of living possibility are directed by environmental circumstance – this is what evolution is all about. It is tempting to ask the impossible question of what the genetic make-up of a living creature needs to be in order for it to develop the level of self-reflective awareness that, as it were, breaks out of the shell of awareness that characterises all life – and all animal life in particular – to question the meaning of its existence.

It is easy enough – comparatively at least! – to travel the earlier stages of this journey backward through time: and to see how much of the philosophical and religious differences that separate us, which evolved in the course of our cultural evolution on different continents, gradually and progressively peels away as the millennia rewind backward in time. This is a theme we can touch on with the broadest of brush strokes only, even when limiting the horizon of our concern to the several millennia of the biblical narrative: in view of the fact that human beings have lived on Earth for many hundreds of thousands of years.

It is not as though we are trying to get back to a certain 'lowest common denominator' in terms of content, but to peel away the cultural accretions in which an essential core *primal insight* has necessarily been clothed. What all cultural traditions attempt to do is anchor their stage of history more concretely, as it were, in that 'something' that was there from a remote beginning: instinctive apprehension of an 'Ultimate'.

The emergence of the Tao

When human consciousness first awoke to self-reflective awareness, can you imagine the shock with which our First Parents saw the Creation about them come into focus? Without any of our distractions to deflect or dim or distort *the sensory experience*? – and they reached to try to touch what was behind it with their newly awakened intellect. All they could know, all they could ever know, lay before them, was all around them, in the thrilling and terrifying creation out of whose womb they had emerged after a gestation of nearly fourteen billion years. All they could ever *come* to know had to grow from that encounter. Their deepest intuition told them (as it tells us) that there was an Ultimate Greatness behind it that manifested itself in the beauty, the joy, the awesomeness, the terror indeed, and which – or was it Who? – must be the source, the font of all those experienced realities.[26]

For the overwhelmingly greater number of all of the generations of humankind, our experience of anything in the nature of 'ultimate meaning' was the created marvel that had come into being through that awesome process of Unfolding that we in our time are the first to know about, to understand, and to stand in amazement before.

Until the emergence of what we call 'civilisation' we were immersed in creation for all of our waking hours and through the hours of our dreaming. Civilisation allows us to withdraw from nature as it were and create the space in our mind that allows us to think about it, and to try to formulate in words and music and ritual what we experience out there under the clouds and stars, and between the trees.

Up to this, all our First Parents and their early descendants could know about what in time they would come to call 'God' lay before them, in Nature: in these others who share the Earth with me: others the same as me in my family and clan and further afield, others who are alive but variously different: and in the seasons and elements in which we all play out our lives – the sun rising in the morning, the stars at night, the round of the year, wind, fire, water, air. What are they saying to me about who and what they are, and where they have come from?

There are no books.

For the longest time there is no language in which to frame our thoughts about it all with each other.

But no words can *stand in for* what such words merely *sign*-ify. It is in the *experience* of creation that God is revealed, is revealing himself: not in the words, the sentences, the treatises that attempt to describe it, to contain it, to hold it down. It cannot *be* described: its being cannot be caught in the description.[27]

This wordless affirmation is the essence of the human spiritual response, common to all traditions. Its very foundation is a sense of meaning and direction running through all that is experienced, as utterly and forever beyond our human grasp: indeed, the nature of our response is carried on this sense of it being utterly and forever beyond our comprehension.

It is out of this wordless affirmation that what would, with the passage of many long Chinese centuries, emerge as the Tao begins to crystallise; the Tao, which struggles to find words to anchor itself, knowing that which is touched will withdraw when spoken of. With the invention of civilisation, of language and writing, and especially once we start to do 'theology', an ever-growing thicket of exegesis begins to accrete around the Tao, which itself just *is*, i.e. it is not a *concept*. Definition, and all that follows, pins it down, but at the same time bleeds it of meaning:

> The way conceals itself in being nameless.
>
> *TAO TE CHING* XLI (92)[28]

> Once the whole is divided, the parts need names.
>
> *TAO TE CHING* (32)[29]

> Only when it is cut are there names.
> As soon as there are names
> One ought to know that it is time to stop.
>
> *TAO TE CHING* (32)

Two books of revelation

When we in the Christian tradition speak of 'revelation', we are talking about how God *reveals* himself to us, how God enables us to come to know Him, to see him in so far as our eyes *can* see God.

In the far eastern world there is no revelation in that sense: no revealing of a hidden Ultimate by drawing back the veil. There is no departure from the primitive awareness that there is nothing to be said. But this is not the 'nothing to be said' of the atheist: it is that nothing can be said of that of which we would speak that in the very act of speaking does not collapse the reality of which we are aware: the reality that is apprehended by the human spirit before speech. 'The Tao that can be spoken is not the real Tao …' The Tao, so far from the possibility of definition by word, that words may catch the echo of it less immediately than sound of itself, in its beauty and harmony: through music for instance.

Written revelation indeed – scripture – is itself no more than a subset of this primal revelation mediated over the time of human history through spiritually attuned human persons of a special kind: themselves always formed and limited by the cultural inheritance of their time, constrained by linguistic limitation, as we too are.

Celtic Christianity and the Tao?

If we look now at the origins of religious belief in this corner of Europe we sometimes speak of as the Celtic Fringe, we find at the heart of it that which, in every essential, is the Tao, that which cannot be named, that which is so far beyond while yet so intimate that no net of words can contain it: it slips between all the distinctions that language can essay to hold it.

When Christianity arrived in this far-flung corner of Europe in the early fifth century, it was not coming into a spiritual vacuum. There was already a highly developed body of earlier spiritual belief and practice that intuited divinity at the very heart of the natural world, onto which Christianity attempted to graft the Good News of Salvation and Redemption. Because of this it was able to develop in a different direction from that centred on Rome.

And so, between the fifth and the ninth centuries in Ireland a form of Christianity prevailed that has been characterised as being more deeply imbued with the sense of, and alertness to, creation as the primary revelation: until the time came when the Roman church felt itself sufficiently anchored politically and theologically to turn its gaze to this northwesternmost fringe of its reach in order to bring it under properly orthodox control. And this earliest 'vision' or 'intuition' was not a matter of doctrine, to be picked up by reading the right books, attending the right courses or practising the proper new rituals; it was a lived absorption in the beauty and pattern, the terror and challenge of the world that called for acclaim and response. The bedrock of this Christian 'faith' was a lived absorption in *the reality of creation as meant* (as word, Tao). 'The incarnation of the divine', Mark Johnston wrote, 'is ubiquitous.'[30]

What Christopher Bamford wrote of this Celtic Christianity – that the heritage we seek to recover in our day 'is that of a beginning' – is equally true of the *Tao Te Ching*. Celtic Christianity,

> which, as beginning, is shrouded in mystery, is quintessentially mysterious: beginning in mystery, continuing in mystery, ending in mystery. One gets the sense, indeed, trying to unravel the different strands of scholarship, legend and archaeology, of entering into relation with a moment of history in which the spiritual is so closely and clearly involved with the phenomenal that all of one's usual means of understanding are wanting.[31]

Where science comes in

Where our modern scientific enquiry fits into all this is in the way in which, with ever increasing depth and scope, it penetrates and elucidates the fabric of reality. We can be misled by our use of that word 'science', identifying it with the hypersophisticated intellectual achievement we see in particle accelerators, sophisticated drugs and medical procedures, in digital technology. And indeed it does include all of this. But what science is, essentially, is fearless and dedicated use of the human intellect we all have. And what that advance has done is to show us a creation great beyond anything we could have imagined. The more deeply the progress of science peers into creation – on every level that science investigates, from mathematics to sociology – the further along the road of understanding its quest takes us, the more awe-inspiring our awareness of complexity, diversity, beauty, intelligibility, becomes; and really, you have to be involved in that progress yourself to truly appreciate the extent to which this is the case.

The more deeply our human sensory and intellectual penetration extends, the more we come to realise how much further beyond our grasp its greatness extends; that, indeed, it is beyond the scope of words like 'extent' or 'depth', and ultimately we find ourselves without words. 'Much speech', the Tao tells us, 'leads inevitably to silence' (V). The more our discernment penetrates the Four Quarters (in the words of the *Tao Te Ching*), the more we become 'capable of not knowing anything' (X). In the classic and characteristic paradox of the Tao such ignorance is the ultimate in wisdom: and being mysterious, fuzzy of definition, is less distorting in its verbal unsettlement of the ultimate truth we struggle to articulate.[32]

The more deeply the gaze of science penetrates reality on any and all of its tiered levels of growing complexity the more we realise how much greater the distance between us and the Ultimate is, augmenting our sense of 'what we are smaller than', as Salman Rushdie put it, but as it does this, so should our growing appreciation of how unique we are keep pace.[33] True spirituality must never be afraid of the discovery science unveils: and indeed it feeds upon it, is enriched by it, matures through it.

The essence of what the Tao seeks to teach rises out of the very heart of scientific advance. The more we come to know, the more we begin to comprehend the extent of the unknowability of what sustains all.

> Is not the space between heaven and Earth like a bellows?
> It is empty without being exhausted:
> The more it works the more comes out.
>
> *Tao Te Ching* V (15)

Here – in science – we all, of whatever culture, speak the same language, and our response to that which reaches up to us from the deepest heart of what we encounter, whether stars or eyes of human souls, *is a response common to every one of us*. Out of this our different individual responses are moulded as our particular endowments permit – cultural, historical, genetic – in our personal attempt to articulate that core response. Our individuality finds its ultimate expression of acclaim in these voices: wordless expression in music and graphic form, or hosted in words (as in poetry or theology): in our shared contemplation of which a further mutual deepening takes place.

I think I am myself most aware of all this, of its immediacy, when I am engaged alone in geological fieldwork.

From time to time I spend a few days in Corraun in eastern Achill in the west of Ireland, where the rocks are late Devonian in age, splendidly exposed along the northern shore of Clew Bay. And with my geologist's eyes I can trace in these rocks the lineaments of the great river system of 365 million years ago in which the vast sheets of sand and mud that went into their making were carried, and laid down layer upon layer over tens of millions of years. And through that geological understanding I become present to that vanished landscape; I can hear the river, reconstruct the pattern of its seasonal flow, of the lives of plants and animals under the hot sun and blue sky that governed its seasons. Here of course there is no presence but my own, except the presence of those ancient plants and animals which are not *alert* presences, alert only to their immediacy. No alert presence except my own, out of its own time transported back through a geological wormhole in time to be *there*. And to be *aware* (in a purer sense perhaps than is possible *here* in our own time), of that *presence* which the deepest spirituality in all the religious traditions of the world is reluctant to name, knowing that any attempt to define it will cause it to retreat, because indeed, it is not to be named, is beyond name.[34]

A new ecumenism

There is talk in theological circles these days of a radical 'New Ecumenism' that takes as its priority the celebration of diversity and engaging in dialogue with other faiths in a spirit of open-mindedness and humility rather than devoting all our energies to the recovery of a dysfunctional unity.[35] What we must strive for is a unity in diversity that echoes and amplifies that of the natural world itself. This New Ecumenism presents us with an immensely fruitful field of exploration, in which we set out to pick up the anchoring threads of that which lies at the heart of our response to the natural world, and try to weave them into the fabric of our time.

A new creation story, common to all races, is unfolded for us in the language of science. In its further progress and elaboration lie the seeds of a future consilience that will catalyse the ultimate ecumenism that will bring us all together in Acclaiming the One God, the One Lord of Heaven. It will take centuries, but that is the way of things.

Nor should the apparently confident certitude of scientism upset or deflect us. As the *Tao Te Ching* reminds us:

> When the worst student hears about the way
> He laughs out loud;
> If he did not laugh
> It would be unworthy of being the way.

XLI (90)

How we apply the knowledge that science endows us with is a separate question, and again one we must wrestle with together, as a human family guided by the ethical instinct that reason nurtures in us all: and this we all seek to do, in our imperfect, stumbling way, as we strive to attain the humaneness so central to the Confucian tradition, in our quest to become *junzi*, the ideal human person, which was dissected in such masterly fashion by Thomas Aquinas in his treatment of 'virtue'.[36]

Raimon Panikkar writes of great philosophies as 'homeomorphic equivalents', of how 'this continuous discontinuity of traditions might constitute a symphony if we could "hear" the ideas of these thinkers in a creative way'.[37] A symphony, but a *concordia discors*; *Tota haec mundi concordia ex discordibus constat*, wrote Seneca (the Roman Stoic philosopher who lived around the time of Christ), 'the entire harmony of the world consists of discordant elements.'[38] The very harmony that is human cultural achievement is constituted by the 'discordant' elements of its individual instruments. We are reminded of Thomas Merton's search for *constantia*: where 'all notes in their perfect distinctness, are yet blended in one'.

This alternative ecumenical approach asks us to take a step back, leaving our differences to one side for the moment – diluting the cocktail of evangelism (at whatever end of the faith spectrum, from atheism to deism) with the dose of humility the advance of human understanding requires of us – and to concentrate our reach on that 'other book' of revelation, because this is an endeavour in which we all share, confident that out of deeper understanding the possibility of that deeper consilience will arise and develop, however long it takes.

It is in exploration of that common experience that the way forward lies: the 'way' now in the sense of the everyday paths our feet follow, the rites to be performed together, now that a globalised world brings us all back together and we can ask each other what we have discovered since we went our separate ways – so many tens of thousands of years ago – and looked at the glory of the world from all the different angles our geographical separation made possible.

> The current religious turmoil may also be a forward move in which the achievements of all the Ways, enlightened by all that the sciences have taught us, can be united in a convincing synthesis. Perhaps such a new faith could provide the conviction and vision required to arouse us to the drastic changes we need in our intellectual life and our relations to the rest of nature.[39]

Laudato Si'

This is the deeper ecumenism to which our energies need in the first and most urgent instance to be directed, because in so many other directions those energies will drain away like water in sand. That common engagement is what Pope Francis urges and hopes for in his encyclical: 'I wish to appeal to every person living on this planet;' 'In this Encyclical, I would like to enter into dialogue with all people about our common home.'[40] This is the 'right living' to which all of us are called, into whatever cultural tradition we are born.[41] In the exhilaration and challenge of its exploration we find common cause. It matters not whether we are Christian or Buddhist or Atheist when we are excavating the fossil beds of northern China or seek to understand the chemistry of soil nitrogen or the genetic defence strategies of bacteria.[42]

And in that common exploration, side by side and hand in hand, (when we can afford to take our eyes from the thrill and challenge of the common task) what our respectful attention should be on is not the doctrinal detail of what divides us, but on *seeking to understand the difference of the other*: not looking in advance for the essence of our distinction to what is *different*, but to what we share. All of what divides us post-dates the fossilisation of language and is part of cultural diversity: however other we may have come to think of it.

Let us agree on that foundation to begin with, and build on the common ethic it grounds: until a deeper maturity enables a more rational consilience. In the meantime, share and enjoy our difference, in a way analogous to that by which we enjoy biological diversity. 'When you meet someone better than yourself,' we are instructed in the *Analects* of Confucius, 'turn your thoughts to becoming his equal. When you meet someone not as good as you are, look within and examine your own self.'

This – in essence – was the approach taken by Matteo Ricci and Michele Ruggieri over the course of their extraordinary missionary encounter with China in the late sixteenth and early seventeenth centuries: and who knows where we might be today if those embryonic possibilities had been allowed to grow from that beginning.[43] It is fascinating to note the complementary theological interpretations of Ricci and Ruggieri. Both passionately believed in the presence of a primordial revelation in Chinese tradition, but Ricci was especially drawn to Confucianism, while Ruggieri looked to a new cultural synthesis between the Tao and the Christian concept of the *Logos*: itself the product of an earlier synthesis between nascent Christianity and the traditions of Greece and Rome.[44]

Central to the encyclical of Pope Francis is the message, grounded in the advance of scientific understanding, that all that we see and understand of living reality, and the broader chemical and physical reality out of which it has been born, all of this has unfolded, continues to unfold; all this *is meant*. To believe otherwise, for all the pseudo-intellectual jargon in which the argument to the contrary is embellished, goes against all reason when reason is understood as the fearless use of all our human capacities of sense, intellect and spirit: through the unflinching use of which we may also come to know how utterly beyond our human capacity is that meaning: even though our human capacity in some sense *is whispered out of it.*

And being *meant*, and therefore with Ultimate Direction, this is *the* Way, whose never-to-be discovered name the Tao attempts to echo. This is before all the ways of approaching it our cultures define for us, ways appropriate to our limits, grounded ways all-important if we are to keep our feet on the ground, which is why performance of ritual, keeping the rites, is so important to us (as it is in the Confucian tradition). The Confucian tradition can be seen to correspond functionally to western religious governance (which is how Matteo Ricci saw it): in order to provide a frame within which response to the unbounded (God, Way of Heaven) can be contained in everyday life.

In concluding

These thoughts are no more than the broadest of brush strokes. The ideas they sketch need to be filled out with deeper exploration of the links between the Tao (as indeed the spiritual traditions of every other part of the world), scientific advance, and the essential message of Christianity.[45] In practice, this comes down to common engagement with creation, with the world around us: most productively, I think, to begin with, at the level of village or commune or parish. I don't need to go beyond the gate of my parish except to understand better what I encounter within its compass, to see it with new eyes, to see it as it were for the first time (in T.S. Eliot's sense)[46], as fresh as Eden. Everything you find outside, beyond, will bring you back here, enrich your encounter with the place your feet walk in every day.

A day spent exploring the flowers or insects of the fields around us together will bring more ecumenical enlightenment, it may be, than a decade of retrospective tinkering with the unwieldy dysfunctional theological architecture that five centuries of division have bequeathed us. In so many ways we are closer to God at the wordless start of it all, in this encounter with the natural world.

The most thoughtful analysts among those who study biodiversity are of one mind that this must be our approach. In a seminally important book he wrote thirty years ago, Edward Wilson acknowledges that by today's ethic, the value of the abundant, scarcely known, natural world may be limited, but that 'as biological knowledge grows the ethic will shift fundamentally so that everywhere, for reasons that have to do with the very fibre of the brain, the fauna and flora of a country will be thought part of the national heritage as important as its art, its language, and that astonishing blend of achievement and farce that has always defined our species'.[47]

He goes on to say:

> To the extent that each person can feel like a naturalist, the old excitement of the untrammeled world will be regained. I offer this as a formula of re-enchantment to invigorate poetry and myth: mysterious and little known organisms live within walking distance of where you sit. Splendour awaits in minute proportions.[48]

How better to conclude than with words of the *Tao Te Ching*.

> Without stirring abroad
> One can know the whole world;
> Without looking out of the window
> One can see the way of heaven.
> The further one goes
> The less one knows.
> Therefore the sage knows without having to stir
> Identifies without having to see,
> Accomplishes without having to ask.[49]

Back to the future?

How much of all this will still be relevant fifty or a hundred years from now is open to question. Like their counterparts everywhere, Chinese millennials are a product of globalisation, and while they are much more alert than their parents to the environmental crises we face, they are as far from traditional religion as their western counterparts. And in spite of the ever-increasing gap between social classes in China, this is probably as true for the rural young who are migrating in such numbers from the countryside to China's burgeoning cities.[50]

The missionary societies that proliferated over the last centuries went abroad to bring the gospel *ad gentes*: to the different non-Christian peoples of the world. The traditional understanding of the mission *ad gentes* was conceived within a world where the *gentes* in question were the different cultural worlds that reached their greatest flowering in an early modern geographical context: Indian, Chinese, African, American, etc. One of the defining aspects of the modern world is the way *human cultural differentiation is turned back inwards upon itself.* In earlier cultures *borrowings* of particular cultural advances were the rule – notably in agriculture and technology. But now there is the interweaving of all except the most isolated cultures we call globalisation, and the cross-fertilisation of earlier distinctiveness by a certain *unification* that results in the extinction of certain elements of the earlier distinctiveness (e.g. genetic, linguistic), and an increasing primacy being given to *reason* in the regulation of human affairs.

One of the effects of this is the need for a redefinition of the concept of *gentes*, especially when we think of introducing a Christian perspective to the young; the geographically conditioned distinctiveness of earlier generations no longer defines these younger generations of humanity, and the Book out of which 'mission' must draw its lessons is the Other Book.

AFTERWORD

On the feast of All Saints in 1517, according to old legends, Martin Luther nailed his ninety-five theses to the door of the Castle Church in Wittenberg, setting in train the revolutionary sequence of events we call the Reformation. When we commemorated the five hundredth anniversary of this great upheaval three years ago, there was a surprising degree of consensus between the leaders of both Protestant and Catholic churches on the necessity for fundamental change in the church at the time, especially in relation to the need to return *ad fontes*, to the sources: the streams that gave rise to Christianity. In our time we are called once again to return to the sources but with the new insight our age of the world allows us into the nature of God's Word, the letters of which we now see in the very fabric of creation all about us, and of which we can make out the odd sentence here and there, decipher even the occasional passage or sonata, against the background of which is framed the marvellous human story the Bible tells in human words, echoing those wordless ones of God.

Increasingly this reach into the time to come is seen as the narrative of our time, both in science and theology: reaching towards a future that holds the promise of fuller being. John Haught identifies with Teilhard de Chardin in postulating the future as a power that *draws* evolution to it rather than a *reach* implied in the progressive realisation of inherent potentiality. 'The narrative of our day is not about having fallen from a perfect state, but about the endless search for a perfect state somewhere in the future.'[1] That future, we need to remind ourselves, is potentially a very long one: tens of thousands, indeed millions, of years. The Teilhardian articulation will in the course of that time doubtless be abandoned for the inadequacy of the metaphor that it is, just as earlier and now outmoded metaphors of heaven and life eternal are now seen as vessels unable to hold the more mature understanding of our time, unable to hold the ultimate meaning the words intend.[2] Between

---

1   Haught (2006).

2   John Feehan (2007).

the Alpha of our origins and the Omega of our final destination we may perhaps still have to traverse and decipher most of the letters in the alphabet of human possibility.

ENDNOTES

Chapter 1 Attending to Creation

1 Perry (ed.) (2000).

2 Houzeau (1887), quoted in Linssen (1951), p. 239.

3 'Advice, addressed to the young clergy of the diocese of Carlisle, in a sermon, preached at a general ordination, holden at Rose Castle, on Sunday July 29, 1781.'

4 Polonnaruwa is an ancient Buddhist monastery in Sri Lanka, a World Heritage Site famed especially for its giant statues, carved out of the living rock. Thomas Merton visited in 1968 and 'Looking at these figures ... was suddenly, almost forcibly, jerked clean out of the habitual, halftied vision of things, and an inner clearness, clarity, as if exploding from the rocks themselves, became evident and obvious.' (*Asian Journal*, pp. 231-236).

5 Drummond (1832), p. 102.

6 McCarthy (2015), p. 17.

7 Louv (2005), p. 16.

8 'The early Christian monks came to recognise that whatever power the Word might have in their lives would depend on their capacity to listen to the silence out of which it rose. "Perfect silence alone proclaims [God]," says Maximus the Confessor' (Christie, [2013], p. 187).

9 See 'A Deeper Mode of Scientific Encounter', Chapter 7 of *The Singing Heart of the World*, pp. 111–124.

10 McCarthy (2015).

Chapter 2 The Evolution of Human Understanding

1 Adelard of Bath, *Perdifficiles Questiones Naturales*, quoted in Ross and McLaughlin, pp. 621-624.

2 Dobell (1958).

3 Margaret Espinasse, M. (1956).

4 Hooke (1665).

5 These are scanning transmission electron holography microscopes.

6 A nanometre is one thousand-millionth of a metre. A picometre is one trillionth of a metre (1/1,000,000,000,000), and is mainly used to measure atoms and subatomic particles.

7 By 2030 common computers will be a million times more powerful than they were in 2000.

8 Rees (2018), p. 137.

9 *Ibid.*, p. 152; 'If a lion could speak, we couldn't understand him' (Wittgenstein, quoted on p. 159).

10 Of course, this is not to deny that there are fundamental differences as well.

11 Wilson (2006), p. 67.

12 Miall (1895), pp. 219-223.

13 Wilson (2006), p. 115.

14 Miall (1895), p. 389.

15 Albert the Great (c.1260).

16 Ray (1743), p. 23.

17 William Paley (1830), p. 510.

18 Barnes (1998).

19 Margulis and Schwartz (1997).

20 Linnaeus (1749-1769), pp. 387-388.

21 In fact, there are many more, but these are the only ones known to us; the rest have never been seen and many will never be.

Chapter 3 The Wonder of the Other Lives

1 See Dawkins and Wong (2017).

2 Grant Watson (1947), p. 192.

3 There are few better introductions to this than the thirty-eight wonderful chapters in Grant Watson's *Wonders of Natural History* (1947); or Eric Duthie's compendium *Wild Company* (1962).

4 In the United States, for which more accurate figures are available than elsewhere, the number of birdwatchers (60 million) far exceeds the combined numbers of those who play basketball (24 million), baseball (23 million) and football (9 million).

5 The experiments of Lee R. Dice summarised in *Wild Company* (1962), p. 319.

6 Randerson (2002), p. 20.

7 *Animal Wonderland* by Frank W. Lane (1948) contains excellent examples.

8 Fenton and Simmons (2014).

9 Birkhead (2012).

10 It looks as if blue-green light has a role to play here; it is believed that this causes a particular protein called cryptochrome to transfer an electron to a small molecule called FAD, causing a molecular re-alignment that allows the bird to sense the orientation of the magnetic field. It is thought that because of the tight alignment between vision and magnetoreception birds may actually be able to *see* magnetic fields.

11 Yong (2010), pp. 42-45.

12 Olson (1987); Gillespie (1987).

13 Brand and Yancy (1980).

14 James Le Fanu gave a selection of some recent discoveries in an article in that iconoclastic read of older people, *The Oldie* (Summer 2013): 'among the more exotic of recently discovered creatures': the Hawaiian bobtail squid that glows in the dark due to the luminescent bacteria in its stomach; a brilliant white flesh-eating 'ghost' slug that preys on earthworms in their burrows; a spiky bright pink dragon millipede that oozes cyanide from its skin to discourage potential predators; the world's largest stick insect at 2 feet, whose eggs possess a distinctive miniature pair of wings, and the world's smallest snake, thinner than a strand of spaghetti, which, curled up, would just cover a ten-cent piece.

15 *The Singing Heart of the World*, p. 88.

16 Muir (1913), p. 41.

17 See Balcombe (2011), Bekoff and Pierce (2009).

18 Williams (2011), pp. 36-39.

19 Mather (2008).

20 Muir (1913), p. 86.

21 Hutto (1995).

22 For a fuller treatment see Chapter 5 in *The Singing Heart of the World*.

23 Moore (1906), p. 328.

24 Muir (1916), p. 10.

25 Paley (1828), p. 504.

26 *The Singing Heart of the World*, p. 89.

27 Muir (1916), p. 66.

28 'Diary', *London Review of Books*, 20 June 2019, p. 41.

29 Quoted in Robinson (2006), p. 326.

30 Barnes (1998), pp. 251-256.

31 Barnes (1998) recognised 90 phyla: 14

bacterial, 32 protistan, 3 fungal, 2 plant and 38 animal (p. xii).

32 L.C. Miall (1896).

33 Miall and Hammond (1900).

34 Humphries (1938), quoted in Murray *et al.* (2018).

35 Murray *et al.* (2018), p. 1.

36 Albert Schweitzer (1875-1965) won the Nobel Peace Prize in 1952 for his philosophy of Reverence for Life. See, e.g. Schweitzer (1965), Barsam (2008).

37 There is an excellent introduction in 'Plants of Greek myth' at theoi.com.

38 This is the Doctrine of Signatures at work again; one of the effects of gout is painful swelling of the joints, of which the swollen nodes of herb Robert were thought to be suggestive. According to one interpretation, the medieval Latin name *herba Roberti* (of which 'herb Robert' is a straight translation) could have originated as *herba rubra* (the red herb), only later developing an association with the eighth-century St Rupert of Salzburg, whose aid was invoked in cases involving erysipelas, bleeding wounds and ulcers, and after whom the plant was named by Linnaeus. Other medicinal uses included the treatment of ophthalmic complaints (because of its gallic acid content) and gout, and a poultice made from it was applied to relieve rheumatism.

39 Many examples in Feehan (2009). *The Wildflowers of Offaly*, Offaly Co. Co., 510 pp.

40 Vanderplank (2000).

41 Paghat's Garden: Passion Flower Symbolism: www.paghat.com/passiflorasymbolism.html

42 Fascinating videos of passion-flower pollination are available on YouTube.

43 Sprengel (1793).

44 *Ibid.*, p. 43.

Chapter 4 Nature as Revelation

1 Buick Knox (1967).

2 The original Latin version – *Annales Veteris Testamenti, a prima mundi origine deducti, una cum rerum Asiaticarum et Aegyptiacarum chronico, a temporis historici principio usque ad Maccabaicorum initia producto* – appeared in 1650. The English translation (*Annals of the Old Testament, deduced from the first origins of the world, the chronicle of Asiatic and Egyptian matters together produced from the beginning of historical time up to the beginnings of Maccabees*) followed eight years later. He had been thinking about his chronology for decades, but started work on it seriously when he got to England; he was reported to be 'spend[ing] constantly all the afternoones' in the Bodleian Library in Oxford during his first summer (1640) in England.

3 Gould (1993). 'Fall of the House of Ussher', in *Eight Little Piggies*.

4 Ussher Chronology (Wikipedia).

5 Ussher's calculation was generally accepted by theologians until the late nineteenth century, although its inadequacy was becoming ever clearer with the progress of geology long before this. It is still accepted in Young Earth creationist circles, where a modern translation (*The Ages of the World*, New Leaf Publishing, 2005) is widely read.

6 Nicholas of Cusa (1453), p. 19 (Chapter 6).

7 *Laudato Si'*, 12, 85.

8 *Laudato Si'*, 85. This last is a quotation from Paul Ricoeur.

9   Browne (1643).

10 St Augustine, *Sermons*, 68, 6.

11 Paley (1802), pp. 420-421.

12 'Christianity ... perceives in the words
    the Word himself, the Logos who
    displays his mystery through this
    complexity and the reality of human
    history.' The Apostolic Exhortation
    Verbum Domini of Benedict XVI (2010)
    builds on the encyclical *Divino afflante
    Spiritu* of Pius XII (1943), which led
    to the beginning of modern Catholic
    biblical scholarship.

13 Friedrich Schleiermacher (1768-
    1834) was a key figure in its early
    development: although some milestones
    are much earlier, notably St Augustine's
    belief that the biblical text should not
    be interpreted literally if it contradicts
    what we know from science and
    reason, 'If anyone, not understanding
    the mode of divine eloquence, should
    find something [about the physical
    universe] in our books, or hear of the
    same from those books, of such a kind
    that it seems to be at variance with the
    perceptions of his own rational faculties,
    let him believe that these other
    things are in no way necessary to the
    admonitions or accounts or predictions
    of the scriptures' (Augustine, *The
    Literal Interpretation of Genesis*, 1:2-9).
    With regard to the 'days' of creation
    he wrote: 'What kind of days these
    were it is extremely difficult, or perhaps
    impossible for us to conceive, and how
    much more to say' (*The City of God*,
    Book 11, Chapter 6).

14 Boyle (1690). More quotations on the
    theme can be found at bookofnature.
    org

15 St Augustine, *Confessions*, Book 10,
    Chapter 6.

16 Cooper (2007), p. 18.

17 *Ipsa actualitas rei est quoddam lumen
    ipsius* (Commentary on the *Liber de
    Causis*, I. 6.).

18 Wallace (1869), p. 342.

19 Hudson (1893).

20 Hopkins, 'The Windhover: To Christ
    our Lord' (Penguin edition, p. 30).

21 Ruse (2003), p. 336.

22 Raven (1953), pp. 112-113.

23 Fenton and Simmons (2014).

24 Genesis 1:1-2; quotations here from the
    New Revised Standard Version Bible.

25 Genesis 1:6-7, 9, 11, 20, 24.

26 Foster (2010), p. 129.

27 This is where A.N. Whitehead's Process
    Philosophy originates.

28 Literally, 'in tasting we are alive in
    God'; Mountford (2011), p. 67.

29 Hopkins, 'Pied Beauty' (Penguin
    edition, pp. 30-31).

30 Ruse (2003), p. 331.

31 Ruse (2003), p. 335.

32 Nicholas of Cusa, *De Visione Dei* (1453)
    9 (Chapter 4).

33 Schleiermacher, quoted in Macintosh
    and Stewart (1989), p. 39.

34 Nicholas of Cusa (1444-1445).

35 *Super Librum Boethii de Trinitate
    Proem.*, q. 1, 2 ad 1. Thomas Aquinas
    wrote his Commentary on Boethius' *De
    Trinitate* in Paris in 1257-1258.

36 *Sed quia de Deo scire non possumus
    quid sit, sed quid non sit, non possumus
    considerare de Deo quomodo sit, set
    potius quomodo non sit. Primo ergo
    considerandum est quomodo non sit;
    secundo, quomodo a nobis cogniscatur;
    tertio, quomodo nominetur* (*Summa
    Theologiae*, 1a, q. 3 prologue).

37 'But suddenly, at the edge of [Mrs Moore's] mind, Religion appeared, poor little talkative Christianity, and she knew that all its divine words from "Let there be light" to "It is finished" only amounted to "boum"' (Forster [1924], Chapter 14).

38 Inge (1899), p. 101.

39 There is an intimation of what became the Christian concept of Word also in the Jewish notion of *Hokmah/Sophia*, the enlivening life force that sustains the 'very structure of the world and the properties of the elements' (Ws 7:17). And we saw earlier how the Stoics of ancient Greece had this notion of *logos spermatikos*, which were envisaged as seeds planted in the divine Logos, waiting to germinate and unfold at some later, divinely ordained moment. Plotinus thought of creation as the *ecstasis* of God, a radiation out of Godself into all the beauty and intelligibility of our material world, in which God is not merely reflected *but somehow embodied*.

40 *The Origin of Species* was published in 1859.

41 *Lehrbuch der Naturphilosophie*, I, 4. Oken's term for 'realisation' is *Realwerden*.

42 Lovejoy (1936), pp. 325-326.

43 Cooper (2007), p. 84.

44 Lamm (2004), p. 150.

45 Watts (1999), p. 69.

46 Dante, *Paradiso*.

47 Wallace (1869), pp. 448-449.

48 Dennett (1995).

49 Haught (2007), p. 2.

50 Matthew 22:36-40 (David Bentley Hart's translation). In Luke 10:27 the same response is followed by the parable of the Good Samaritan.

51 Wilson (2006), p. 12.

52 Cobb (1998), p. 65. Northrop's book was published in 1946.

53 Cobb (1998), p. 66.

54 *Laudato Si'*, 217.

55 *Laudato Si'*, 218.

56 *Laudato Si'*, 219 (my italics).

57 'Cosmic Christ' terminology originated among nineteenth-century German and British theologians, but has been popularised in more recent times by Matthew Fox (Fox, 1988). The idea that there is a cosmic dimension to the Incarnation was central to Teilhard de Chardin's belief that Christ is the unifying centre of the universe and its goal. Teilhard may have been influenced by something in the writings of Origen (c. AD 185-254), whose wide-ranging speculations on the meaning of Christ were as breathtakingly inventive as Teilhard's own, and brought comparable condemnation from Church councils in the fifth and sixth centuries.

58 Jäger (2006).

Chapter 5 The Theology of Biodiversity in *Laudato Si'*

1 An earlier version of this chapter was delivered at a conference on '*Laudato Si'* and the importance of biodiversity' in St Columban's, Dalgan, 19 March 2016.

2 Unknown ninth–tenth-century Irish author: Stokes (1905), *The Martyrology of Oengus the Culdee*, p. 56; printed (no. 234) in Jackson (1971), p. 296. The 'Life' of Molua probably dates to the early twelfth-century.

3 Genesis 1:26; as also Genesis 1:28: 'And God blessed them, and God said unto them, Be fruitful, and multiply, and replenish the Earth, and subdue it; and

have dominion over the fish of the sea, and over the fowl of the air, and over every living thing that moveth upon the Earth.'

4   Quoted in Dermot Moran, 'Towards a Philosophy of the Environment' in Feehan (ed.) (1995), pp. 45-67.

5   Rickaby (1901), pp. 2, 199.

6   *Catechism of the Catholic Church* (1994), paragraphs 299 and 2415. See Linzey (2009).

7   Ray (1743, 1826).

8   Raven (1942), p. 467.

9   Darwin, F. (1887), vol. II, p. 219.

10 Ray (1743, 1826), pp. ix-x.

11 18,000 plants, 150 'beasts', 500 birds, 500 fishes 'secluding shell-fish', 'but if the shell-fish be taken in, more than six times the number'; and 20,000 insects (*Wisdom of God*).

12 *Ibid.*, p. 24.

13 Peattie (1948), p. 46.

14 Barnes (1998).

15 Margulis and Schwartz (1997).

16 Among other key passages are the following:

    'Saint John of the Cross taught that all the goodness present in the realities and experiences of this world "is present in God eminently and infinitely, or more properly, in each of these sublime realities is God"' (*Laudato Si'*, 234).

    Creation is 'a precious book, "whose letters are the multitude of created things present in the universe"' (*Laudato Si'*, 85; quoting John Paul II).

    The Japanese bishops write of how every creature sings 'the hymn of its existence' (*Laudato Si'*, 85).

17 *Laudato Si'*, 84.

18 *Laudato Si'*, 83.

19 *Laudato Si'*, 233. In the prayer for the Earth at the end of the encyclical God is addressed as 'present in the whole universe and in smallest of your creatures'.

20 *Laudato Si'*, 9; quoting Patriarch Bartholomew.

21 *Laudato Si'*, 233.

22 The *Summa* was written between 1266 and 1273.

23 Albert the Great (c.1260).

24 477 numbered species: 113 quadrupeds, 114 flying animals, 140 swimming animals, 61 crawling animals and 49 'vermes'; Albert the Great, *Man and the Beasts*, Scanlan (tr.) (1987), p. 16.

25 'My Brothers, we begin with the most important thing of all to us, our faith in God. About God we believe what he himself has revealed to us: that he is one, existing as the Trinity of Father, Son and Holy Spirit, infinite and eternal, utterly vast, yet present to even the smallest creature; he is both immeasurably far off and inconceivably close. Believing this gives us enough to live the life of Faith. How arrogant it would be to seek to know God's inner secrets, mysteries of his life power and way of existence. And how futile! Our small minds are not made for that. Think of this world our familiar Earth and sea: familiar indeed, and how much we know of them, and how little. What do we know of the teeming life beneath the waves, or even on much of the surface of the Earth?' (Sermons of St Columban, in Walker [1957]).

26 *Summa Theologiae*, 1a, q. 47, a. 1. See also *Summa Contra Gentiles*, II, XLV.

27 Johnson (2015a), p. 41.

28 A koan is a Zen Buddhist riddle used to focus the mind during meditation, and to develop intuitive thinking.

29 'Flower in the crannied wall' (1863).

30 'Peter Bell: A Tale in Verse', *Poems of the Imagination* (1819).

31 'Those of us who are theologically inclined may wish to reflect on the way all of this deepens and extends the meaning of incarnation' (Feehan [2015], pp. 21-22); for the background see Gregersen (2001, 2013).

32 Raven (1953), p. 102.

33 Pieper (1953), p. 92.

34 Commentary on the *Liber de Causis*, I. 6.

35 Pieper (1953), p. 59.

36 Feehan (2015), pp. 16-17.

37 Quoted in Mabey (2015), Chapter 27.

38 The story is probably apocryphal. See Feehan *et al.* (2008), pp. 222-223.

39 'The Earth Community' in Berry (2015), p. 8.

40 *Ibid.*, quoted in Tucker, Grim and Angyal (2019), p. 259.

41 Feehan (2016a), pp. 167–168.

42 D.H. Lawrence, 'God is Born'.

43 Feehan (2015), p. 22.

44 Henry David Thoreau, 'Walking'.

Chapter 6 Purpose, Design and Meaning

1 Quoted in Raven (1962), p. 136.

2 News (1981). 'Hoyle on Evolution', *Nature*, 294, p. 105.

3 Hoyle (1982).

4 Hands (2015), p. 245.

5 Hannam (2009).

6 He died in 1913 at the age of ninety, more than thirty years after Darwin, who was fourteen years older than him.

7 Raby (2002), p. 206.

8 Our notions of heaven and hell, time and eternity still carry vestiges of the geocentric cosmology.

9 de Duve (2002), p. 100.

10 Hamilton (2005).

11 Conway Morris (2007).

12 Behe (2019).

13 *Ibid.*, p. 36.

14 Fabre (1923), p. 208.

15 Wilson (1997), p. 279.

16 Barrow and Tipler (1988), p. 5.

17 Dyson (2007), p. 44.

18 Davies (1992, 1988, 1999, 2007).

19 Hawking and Mlodinow (2010), p. 161.

20 Adler (2011).

21 Davies (2006), pp. 166-170.

22 Chaisson (2000), pp. 126-127.

23 Davies (1999).

24 '... per the speculations of physicists desperate to keep the divine foot out of the door the Big Bang seems to have opened' (Feser [2008], p. 103).

25 Davies (1992), p. 173.

26 Maxwell (2013).

27 S.A. and M.L. Ionides, 'Looking Forward' in Beebe (1944), p. 382. From *Stars and Men*, 1939.

28 'The Proofs for God's Existence', General Audience of Pope John Paul II, 10 July 1985.

29 Darwin (1859), p. 188.

30 Huxley (1903), vol. 1, p. 311.

31 Darwin (1862).

32 Foster (2010), p. 222.

33 Mesle (2008).

34 For further details see Grassie (2010).

35 Rifkin (2009).

36 Newman (1864), pp. 217-218.

37 In Southern Bahia where the Atlantic Rainforest Institution has its base camp 270 species of mammals (90 endemic), 372 species of amphibians (260 endemic), 197 reptiles (60 endemic), 849 birds (188 endemic), 2120 butterflies (948 endemic) and 456 species of trees were recorded in an area no bigger than a football field (ARI Website).

38 Quoted in Speziali (1972).

39 Wilson (1997), p. 279.

40 Carson (1955).

41 Mountford (2011), p. 19.

42 Tudge (2013), pp. 254-255.

43 *Laudato Si'*, 233; quoting Eva de Vitray-Meyerovitch (1978), p. 200.

44 Michelson (1903), pp. 23-24.

45 Wilson (1998), pp. 40-41.

46 Quoted in de Duve and Patterson (2010), p. 178.

47 de Duve and Patterson (2010), pp. 175-176.

48 See Plato, *Phaedo*, 96a.

49 Inge (1899), p. 300.

50 See Inge (1899), p. 159: '[Eckhart] asserts the absolute supremacy of reason more strongly than anyone since Erigena.'

51 'Faith, Reason and the University: Memories and Reflections', Lecture of the Holy Father Benedict XVI, Aula Maxima, University of Regensburg, 12 September 2006. Infamous for its impolitic but justified use of language in relation to violence and religion, but startling in its emphasis on the priority of Reason.

52 'The reference to the Word at the beginning of the Gospel of John suggests that the Logos as pre-eminent rational intelligibility is essentially communicated in the unfolding of the universe and in human history, and it is because of this that pre-eminent rational intelligibility deserves the name of "intelligible speech" or "Word". So in the revelation of the Highest One as Logos, the Highest One is revealed as communicating himself in creation and in us' (Johnston [2009], pp. 117-118).

53 Tillich (2009), pp. 8-9.

54 Freud (1927), p. 85.

55 Thomas Aquinas, *Summa Theologiae*, 1, q. 2.

56 Feser (2008); Stenger (2007).

57 'A small error in the beginning of something is a great one at the end' (Thomas Aquinas, paraphrasing Aristotle; preface to On Being and Essence, in Goodwin [1965]).

58 Baggini (2003), p. 106.

59 Feser (2008).

60 There is what Alan Watts (1999) called 'atheism in the name of God'. 'We still envision that fellow up there with a beard' (p. 55).

61 Feehan (2010), p. 178.

62 Miall (1895), pp. 388-389.

63 Letter to Hooker 13 July 1856; www.darwinproject.ac.uk; letter no. 1924.

64 Stephen Fry interviewed by Gay Byrne on 'The Meaning of Life' on RTE1, 31 January 2015.

65 David Attenborough, quoted in Simon Barnes (2014), pp. 72-73.

66 Interview with David Attenborough, *New Scientist*, 16 May 2009, pp. 28-29.

67 Arthur Peacocke, 'The Cost of New Life' in Polkingthorne (2001), p. 34.

68 Moltmann adds the difficult notion that suffering is redemption, but without any real explanation as to why this needs to be the case in the first place.

69 Peacocke (2001), p. 37.

70 Whitehead (1933, 1967), p. 249.

71 Goethe, *Faust*, Part I.

72 Egan (1998), p. 67.

73 Job 40:15, 19; 41:18, 24, 33, 34 (King James Bible).

74 The index to Groups of Organisms in Barnes' *Diversity of Living Organisms* has some 1,500 entries, of which fewer than 100 would be familiar to most people.

75 Lovejoy (1936), p. 211.

76 King (1732), pp. 109-113.

77 Jenyns (1757), p. 104.

78 Saint Augustine was a Manichean before his conversion.

79 Fox and Sheldrake (1997), p. 191.

80 Schillebeeckx (1983), p. 112.

81 'There is need of one thing only' (Luke 10:42).

82 de Duve and Patterson (2010).

83 Lorenz (1988), p. 64.

84 Hume (1977), p. 55.

85 The phrase was first used by Karl Barth in 1947 (apparently deriving from something St Augustine said), and in Catholic circles by Hans Küng and others during Vatican II in the 1960s; see Mahlmann (2010), pp. 384-388.

86 Johnson (2015a), p. 207.

87 Casey (2010).

88 See Inge (1899), pp. 138-139.

89 Cooper (2007), p. 176.

90 Cooper (2007), p. 200.

91 Emily Dickinson, 'Hope is the thing with feathers' (314).

92 Thomas Aquinas insists that *sacra doctrina* is essential for salvation. Then what about the illiterate old lady at the back of the church (*una vetula*) during morning Mass: who doesn't have a degree in theology? But 'since the source of *sacra doctrina* is God's infinite self-knowledge, the difference between all our finite receptions of such knowledge, whether those of Thomas and his students or of the old lady at the back of the church, sink into insignificance. For Thomas what they (and we) all need to have in order to be saved is willingness to be instructed.' The *una vetula* comes from a text in Thomas's *Sermons on the Apostles Creed* in which he says that none of the ancient philosophers before Christ knew as much 'as one old woman [*vetula*] knows by faith after Christ's coming' (McGinn [2014], p. 55 and endnote 40). Similarly! of the difference between those who ardently believe in God, and those who cannot, for whatever reason, profess faith.

Although the genetic difference between us may be little more than a few nucleotide base pairs, it may appear to me as though the distance in mental capacity between Thomas Aquinas and myself must be measured in intellectual light years. At the same time! ... there may be equally great differences in physical, empathetic or spiritual capacity in the opposite direction. But these differences are as nothing – less than millimetres compared to light years – compared with the distance between any of us and God.

93 When talking about life after death Teilhard de Chardin uses language that makes it impossible to know what he means in any sort of concrete way. 'In the human', he wrote, 'the radial escapes the tangential and is freed from it. ... One by one ... "souls" break away around us, carrying their incommunicable charge of consciousness towards what is above' (Teilhard de Chardin [1955], p. 194).

94 All of this can provide us with a deeper and purer understanding of Meister Eckhart's concept of *Gelassenheit*: the pure detachment in which the soul can meet God in the ground (*Grunt*) of All Reality: or of the *apatheia* of Evagrius of Pontus, or the much older mystical concept. Or we may see in it the essential flame at the heart of Quietist piety.

95 Sermon 25:7 in Pelikan (1971-1989), IV, p. 163.

96 Koestler (1985).

97 Mark 2:22; Luke 5:37-38.

98 T.S. Eliot, 'Little Gidding', II.

Chapter 7 Living as Part of the Whole

1 Feehan (1979), p. 98.

2 Feehan (2010), pp. 164-174 (quotations from pp. 166, 168).

3 Williams (1972).

4 Wilson (2006), pp. 4-5.

5 Birch (1990), p. 132.

6 McCarthy (2015).

7 Rifkin (2010).

8 Armstrong (2009).

9 Feehan (2010), pp. 144-161.

10 Aldo Leopold (1933), p. 184.

11 Wallace (1864).

12 Wikipedia: solar storm of 1859 is named after Richard Carrington, one of the scientists who studied it at the time.

13 Kanipe (2008).

14 The journal *Advances in Space Research* devoted an entire issue to the Carrington Event, entitled 'The Great Historical Geomagnetic Storm of 1859: A Modern Look' (vol. 38 [2] [2006], pp. 115–388).

15 Ambrose (1998).

16 Leopold (1924), in Flader and Callicott (eds).

17 Leopold (1939), in Flader and Callicott (eds).

18 Leopold (1941). Leopold is referring to a university course (Wildlife Ecology 118) that he was giving at this time.

19 *Laudato Si'*, 217.

20 *Laudato Si'*, 3.

21 For an excellent introduction see Andrews (1993).

22 The Ordnance Survey maps were prepared on a number of different scales, to suit different purposes: one-quarter inch to a mile, one inch to a mile, six inches to a mile, twenty-five inches to a mile, and scales still larger for towns and cities. Of them all, the most important, as well as the earliest to be published, was the six-inch map, which was intended to serve as the base map for the proposed land valuation as plans were drawn up to reform the county's local taxation system, to provide a base map for the census of population and for the geological survey of Ireland, as well as for military and other purposes.

23 See the discussion of virtue in Feehan (2010), Chapter 9.

24   Act IV, Scene 1:

These our actors,

As I foretold you, were all spirits and

Are melted into air, into thin air:

And, like the baseless fabric of this vision,

The cloud-capp'd towers, the gorgeous palaces,

The solemn temples, the great globe itself,

Ye all which it inherit, shall dissolve

And, like this insubstantial pageant faded,

Leave not a rack behind. We are such stuff

As dreams are made on, and our little life

Is rounded with a sleep.

25   And so too for other dichotomies: matter and form, mind and body, body and soul: and the conceptual framework of a primitive biology. Why so many young educated people abandon the religious ethos in which they were brought up is that they are confronted with an either/or: either you believe this outmoded stuff or nothing. The quest to reconcile by a deeper probing and unfolding is the true solution. Faith is not one side of a two-sided coin, the other side being denial. It is a spectrum. The important thing is to know you're on it, even if you don't quite know where!

26   Thomas Aquinas, *De Veritate* II, q.14, a.11.

27   Tillich (1952), p. 28.

28   Interestingly, athletes do not look with envy at the top athletes in disciples other than their own!

29   Taking twenty-five years as one human generation. Jared Diamond gives a figure of 7 million years.

30   The transition to full human consciousness does not appear to have been sudden and sharp. For example, what are we to make of *Homo naledi*, recently discovered in South Africa, 'an animal that appears to have had the cognitive ability to recognize its separation from nature' (Shreeve [2015], p. 53).

31   It is thought that Eurasians and Americans today have inherited 2.5 per cent of their DNA from Neanderthals, and Aboriginal Australasians have 5 per cent of Denisovan-derived DNA in addition to this Neanderthal 2.5 per cent.

32   Coughlan (2015).

33   Feehan (2012), pp. 11-13.

34   Leopold (1933), p. 183.

35   See Storr (2013).

36   Storr (2013).

37   Lindberg (2006).

38   Ingold (1994).

39   Harari (2016).

Chapter 8 Evolution – Life Unfolding

1   Virgil, *Georgics*, 2, pp. 476-482.

2   Marcus Manilius, *Astronomica*, 1.

3   Quoted in Purcell (2012), p. 270. Earth was thought to be surrounded by a series of otherwise *insensible* concentric spheres composed of a tenuous crystalline 'fifth element' (distinct from Earth, air, fire or water); music was produced by vibration within these crystalline spheres.

4   Aristotle: *De Anima*, III, 7.

5   Quoted in Lovejoy (1936), p. 294.

6   Locke (1690), vol. III, chapter vi, p. 12.

7   Lovejoy (1936), p. 186.

8   *Ibid.*

9   Letters of Schiller, *ed.* Cotta, 189, 188, quoted in Lovejoy (1936), p. 299.

10   Francis Bacon, *De sapientia veterum,* quoted in Spedding, Ellis and Heath (eds) (c.1900), VI, p. 747.

11   More (1653), II, Chapter 9, 8, quoted in Lovejoy (1936), p. 188.

12   Locke (1690), *loc. cit.*

13   Jenyns (1790), pp. 179-185.

14   Jenyns (1757), pp. 165-167.

15   It had originally been discovered by Leeuwenhoek.

16   Quoted in Hahm (1977), p. 60. Stoicism was a philosophical movement that flourished in the Greek and Roman worlds between 300 BC and AD 200, which taught that detachment and discipline are the key to truth and happiness.

17   Picknett and Prince (2011), p. 213.

18   Tuveson (1982), p. xi.

19   See Horan (2007).

20   Even the notion of stellar evolution can be traced back to ancient Greece, where the idea that stars are born and die can be found in the speculations of Hipparchus (*floruit* 146-127 BC), who mapped and catalogued hundreds of stars. And nearly two thousand years before Copernicus, Aristarchus of Samos (c. 310-230 BC) speculated that all the planets revolve around the sun, and that the Earth rotates on its axis once a day: but these are all *speculations*, not based on evidence.

21   Armstrong (2009), pp. 197-202.

22   Yet the Cotton Mather who wrote *The Christian Philosopher*, expounding this view in 1721, was also the author of *Memorable Providences relating to Witchcraft and Possessions* in 1689, and was a leading figure in the Salem witch trials of 1692.

23   The earliest fossils are 3.5 billion years old: 1 billion years after the Earth formed.

24   Buffon, Comte de (1749-1789).

25   Mayr (1982).

26   Chaisson (2000), p. 94.

27   Huxley (1873), pp. 272-274.

28   Laplace (1896), p. vi.

29   On the other hand, Stephen J. Gould (1989) famously postulated that if the course of evolution were to play all over again it would have an entirely different outcome, independently of any consideration of the radical uncertainty embedded in the operation of subatomic realities. However, the same laws of physics and chemistry would still govern that alternative; its biology would still be carbon-based, still dependent on the same unique properties of individual other elements, so that its biochemistry, physiology and morphology might not be radically different.

30   Hutton (1794), Chapter 3 (Section 13) of vol. 1, quoted in Hands (2015), p. 250.

31   Kühn (1996).

32   There are some 800 million stars in our galaxy, the Milky Way, which is 100,000 light years across and 1,000 light years thick.

33   Küng and Tracy (eds) (1989).

34   The Wikipedia entry on 'history of technology' is a good introduction.

35 Bryson (2003), p. 463.

36 Joseph Hooker (1817-1911), Director of Kew (1865) and President of the Royal Society 1872-1877, perhaps the most eminent botanist of his day. Asa Gray (1810-1888) was Professor of Natural History at Harvard, and America's leading botanist at the time.

37 Hands (2015), p. 253; the text can be accessed at http://www.linnean.org/incex.php?id=380

38 Wallace died in 1913 at the age of ninety, more than thirty years after Darwin, who was fourteen years older than him.

39 Henig (2000), p. 83.

40 Henig (2000), pp. 250-251.

41 For a gripping (if somewhat biased) account, see Watson (1968).

42 Hands (2015), p. 276.

43 Paraphrased on Hands (2015), pp. 276-277, which is based on Coyne's summary.

44 Dawkins and Wong (2017).

45 We have no idea for example how out of the five hundred or so different amino acids there are only twenty should be involved in the formation of proteins, and of these only their left-handed forms are involved (amino acids come in two forms that are mirror images of each other).

46 For a succinct critique of Darwinism see Hands (2015), pp. 256-274.

47 Darwin (1859), p. 134.

48 Darwin (1882), p. v.

49 Quoted in Hands (2015), p. 264.

50 Our own view is that what is pre-determined, implicate in matter, is the *potential* for the complexity and diversity of life to unfold.

51 Hands (2015), p. 278.

52 Kropotkin (1914), p. 30.

53 Darwin (1958), p. 85.

54 Darwin, F. (1888), vol. 2, p. 312, quoted in Birch (1990), p. 40.

55 Charles Darwin, letter to Athenaeum, 9 May 1863 (written 5 May). In Burkhardt *et al.* (eds) (1985), vol. 11, pp. 380.

56 This is one of the areas explored by Stuart Kaufmann in his books *Origins of Order* (1993), *At Home in the Universe* (1995).

57 Paragraph 81 of *Laudato Si'* begins, 'even if we postulate a process of evolution.' Pope Francis knows perfectly well that evolution is the way in which God brings about his purpose in creation (it is implicit in the phrase 'God's own unfolding plan for Creation'), but he knows equally well the storm such an acknowledgement on his part in an encyclical would generate.

58 Inge (1899), pp. 73, 115-116.

59 Paragraphs 4, 217 (twice), 218 (three times), 219 (twice), 220 (twice), 221 (twice) and the title of Section III (Ecological Conversion).

60 Tillich (1959), p. 5.

Chapter 9 Deep Ecumenism: Actions and Directions

1 Panikkar (2010), p. 9.

2 Darwin, in Burkhardt (1996).

3 Punctuated equilibrium is the idea that evolutionary change occurs in bursts, separated by intervals where nothing much is happening.

4 Panikkar (2010), pp. xxv-xxxii.

5 Grassie (2010), p. 187.

6 Rorty and Vattimo (2007).

7   Jaspers (1953).

8   Grassie (2010), p. 175.

9   Armstrong (2009), p. 234.

10 Armstrong (2009), pp. 241-242.

11 Berger *et al.* (1999).

12 Grassie (2010), p. 109.

13 Schleiermacher, *Reden*, V, quoted in Lovejoy (1936), p. 310.

14 Schleiermacher, *Reden*, V, quoted in Lovejoy (1936), p. 311. The final sentence translates: 'Only in the totality of all such possible forms can one truly receive the totality of religion.'

15 Joint statement of Pope Francis and Ahmed el-Tayeb, Grand Imam of al-Azhar: 'A Document on Human Fraternity for World Peace and Living Together', February 2019.

16 Agenda for the Synod of the Amazon, paragraphs 120-121. 'There are calls for indigenous theology to be taught in seminaries, and for an evangelisation based on dialogue that is not impeded by "fossilised doctrines". This seems to be taking the idea of "inculturating" the Gospel to a new level, and one can almost see eyebrows being raised in theology faculties around the world' (Francis McDonagh, 'Can Latin America lead the way?', *The Tablet*, 28 September 2019, pp. 6-7).

17 Dorr (2018), p. 154.

18 Cuenot (1962), pp. 368-369.

19 Cuenot (1962), pp. 325-326.

20 Raven (1962), p. 98. The Jade Buddha is a great statue of grey limestone in a tiny Buddhist temple north-west of the Imperial Palace in Beijing.

21 Adapted from Feehan (2016b).

22 Allen, Allen and Garrod (1906-1958), vol. 2, p. 284.

We can think of what we are about here as an extension of one of one of the driving influences behind the European Renaissance, and ultimately of the Reformation: the desire to revert to a purer original Christianity by going back to the Hebrew scriptures and the early Church Fathers, bypassing the corruption and distortion with which it had been overgrown and distorted over the centuries.

Another renaissance influence is the quest for a deeper, more 'mystical' element in religious life than the more superficial devotion convention encouraged or allowed; an element exemplified above all (before the dam burst or the match was applied to the powder keg) by Erasmus.

23 Pico della Mirandola (1486).

24 Dawkins (2004), *The Ancestor's Tale*.

25 'Intuitive sensibility' is also a factor that featured centrally in Laozi's approach to the Tao.

26 Feehan (2015), p. 5.

27 Feehan (2015), p. 6.

28 Lau (1963).

29 Twenty-four centuries of Chinese scholarship have been devoted to separating the essence of the Tao from its Warring States context, and the limit in our degree of human understanding of cosmic and historical reality attained by that time. All the more difficult for me then, even though I have the benefit of that scholarship to prevent me straying too far! So much has to be abstracted it seems an almost impossible task to make it relevant to modern concern.

30 Johnston (2009), p. 121. See also Feehan (2015).

31   Bamford (1982).

32   In looking for the common chord we
      have to go back to before the attempts
      in subsequent centuries to commandeer
      it and to harness it to other agendas.
      We have to peel away the subsequent
      layers of the several attempts to
      appropriate it in later centuries, in the
      process distorting and mythifying it.
      Any rediscovery of earlier spirituality
      is necessarily re-invention. See Bradley
      (1999).

      In one sense, the Celtic spirituality
      that I have described is not simply a
      rediscovery but a *reinvention*. There
      is a danger that either we force the
      history and tradition of particular
      spiritualities into the shape of other,
      modern experiences or we seek to shape
      our own contemporary spiritual quest
      naively in terms of some presumed
      golden age. Sheldrake (1995), pp. 93-94.

      Of course, in all of this we have to
      beware of simplistic interpretation
      and of projecting our preconceptions
      back onto a culture whose unmediated
      encounter with the world was so utterly
      different from ours. We bring our
      stage in history with us because it is
      embodied in us, and our appropriation
      of that earlier time is a sort of
      elutriation: a process of straining our
      modern selves through the sieve of our
      scholarly apprehension of any earlier
      time; and that sieve has a very wide
      mesh.

33   Rushdie (1990), p. 8.

34   Feehan (2015), pp. 5-6.

35   Bradley (2010).

36   'To be able to practise five things
      everywhere under heaven constitutes
      perfect virtue … gravity, generosity of
      soul, sincerity, earnestness, and kindness'

      (Confucius [K'ung Fu-tzu, 441-479
      BC], *Analects*).

37   Panikkar (2010), p. 7. He lists – among
      others – Aristotle, Augustine, Thomas
      Aquinas, Ibn Rushd, Kant, Heidegger
      and the neo-Thomists.

38   Seneca, *Naturalium quaestiones*, VII, 27,
      4.

39   Birch and Cobb (1981), p. 138.

40   *Laudato Si'*, paragraph 3. *Laudato Si'*
      embeds this ancient principle for right
      living (found in one shape or another
      in all the great religious traditions) in
      the soil of modern life (countering the
      current of the time): cf. *Laudato Si'* 220-
      225.

41   The single word that can serve as the
      guide to conduct (in action) through
      all one's life is 'shu': do not impose on
      others what you would not impose
      on yourself (*Analects* 15.24). This is
      the unadorned, unbreakable common
      thread that runs through all traditions:
      the single thread around which, with
      which, Confucius binds all that he
      learns (*Analects* 15.3).

42   We will not overnight convert the
      majorities in our churches to the belief
      that creation is the living Word of
      God, before and beyond and beneath
      all written scriptures, indeed the anvil
      on which these scriptures were forged.
      In the long term (in God's own time)
      this way of thinking must become part
      of the fundamental change: change
      of direction, change of heart we,
      humankind, must take. But if the Earth
      is to survive to that future, our first
      line of argument has to be the one that
      will convince the majority at the most
      immediate and selfish level.

43   Albeit with the 'ulterior' motive
      inseparable from the missionary

effort of the age: and underlain by a conviction of superiority which, while thinking of this as *spiritual* in nature was intertwined with a sense (conscious or unconscious) of cultural superiority.

44 'Interestingly, the official Chinese translation of the Gospel of John renders its opening sentence as, "In the beginning was *Dao*." Even if any transcultural translation is risky, this alignment of Logos/Wisdom with *Dao* succeeds in bringing forward the Johannine point that the divine Logos is both the generative principle of creation and the Way (*Dao*) to follow: "I am the way, and the truth, and the life" (John 14:6)' (Gregersen [2015], p. 362).

45 Much of the work done in this area is academic in nature, rather than in the nature of sympathetic exploration of spiritual content. See Herzman (2013), pp. 3-16 and references therein.

46 We shall not cease from exploration
And the end of all our exploring
Will be to arrive where we started
And know the place for the first time.
    T.S. Eliot, 'Little Gidding', 239-243.

47 Wilson (1984).

48 Wilson (1984), p. 139.

49 *Tao Te Ching* XLVII.

50 Kan (2019), Fish (2015).

BIBLIOGRAPHY

Adelard of Bath, *Perdifficiles Questiones Naturales: Questions on Nature* in *The Portable Medieval Reader*, J. Ross and M. McLaughlin (eds) (1977), London: Penguin Books.

Adler, R. (2011). 'Ultimate guide to the multiverse', *New Scientist*, 26 November.

Albert the Great (c.1260). *Man and the Beasts (De Animalibus, Books 22-26)*, James J. Scanlan (tr.) (1987), New York: Medieval and Renaissance Texts and Studies.

Allen, P.S., Allen, H.M. and Garrod, H.W. (eds) (1906-1958). *Opus epistolarum Des. Erasmi Roterodami: denuo recognitum et auctum*, Clarendon Press.

Ambrose, S.H. (1998). 'Late Pleistocene Human Population Bottlenecks, Volcanic Winter, and Differentiation of Modern Humans', *Journal of Human Evolution*, 34 (6), pp. 623-651.

Andrews, J.H. (1993). *History in the Ordnance Map: An Introduction for Irish Readers*, 2nd edn, David Archer.

Anscombe, G.E.M. and Geach, P.T. (1961). *Three Philosophers*, Oxford: Basil Blackwell.

Aquinas, Thomas. *De Veritate* II.

Aquinas, Thomas. *Summa Theologiae*.

Aquinas, Thomas. *Super Librum Boethii de Trinitate Proem.*

Ariga, T. (1959). *An Enquiry into the Basic Structure of Christian Thought*, Tokyo: Maruzen.

Aristotle, *Astronomica* I, 483-450. G.P. Goold (tr.).

Aristotle, *De Anima* III, 7.

Armstrong, K. (1993). *A History of God: The 4000-year Quest of Judaism, Christianity and Islam*, New York: Ballantine Books.

Armstrong, K. (2009). *The Case for God: What Religion Really Means*, London: The Bodley Head.

Atherton, I., Bosanquet, S. and Lawley, M. (2010). *Mosses and Liverworts of Britain and Ireland: A Field Guide*, London: British Bryological Society.

Augustine, St, *Confessions*, see Chadwick (2008).

Baggini, J. (2003). *Atheism: A Very Short Introduction*, Oxford: Oxford University Press.

Balcombe, J. (2011). *The Exultant Ark: A Pictorial Tour of Animal Pleasure*, Berkeley: University of California Press.

Ball, S. and Morris, R. (2015). *Britain's Hoverflies*, 2nd edn, Princeton: Princeton University Press, WILDGuides.

Bamford, C. (1982). 'Ecology and holiness: The heritage of Celtic Christianity' in *Celtic Christianity: Ecology and Holiness*, W.P. Marsh and C. Bamford (eds), New York: Lindisfarne Press.

Barnes, R.S.K. (ed.) (1998). *The Diversity of Living Organisms*, London: Blackwell Science.

Barnes, S. (2014). *Ten Million Aliens: A Journey Through the Entire Animal Kingdom*, London: Short Books.

Barrow, J.D. and Tipler, F.J. (1988). *The Anthropic Cosmological Principle* (revised edn), Oxford: Oxford University Press.

Barsam, A.P. (2008). *Reverence for Life: Albert Schweitzer's Great Contribution to Ethical Thought*, Oxford: Oxford University Press.

Beebe, W. (ed.) (1944). *The Book of Naturalists: An Anthology of the Best Natural History*, London: Robert Hale.

Behe, M. (2019). *Darwin Devolves: The New Science About DNA That Challenges Evolution*, New York: HarperOne.

Behe, M. (2006). *Darwin's Black Box: The Biochemical Challenge to Evolution*, 2nd edn, New York: Free Press.

Bekoff, M. and Pierce, J. (2009). *Wild Justice: The Moral Lives of Animals*, Chicago: University of Chicago Press.

Belloc, H. (1902). *The Path to Rome*.

Benedict XVI (2006). 'Faith, Reason and the University: Memories and Reflections', Lecture of the Holy Father Benedict XVI, Aula Maxima, University of Regensburg, 12 September.

Benedict XVI (2010). *Verbum Domini: Apostolic Exhortation on the Word of God in the Life and Mission of the Church*.

Berger, P.L., Sachs, J., Martin, D., Weiming, T., Weigel, G., Davie, G. and An-Na'im, A.A. (1999). *The Deserialization of the World: Resurgent Religion and World Politics*, Michigan: Eerdmans Publishing Co.

Bergson, H. (1911). *Creative Evolution*, Arthur Mitchell (tr.), Random House, the Modern Library of New York.

Bergson, H. (1935). *The Two Sources of Morality and Religion*, R. Ashley Audra and Cloudesley Brereton (trs), New York: Henry Holt.

Berry, T. (2015). *The Dream of the Earth*, Berkeley: Counterpoint Press; first published San Francisco: Sierra Club Books, 1988.

Birch, C. (1990). *A Purpose for Everything: Religion in a Postmodern Worldview*, Connecticut: Twenty-Third Publications.

Birch, C. and Cobb, J.B. (1981). *The Liberation of Life: From the Cell to the Community*, Cambridge: Cambridge University Press.

Birkhead, T. (2012). *Bird Sense: What It's Like to Be a Bird*, London: Bloomsbury.

Birkhead, T. (2013). 'Bird Senses', *New Scientist* Instant Expert, 3 August 2013.

Bosio, J. (1610). *La trionfante et gloriosa croce*.

Boyle, R. (1690). *The Christian Virtuoso*.

Bradley, I. (1999). *Celtic Christianity: Making Myths and Chasing Dreams*, Edinburgh: Edinburgh University Press.

Bradley, I. (2010). 'Liberals must stand together', *The Guardian*, 29 May.

Brand, P. and Yancy, P. (1980). *Fearfully and Wonderfully Made*, Michigan: Zondervan Publishing House.

Briggs, A., Halvorson, H. and Steane, A. (2018). *It Keeps Me Seeking: The Invitation from Science, Philosophy and Religion*, Oxford: Oxford University Press.

Browne, Sir T. (1643). *Religio Medici*.

Bryson, B. (2003). *A Short History of Nearly Everything*, London: Doubleday Black Swan.

Buick Knox, R. (1967). *James Ussher, Archbishop of Armagh*, Cardiff: University of Wales Press.

Bunyan, J. (1666). *Grace Abounding to the Chief of Sinners, or, The Brief Relation of the Exceeding Mercy of God in Christ, to his Poor Servant John Bunyan* in *John Bunyan: Grace Abounding, with other Spiritual Autobiographies*, J. Stachniewski and A. Pacheco (eds), Oxford: Oxford University Press, 1998.

Burkhardt, F. (ed.) (1996). *Charles Darwin's Letters: A Selection*, Cambridge: Cambridge University Press.

Burkhardt, F. and Smith, S. *et al.* (eds) (1985). *The Correspondence of Charles Darwin*, 11 vols, Cambridge: Cambridge University Press.

Burwick, F. (ed.) (1987). *Approaches to Natural Form: Permutations in Science and Culture*, Dordrecht: Reidel.

Butler, J. (1824) [1736]. *The Analogy of Religion, Natural and Revealed, to the Constitution and Course of Nature*, London: Longman, Hurst, Rees, Orme.

Caputo, J.D. and Vattimo, G. (2006). *After the Death of God*, New York: Columbia University Press.

Carson, R. (1955). *The Edge of the Sea*, London: Staples Press.

Casey, J. (2010). *After Lives: A Guide to Heaven, Hell and Purgatory*, Oxford: Oxford University Press.

Catechism of the Catholic Church (1994), London: Geoffrey Chapman.

Chadwick, H. (2008). *Saint Augustine: Confessions*, Oxford: Oxford University Press.

Chaisson, E. (2000). *The Life Era: Cosmic Selection and Conscious Evolution*, Indiana: iUniverse.

Christie, D.E. (2013). *The Blue Sapphire of the Mind: Notes for a Contemplative Ecology*, Oxford: Oxford University Press.

Clayton, P. and Davies, P. (eds) (2006). *The Re-Emergence of Emergence: The Emergentist Hypothesis from Science to Religion*, Oxford: Oxford University Press.

Cobb, J.B. (1998). *Beyond Dialogue: Toward a Mutual Transformation of Christianity and Buddhism*, Oregon: Wipf and Stock.

Cobb, J.W. and Griffin, D.R. (1976). *Process Theology: An Introductory Exposition*, Philadelphia: The Westminster Press.

Conniff, R. (2016). *House of Lost Worlds: Dinosaurs, Dynasties and the Story of Life on Earth*, Connecticut: Yale University Press.

Cooper, J.W. (2007). *Panentheism: The Other God of the Philosophers: From Plato to the Present*, London: Apollos.

Coughlan, A. (2015). 'First humans to leave Africa went to China', *New Scientist*, 17 October.

Coyne, J.A. (2009). *Why Evolution is True*, Oxford: Oxford University Press.

Cuénot, C. (1962). *Teilhard de Chardin*, Bourges: Éditions Du Seuil.

Darwin, C. (1859). *On the Origin of Species by Means of Natural Selection, or the Preservation of Favoured Races in the Struggle for Life*, London: John Murray.

Darwin, C. (1868). *The Variation of Plants and Animals under Domestication*, London: John Murray.

Darwin, C. (1872). *On the Origin of Species by Means of Natural Selection, or the Preservation of Favoured Races in the Struggle for Life*, 6th edn, London: John Murray.

Darwin, C. (1882). *The Descent of Man, and Selection in Relation to Sex*, 2nd edn, London: John Murray.

Darwin, C. (1958). *The Autobiography of Charles Darwin 1809-1882: With Original Omissions Restored*, London: Collins.

Darwin, C. (1862). *The various contrivances by which orchids are fertilized by Insects*, 2nd edn (1890), London: John Murray.

Darwin, F. (1887). *The Life and Letters of Charles Darwin*, London: John Murray.

Davies, O. (1988). *God Within: The Mystical Tradition of Northern Europe*, London: Darton, Longman and Todd.

Davies, P. (1999). *The Fifth Miracle: The Search for the Origin of Life*, London: Allen Lane, Penguin Books.

Davies, P. (1992). *The Mind of God: Science and the Search for Ultimate Meaning*, New York: Simon and Schuster; Penguin (1998).

Davies, P. (2007). *The Goldilocks Enigma: Why is the Universe Just Right for Life?*, London: Allen Lane, Penguin Books.

Davies, P. (2019), *The Demon in the Machine: How Hidden Webs of Information Are Finally Solving the Mystery of Life*, London: Allen Lane.

Dawkins, R. and Yan Wong (2017). *The Ancestor's Tale: A Pilgrimage to the Dawn of Life*, London: Weidenfeld and Nicolson.

de Buffon, Comte, G.L. Leclerc (1749-1889). *Histoire naturelle, générale et particulière*, 37 vols.

de Duve, C. (2002). *Life Evolving: Molecules, Mind, and Meaning*, Oxford: Oxford University Press.

de Duve, C. with Patterson, N. (2010). *Genetics of Original Sin: The Impact of Natural Selection on the Future of Humanity*, Connecticut: Yale University Press.

de Vitray-Meyerovitch, E. (ed.) (1978). *Anthologie du Soufisme*, Paris.

Dennett, D.C. (1995). *Darwin's Dangerous Idea: Evolution and the Meanings of Life*, New York: Simon and Schuster.

Descartes, R. (1644). *Principia Philosophiae*.

Dickinson, E. (2016). *The Complete Poems*, London: Faber and Faber.

Dickson White, A. (1896). *A History of the Warfare of Science and Theology in Christendom*.

Dobell, C. (1958). *Antony van Leeuwenhoek and His Little Animals*, 2nd edn.

Dorr, D. (2018). 'Pope Francis on Falling in Love with Nature', *The Furrow*, March, pp. 149-158.

Draper, J.W. (1874). *The History of the Conflict between Religion and Science*.

Drummond, J.L. (1832), *Letters to a Young Naturalist*.

Duthie, E. (1962). *Wild Company: Encounters between Man and Beast*, New Hampshire: Heinemann.

Dyson, F.J. (2007). *A Many-Colored Glass: Reflections on the Place of Life in the Universe*, Charlottesville: University of Virginia Press.

Egan, H.D. (1998). *Karl Rahner: Mystic of Everyday Life*, New York: Crossroad Publishing.

Einstein, A. in *Conjectures and Refutations*, K. Popper (1963), London: Routledge.

Endean, P. (ed.) (2004). *Spiritual Writings of Karl Rahner*, Modern Spiritual Masters Series, New York: Orbis Books.

Espinasse, M. (1956), *Robert Hooke*, London: Heinemann.

Fabre, J.H. (1923). 'The Pentatomae and their Eggs' in 'Some Plant Lice' in *The Life of the Scorpion*, New York: Dodd, Mead and Co.

Feehan, J. (1979). *The Landscape of Slieve Bloom*, Dublin: Blackwater Press; reprinted 2009, Slieve Bloom Development Association.

Feehan, J. (2001). 'Towards a Greener Theology', *The Furrow*, January, pp. 54-56.

Feehan, J. (2007). 'Beyond Omega', *Studies: An Irish Quarterly Review*, 96 (383), pp. 283-294.

Feehan, J. (2010). *The Singing Heart of the World*, Dublin: Columba Press.

Feehan, J. (2012). 'Foreword' in *Eucharist and the Living Earth*, H. O'Donnell, Dublin: Columba Press, pp. 11-13.

Feehan, J. (2015). *Creation, Evolution and Faith: Reflections on the Presence of God in Creation* (privately printed).

Feehan, J. (2016a). *The Dipper's Acclaim and Other Essays* (privately printed).

Feehan, J. (2016b). 'Celtic Spirituality, Scientific Enquiry and the Tao: In Search of a Lost Chord' in *A Sino-Celtic Perspective on the Cry of the Earth, Cry of the Poor; thinking beyond Capitalist Globalisation, War on Terror and Terrorism*, pp. 65-75. International Symposium organised by the Irish School of Ecumenics and the Columban Missionaries, Trinity College Dublin, 14-15 December.

Feehan, J. (2017). 'Creation as Incarnation: Reflections on Biodiversity in *Laudato Si''* in *Laudato Si': An Irish Response: Essays on the Pope's Letter on the Environment*, S. McDonagh (ed.), Dublin: Veritas Publications, pp. 55-82.

Feehan, J. (ed.) (1995). *Educating for Environmental Awareness*, Dublin: UCD, Environmental Institute.

Feehan, J., O'Donovan, G., Renou-Wilson, F. and Wilson, D. (2008). *The Bogs of Ireland: An Introduction to the Natural, Cultural and Industrial Heritage of Irish Peatlands* (revised edn), Dublin: UCD, School of Biology and Environmental Science.

Fenton, M.B. and Simmons, N.B. (2014). *Bats: A World of Science and Mystery*, Chicago: University of Chicago Press.

Feser, E. (2008). *The Last Superstition: A Refutation of the New Atheism*, Indiana: St Augustine's Press.

Fish, E. (2015). *China's Millennials: The Want Generation*, London: Rowman and Littlefield.

Fisher, R.Q. (1930). *The Genetical Theory of Natural Selection*, Oxford: Oxford University Press.

Flader, S.L. and Baird Callicott, J. (eds) (1991). *The River of the Mother of God and Other Essays by Aldo Leopold*, Madison: University of Wisconsin Press.

Flower, R. (1932), 'Religion and Literature in Ireland in the Eighth and Ninth Centuries', *Report of the Church of Ireland Conference*, Dublin.

Forster, E.M. (1924). *A Passage to India*, London: Edward Arnold.

Foster, C.A. (2010). *The Selfless Gene: Living with God and Darwin*, Nashville: Thomas Nelson.

Foster, M. and Lankester, E.R. (eds) (1903). *The Scientific Memoirs of Thomas Henry Huxley*, London: Macmillan.

Fox, M. (1988). *The Coming of the Cosmic Christ*, New York: HarperOne.

Fox, M. and Sheldrake, R. (1997). *Natural Grace: Dialogues on Creation, Darkness, and the Soul in Spirituality*, New York: Image.

Francis, Pope (2015). *Laudato Si'*.

Frank, A. (2009). *The Cosmic Fire: Beyond the Science vs. Religion Debate*, Berkeley: University of California Press.

Franklin, R.W. (ed.) (1999). *The Poems of Emily Dickinson*, Cambridge: Harvard University Press.

Freud, S. (1927). *The Future of an Illusion*, James Strachey (tr. and ed.), New York: Norton (1961).

Gatti, H. (1999). *Giordano Bruno and Renaissance Science*, Ithaca: Cornell University Press.

Gillespie, N.C. (1987). 'Natural history, natural theology and social order: John Ray and the "Newtonian ideology"', *Journal of the History of Biology*, 20, pp. 1-49.

Goodwin, P. (tr.) (1965), *Selected Writings of St Thomas Aquinas*, New Jersey: Prentice-Hall.

Gore, C. (1922). *The Incarnation of the Son of God*, London: John Murray.

Gould, S.J. (1989). *Wonderful Life*, New York: W.W. Norton and Co.

Gould, S.J. (1993). *Eight Little Piggies*, London: Penguin Books.

Grant Watson, E.L. (1947). *Wonders of Natural History*, London: Pleiades Books.

Grassie, W. (2010). *The New Sciences of Religion: Exploring Spirituality from the Outside In and Bottom Up*, London: Palgrave Macmillan.

Gregersen, N. (2001). 'The Cross of Christ in an Evolutionary World', *Dialog: A Journal of Theology*, 40, pp. 192-207.

Gregersen, N. (2013). *Incarnation: On the Scope and Depth of Christology*, Minneapolis: Fortress Press.

Gregersen, N. (2015). 'Deep Incarnation: Opportunities and Challenges' in *Incarnation: On the Scope and Depth of Christology*, Gregersen (ed.), Minneapolis: Fortress Press.

Hahm, D.E. (1977). *The Origins of Stoic Cosmology*, Columbus: Ohio State University Press.

Haldane, J.B.S. (1927). *Possible Worlds and Other Essays*, London: Chatto and Windus.

Hamilton, G. (2005). 'Looking for LUCA – the Mother of All Life', *New Scientist*, 2515, 3 September, p. 29.

Hands, J. (2015). *Cosmosapiens: Human Evolution from the Origin of the Universe*, New York: Overlook Duckworth.

Hannam, J. (2009). *God's Philosophers: How the Medieval World Laid the Foundations of Modern Science*, London: Icon Books.

Harari, Y.N. (2016). *Homo Deus: A Brief History of Tomorrow*, London: Vintage.

Hart, D.B. (2009). *Atheist Delusions: The Christian Revolution and Its Fashionable Enemies*, Connecticut: Yale University Press.

Hart, D.B. (2017). *The New Testament: A Translation*, Connecticut: Yale University Press.

Hart, D.B. (2018). 'The Word made Fresh', *The Tablet*, 13 January, pp. 11-13.

Hartshorne, C. (1967). *A Natural Theology for our Time*, La Salle: Open Court (1992).

Haught, J.F. (1984). *The Cosmic Adventure: Science, Religion and the Quest for Purpose*, New York: Paulist Press.

Haught, J. (2007). *God After Darwin: A Theology of Evolution*, 2nd edn, New York: Routledge.

Haught, J.F. (2006). *Is Nature Enough? Meaning and Truth in the Age of Science*, Cambridge: Cambridge University Press.

Hawking, S. and Mlodinow, L. (2010). *The Grand Design*, London: Bantam Press.

Hay, D. (2006). *Something There: The Biology of the Human Spirit*, London: Darton, Longman and Todd.

Henig, R.M. (2000). *The Monk in the Garden: The Lost and Found Genius of Gregor Mendel, the Father of Genetics*, Boston and New York: Houghton Mifflin Co.

Herzman, R.B. (2013). 'Dante: Cafeteria Catholic?' in *Unruly Catholics from Dante to Madonna: Faith, Heresy and Politics in Cultural Studies*, M. Di Paolo (ed.), Lanham: The Scarecrow Press.

Holland, T. (2019). *Dominion: The Making of the Western Mind*, London: Little, Brown.

Hooke, R. (1665). 'Observation LIII, Of a Flea', *Micrographia*.

Horan, D. (2007). 'Light and Love: Robert Grosseteste and Duns Scotus on the How and Why of Creation', *Cord*, 77 (3), pp. 246-247.

Houzeau, J.C. (1887). *Bull. Séances Soc. Belge Microscopie*, in *Nature Interludes: A Book of Natural History Quotations*, E.F. Linssen (1951), London: Williams and Norgate.

Hoyle, F. (1982). *Evolution from Space: The Omni Lecture Delivered at the Royal Institution, London, on 12 January 1982*, Cardiff: University College of Cardiff Press.

Hudson, W.H. (1893). *Idle Days in Patagonia*.

Hume, B. (1977). *Searching for God*, London: Hodder and Stoughton.

Humphries, C.F. (1938). 'The chironomid fauna of the Grosser Plöner See, the relative density of its members and their emergence period', *Archiv fur Hydrobiologie*, 33, pp. 535-584.

Hutto, J. (1995). *Illumination in the Flatwoods: A Season with the Wild Turkey*, New York: Lyons and Burford.

Hutton, J. (1794). *An Investigation of the Principles of Knowledge*, 3 vols.

Huxley, T. (1903). *The Scientific Memoirs of Thomas Henry Huxley*, 4 vols, M. Foster and E.R. Lankester (eds), London: Macmillan.

Huxley, T.H. (1863). *Man's Place in Nature*.

Huxley, T.H. (1873). *Critiques and Addresses*, New York: Appleton.

Inge, W.R. (1899). *Christian Mysticism*, London: Methuen.

Ingold, T. (1994). 'From Trust to Domination: An Alternative History of Human-Animal Relations' in *Animals and Human Society: Changing Perspectives*, A. Manning and J. Serpell (eds), New York: Routledge.

Ionides, S.A. and Ionides, M.L. (1944). 'Looking Forward' in *The Book of Naturalists*, William Beebe (ed.), New York: Alfred A. Knopf.

Jackson, K. (tr.) (1971). *A Celtic Miscellany* (revised edn), London: Penguin Books.

Jackson, K. (1935), *Studies in Early Celtic Nature Poetry*, Cambridge: Cambridge University Press.

Jacobs, L. (1968). *Faith*, New York: Basic Books.

Jäger, W. (2006). *Mysticism for Modern Times: Conversations with Willigis Jäger*, Christoph Quarch (ed.), Missouri: Liguori Publications.

Jaspers, K. (1953). *The Origin and Goal of History*, Michael Bullock (tr.), New York: Routledge Revivals, 2011.

Jenyns, S. (1757). *A Free Inquiry into the nature and Origin of Evil*.

Jenyns, S. (1790). 'On the Chain of Universal Being' in *Disquisitions on Several Subjects*, I.

Johnson, E.A. (2007). *Quest for the Living God: Mapping Frontiers in the Theology of God*, New York, London: Continuum.

Johnson, E.A. (2015a). *Ask the Beasts: Darwin and the God of Love*, London: Bloomsbury.

Johnson, E.A. (2015b). 'Jesus and the Cosmos: Soundings in Deep Christology' in *Incarnation: On the Scope and Depth of Christology*, N. Gregersen (ed.), Minneapolis: Fortress Press, pp. 133-156.

Johnston, M. (2009), *Saving God: Religion after Idolatry*, Princeton: Princeton University Press.

Kan, K. (2019). *Under Red Skies: The Life and Times of a Chinese Millennial*, London: Hurst and Co.

Kanipe, J. (2008). *The Cosmic Connection: How Astronomical Events Impact Life on Earth*, New York: Prometheus Books.

Kaufmann, S. (1993). *Origins of Order: Self-Organization and Selection in Evolution*, Oxford: Oxford University Press.

Kaufmann, S. (1995). *At Home in the Universe: The Search for the Laws of Self-Organization and Complexity*, Oxford: Oxford University Press.

Keynes, G. (ed.) (1966). *William Blake: Complete Writings with Variant Readings*, New York: Oxford University Press.

King, W. (1732). *An Essay on the Origin of Evil by Dr William King, translated from the Latin with Notes and a Dissertation concerning the Principle and Criterion of Virtue and the Origin of the Passions; by Edmund Law, M.S., Fellow of Christ College in Cambridge*, 2nd edn, London.

Kingsley, C. (1882-1883). *The Water Babies*.

Kingsley, C. (n.d.). *The Hermits*.

Klapwijk, J. (2008). *Purpose in the Living World? Creation and Emergent Evolution*, H. Cook (ed. and tr.), Cambridge: Cambridge University Press.

Koestler, A. (1985). *The Watershed: A Biography of Johannes Kepler*, Maryland: University Press of America (Science Study Series).

Kropotkin, P. (1914). *Mutual Aid: A Factor of Evolution*, London: Allen Lane (1972).

Kühn, T. (1996). *The Structure of Scientific Revolutions*, 3rd end, Chicago: University of Chicago Press.

Küng, H. (1990). *Theology for the Third Millennium: An Ecumenical View*, New York: Anchor Books.

Küng, H. and Tracy, D. (eds) (1989). *Paradigm Change in Theology*, New York: Crossroad.

Lamm, J.A. (2004). *The Living God, Schleiermacher's Theological Appropriation of Spinoza*, Pennsylvania: Pennsylvania State University Press.

Lane, F.W. (1948). *Animal Wonderland*. Country Life.

Lao Tzu. *Tao Te Ching*, D.C. Lau (tr. and introduction), London: Penguin Classics (1963).

Laplace, P.S. (1896). *Introduction à la théorie analytique des probabilités*, Paris.

Lau, D.C. (1963), *Lao Tzu: Tao Te Ching*, London: Penguin Classics.

Leopold, A. (1924). 'The River of the Mother of God' in Flader and Callicott (eds) (1991), pp. 123-127.

Leopold, A. (1933). 'The Conservation Ethic', reworked as 'The Land Ethic' in *A Sand County Almanac: And Sketches Here and There*, Oxford: Oxford University Press (1949).

Leopold, A. (1939). 'The Farmer as a Conservationist' in Flader and Callicott (eds) (1991).

Leopold, A. (1941). 'Ecology and Politics' in Flader and Callicott (eds) (1991).

Leopold, A. (1949). *A Sand County Almanac: And Sketches Here and There*, Oxford: Oxford University Press.

Lewes, G.H. (1864). *Aristotle: A Chapter from the History of Science, including Analyses of Aristotle's Scientific Writings*, London: Smith Elder.

Lewis-Stempel, J. (2016), *The Running Hare: The Secret Life of Farmland*, London: Doubleday.

Lewontin, R.C., Rose, S. and Kamin, L.J. (1984). *Not in Our Genes: Biology, Ideology and Human Nature*, New York: Pantheon Books.

Lindberg, D.C. (2006). 'Exploring Science and Religion's Past', *Science and Theology News*, 21 April.

Linnaeus, C. (1749-1769). *Amoenitates Academicae*.

Linssen, E.F. (1951). *Nature Interludes: A Book of Natural History Quotations*, London: Williams and Norgate.

Linzey, A. (2009). *Creatures of the Same God: Explorations in Animal Theology*, New York: Lantern Books.

Locke, J. (1690). *Essay concerning Human Understanding*, III.

Lopez, B. (1992). *The Rediscovery of North America*, New York: Vintage Books.

Lorenz, K. (1988). *The Waning of Humaneness*, London: Unwin Paperbacks.

Louv, R. (2005). *Last Child in the Woods: Saving our Children from Nature-Deficit Disorder*, Chapel Hill: Algonquin Books.

Lovejoy, A.O. (1936). *The Great Chain of Being: A Study of the History of an Idea*, New York: Harper Torchbook (1960).

Luckert, K.W. and Schmidt, K. (2013). *Stone Age Religion at Göbekli Tepe*, UK: Tiplehood.

Lyons, J.A. (1982). T*he Cosmic Christ in Origen and Teilhard de Chardin: A Comparative Study*, Oxford: Oxford University Press.

Mabey, R. (2015). *The Cabaret of Plants: Botany and the Imagination*, London: Profile Books.

Mahlmann, T. (2010). '"Ecclesia semper reformanda". Eine historische Aufarbeitung. Neue Bearbeitung' in *Hermeneutica Sacra: Studies of the Interpretations of Holy Scripture in the Sixteenth and Seventeenth Centuries*, T. Johansson, R. Kolb and J. Anselm Steiger (eds), Walter de Gruyter: Berlin-New York, pp. 382-441.

Marcus Manilius, *Astronomica*, G.P. Goold (ed. and tr.), Loeb Classical Library, Cambridge: Harvard University Press (1977).

Margulis, L. and Schwartz, K.V. (1997). *Five Kingdoms: An Illustrated Guide to the Phyla of Life on Earth*, 3rd edn, New York: W.H. Freeman and Company.

Marmion, D. (1998). *A Spirituality of Everyday Faith: A Theological Investigation of the Notion of Spirituality in Karl Rahner*, Louvain Theological and Pastoral Monographs 23, Louvain: Peeters Press, WB Eerdmans.

Martini, Cardinal (2012). *National Catholic Reporter*, translation of final interview (published in *Corriere della Sera*), 4 September.

Maslow, A.H. (1966). *The Psychology of Science: A Renaissance*, Indiana: Gateway Editions.

Mather, C. (1721). *The Christian Philosopher*.

Mather, J. (2008). 'Cephalopod consciousness: Behavioural evidence', *Consciousness and Cognition*, 17, pp. 37-48.

Maxwell, J.C. (2013). *The Scientific Papers of James Clerk Maxwell*, vol. 2, W.D. Niven (ed.), Cambridge: Cambridge University Press.

Mayr, E. (1982). *The Growth of Biological Thought*, Cambridge: Harvard University Press.

McCarthy, M. (2015). *The Moth Snowstorm: Nature and Joy*, London: John Murray.

McGinn, B. (2014). *Thomas Aquinas's Summa Theologiae: A Biography*, Princeton: Princeton University Press.

McGrath, A. (2015). *Inventing the Universe: Why We Can't Stop Talking about Science, Faith and God*, London: Hodder and Stoughton.

Mendel, J.G. (1866). 'Versuche über Pflanzenhybriden. Verhandlüngen des naturforschenden Vereines' in Brunn, Bd. IV fur das Jahr 1865, *Abhandlungen*: 3-47. For English translation see C.T. Druery, 'William Bateson (1901), Experiments in plant hybridization', *Journal of the Royal Horticultural Society*, 26, pp. 1-32.

Merton, T. (1973). *The Asian Journal of Thomas Merton*, New York: New Directions.

Merton, T. (2004). *The Way of Chuang Tzu*, Colorado: Shambhala.

Mesle, C.R. (2008). *Process-Relational Philosophy*, West Conshohocken, PA: Templeton Foundation.

Miall, L.C. (1895). *The Natural History of Aquatic Insects*, London: Macmillan.

Miall, L.C. (1896). *Round the Year: A Series of Short Nature-Studies*, London: Macmillan.

Miall, L.C. and Hammond, A.R. (1900). *The Structure and Life-history of the Harlequin Fly (Chironomus)*, Oxford: Clarendon Press.

Michelson, A.A. (1903). *Light Waves and Their Uses*, Charleston: Nabu Press (2011).

Moore, J.H. (1906). *The Universal Kinship*, Chicago: C.H. Kerr.

Moran, D. (2005). 'Towards a Philosophy of the Environment' in *Educating for Environmental Awareness*, J. Feehan (ed.), Dublin: UCD Environmental Institute.

More, H. (1653), *An Antidote against Atheism* in Lovejoy (1936), *The Great Chain of Being*.

Morowitz, H. (2002). *The Emergence of Everything: How the World Became Complex*, Oxford: Oxford University Press.

Morris, S.C. (2007). Gifford Lecture 'Life's Solution: The Predictability of Evolution Across the Galaxy (and Beyond)' given at the University of Edinburgh, 19 February. Audio file available at: www.hss.ed.ac.uk/giffordexemp/2000/details/ProfessorSimonConwayMorris.html

Mountford, B. (2011). *Christian Atheist: Belonging without Believing*, UK: Christian Alternative.

Muir, J. (1913). *The Story of My Boyhood and Youth* in *The Wilderness Journeys*, Edinburgh: Canongate Classics (1996).

Muir, J. (1916). *A Thousand-Mile Walk to the Gulf*.

Murphy, G. (1956). *Early Irish Lyrics: Eighth to Twelfth Century*, Oxford: Oxford University Press.

Murphy, N. and Stoeger, W.R. (eds) (2007). *Evolution and Emergence: Systems, Organisms, Persons*, Oxford: Oxford University Press.

Murray, D.A., O'Connor, J.P. and Ashe, P.J. (2018). *Chironomidae (Diptera) of Ireland – A Review, Checklist and their Distribution in Europe*, Occasional Publication of the Irish Biogeographical Society No. 12.

Nagel, T. (1974). 'What Is It Like to Be a Bat?', *The Philosophical Review*, 83 (4), October.

Newman, J.H. (1864). *Apologia Pro Vita Sua*, Everyman's Library edition (1934).

Newman, J.H. (1989) [1845]. *An Essay on the Development of Christian Doctrine*.

Newman, J.H. (1852). *The Idea of a University*.

Nicholas of Cusa (1444-1445). *Dialogus de Deo abscondito*.

Nicholas of Cusa (1453). *De Visione Dei*.

Northrop, F.S.C. (1946). *The Meeting of East and West*, New York: Macmillan.

O'Donnell, H. (2012). *Eucharist and the Living Earth*, new edn, Dublin: Columba Press.

O'Hanlon, Canon J. (1875). *Lives of the Irish Saints*, vol. 1.

Oldroyd, H. (1964). *The Natural History of Flies*, London: Weidenfeld and Nicolson.

Olson, R. (1987). 'On the nature of God's existence, wisdom and power: the interplay between organic and mechanistic imagery in Anglican natural theology – 1640-1740' in Burwick (ed.) (1987), pp. 1-49.

Ornstein, P.H. (2011). *The Search for the Self: Selected Writings of Heinz Kohut: 1950-1978*, 4 vols, London: Routledge.

Paley, W. (1802). *Natural Theology, or Evidences of the Existence and Attributes of the Deity collected from the Appearances of Nature*, Oxford: Oxford University Press (2006).

Panikkar, R. (2010). *The Rhythm of Being: the Gifford Lectures*, New York: Orbis Books.

Peacocke, A. (2007). *All that Is: A Naturalistic Faith for the Twenty-First Century*, Minneapolis: Fortress Press.

Peacocke, A. (1987). *God and the New Biology*, New York: HarperCollins.

Peattie, D.C. (1948). *Flowering Earth*, Scientific Book Club edition.

Pelikan, J. (1971-1989). *The Christian Tradition: A History of the Development of Doctrine*, 5 vols, Chicago: Chicago University Press.

Perry, S. (ed.) (2000). *Coleridge's Notebooks: A Selection*, New York: Oxford University Press.

Picknett, L. and Prince, C. (2011). *The Forbidden Universe*, London: Constable.

Pico della Mirandola, G. (1486). *Oration on the Dignity of Man*, in *The Renaissance Philosophy of Man*, E. Cassirer (ed.), Chicago and London: University of Chicago Press.

Pieper, J. (1953). *The Silence of St Thomas: Three Essays*, Indiana: St Augustine's Press.

Polkingthorne, J. (ed.) (2001). *The Work of Love: Creation as Kenosis*, London: SPCK.

Praeger, R.L. (1930). *Beyond Soundings*, Dublin: Talbot Press.

Praeger, R.L. (1941). *A Populous Solitude*, Dublin: Hodges Figgis.

Praeger, R.L. (1937). *The Way that I Went*, London: Methuen.

Purcell, B. (2012). *From Big Bang to Big Mystery: Human Origins in the Light of Creation and Evolution*, New York: New City Press.

Quammen, D. (2018). *The Tangled Tree: A Radical New History of Life*, London: William Collins.

Raby, P. (2002). *Alfred Russel Wallace: A Life*, Princeton: Princeton University Press.

Rahner, K. (1971), 'Christian Living Formerly and Today' in *Theological Investigations VII*, D. Bourke (tr.), New York: Herder and Herder.

Rahner, K. (1974). 'On the theology of the Incarnation' in *Theological Investigations*, New York: Seabury.

Rahner, K. (1975). 'Christology within an Evolutionary View of the World,' in *Theological Investigations V*, New York: Seabury.

Rahner, K. (2010). *The Mystical Way in Everyday Life: Sermons, Prayers and Essays*, A.S. Kidder (tr.), New York: Orbis Books.

Randerson, J. (2002). 'Wasps sniff out danger', *New Scientist*, 10 August.

Raven, C.E. (1942). *Experience and Interpretation: The Second Series of the 1951-2 Gifford Lectures: Natural Religion and Christian Theology*, Cambridge: Cambridge University Press.

Raven, C.E. (1942). *John Ray, Naturalist: His Life and Work*, Cambridge: Cambridge University Press.

Raven, C.E. (1953). *Experience and Interpretation: The second series of the 1951–2 Gifford Lectures: Natural Religion and Christian Theology*, Cambridge: Cambridge University Press.

Raven, C.E. (1962). *Teilhard de Chardin: Scientist and Seer*, London: Collins.

Ray, J. (1743, 1826). *The Wisdom of God Manifested in the Works of the Creation*, The Ray Society, facsimile edition of the 1826 edition (2005).

Rees, M. (2018). *On the Future: Prospects for Humanity*, Princeton: Princeton University Press.

Rickaby, J. (1901). *Moral Philosophy (Ethics and Natural Law)*, London: Longmans.

Riedweg, C. (2005). *Pythagoras: His Life, Teaching and Influence*, S. Rendall (tr.), Ithaca: Cornell University Press.

Rifkin, J. (2009). *The Empathic Civilization: The Race to Global Consciousness in a World of Crisis*, Cambridge: Polity Press.

Robinson, T. (2006). *Connemara: Listening to the Wind*, Dublin: Penguin Ireland.

Rorty, R. and Vattimo, G. (2007). *The Future of Religion*, New York: Columbia University Press.

Ross, J.B. and McLaughlin, M. (1977). *The Portable Medieval Reader*, London: Penguin Books.

Rotheray, G.E. and Gilbert, F. (2011). *The Natural History of Hoverflies*, Cardigan: Forrest.

Rovelli, C. (2015). *Seven Brief Lessons on Physics*, London: Allen Lane.

Ruse, M. (2003). *Darwin and Design: Does Evolution Have a Purpose?*, Cambridge: Harvard University Press.

Rushdie, S. (1990). *Is Nothing Sacred?*, Herbert Read Memorial Lecture.

Ruskin, J. (1862). *Unto This Last: Essays from The Cornhill Magazine* (1860).

Ryder, R. (2000). *Animal Revolution: Changing Attitudes Towards Speciesism*, Oxford: Berg Publishers.

Sachs, J. (2012). *The Great Partnership: Science, Religion and the Search for Meaning*, New York: Schocken Books.

Schweitzer, A. (1965). *The Teaching of Reverence for Life*, New York: Holt, Rinehart and Wilson.

Schillebeeckx, E. (1983). *God is New Each Moment: In conversation with Huub Oosterhuis and Piet Hoogeveen*, London and New York: Continuum.

Schleiermacher, F. (1989). *The Christian Faith*, H.R. Macintosh and J.R. Stewart (eds), Edinburgh: T. and T. Clark.

Sheldrake, P. (1995). *Living Between Worlds: Place and Journey in Celtic Spirituality*, London: Darton, Longman and Todd.

Shortt, R. (2016), *God Is No Thing: Coherent Christianity*, London: Hurst and Co.

Shreeve, J. (2015). 'Mystery Man', *National Geographic*, October.

Spedding, J., Ellis, R.L. and Heath, D.D. (eds) (c.1900), *Works of Francis Bacon*, 15 vols, Boston: Houghton, Mifflin and Co.

Speziali, P. (1972). *Albert Einstein–Michele Basso Correspondence, 1903-1955*, Paris: Herman.

Sprengel, C.K. (1793). *Das entdeckte Geheimnis der Natur im Bau und in der Befruchtung der Blumen* (The Newly Revealed Mystery of Nature in the Structure and Fertilization of Flowers), Berlin.

Walker, G.S.M. (ed.) (1957), *Sancti Columbani Opera*, Dublin: DIAS.

Stapleton, O. (1930). *Last and First Men: A Story of the Near and Far Future*, London: Methuen.

Stenger, V.J. (2007). *God: The Failed Hypothesis: How Science Shows that God Does Not Exist*, New York: Prometheus.

Stokes, W. (1905). *The Martyrology of Oengus the Culdee,* London: Harrison.

Storr, W. (2013). *The Heretics: Adventures with the Enemies of Science*, London: Picador.

Tanaka, T. (1984). 'Hyatology and Whitehead's Process Thought' in *Process and Reality East and West* (7-21), unpublished collection of papers of the Japanese Society for Process Studies.

Teilhard de Chardin, P. (1955). *The Human Phenomenon*, S. Appleton-Weaver (tr.), Portland: Sussex Academic Press (1999).

Teilhard de Chardin, P. (1957). *Le Milieu Divin*, London: Collins, Collins Fontana edition (1964).

Teilhard de Chardin, P. (1962). *Letters from a Traveller*, New York: Harper.

Teilhard de Chardin, P. (1968). *Writings in Time of War*, London: Collins.

Thompson, F. (1946). *The Poems of Francis Thompson (Collected Edition)*, London: Hollis and Carter.

Thoreau, H.D. (1849). *A Week on the Concord and Merrimack Rivers*, Boston and Cambridge: James Munroe and Co.

Thoreau, H.D. (1862). 'Walking', *Atlantic Monthly*.

Tillich, P. (1952). *The Courage to Be*, Connecticut: Yale University Press.

Tillich, P. (1959). *Theology and Culture*, Oxford: Oxford University Press.

Tillich, P. (2009). *Dynamics of Faith*, New York: HarperCollins.

Tucker, M.E., Grim, J. and Angyal, A. (2019). *Thomas Berry: A Biography*, New York: Columbia University Press.

Tudge, C. (2013). *Why Genes are not Selfish and People are Nice*, Edinburgh: Floris Books.

Turner, D. (1995). *The Darkness of God: Negativity in Christian Mysticism*, Cambridge: Cambridge University Press.

Tuttle, M. (2015). *The Secret Lives of Bats: My Adventures with the World's Most Misunderstood Mammals*, New York: Houghton Mifflin Harcourt.

Tuveson, E.L. (1982). *The Avatars of Thrice Great Hermes*, London: Bucknell University Press.

Ussher, J. (1658). *Annals of the Old Testament, deduced from the first origins of the world, the chronicle of Asiatic and Egyptian matters together produced from the beginning of historical time up to the beginnings of Maccabees.*

Van Arnim, H. (1903-1905). *Stoicorum Veterum Fragmenta*, Leipzig: Teubner (1964).

Van Dyke, F. (2010). *Between Heaven and Earth: Christian Perspectives on Environmental Protection*, Santa Barbara: Praeger.

Vanderplank, J. (2000). *Passion Flowers*, 3rd edn, Cambridge: MIT Press.

Vickers, B. (ed.) (2008). *Francis Bacon: The Major Works*, Oxford: Oxford World's Classics.

Virgil, *The Georgics*. L.P. Wilkinson (tr.), London: Penguin (1982).

Von Hugel, F. (1908). *The Mystical Element of Religion*, London: Aeterna Press (2015).

Von Humboldt, A. (1850). *Cosmos: A Sketch of a Physical Description of the Universe*, Baltimore: John Hopkins University Press (1997).

Walker, G.S.M. (ed.) (1957). *Sancti Columbani Opera: Scriptores Latini Hiberniae*, vol. 2, Dublin: School of Celtic Studies, DIAS.

Wallace, A.R. (1864). 'The Origin of Human Races from the Theory of Natural

Selection', *Journal of the Anthropological Society of London*, 2, clviii-clxxxvii.

Wallace, A.R. (1869). *The Malay Archipelago: The Land of the Orang-utan and the Bird of Paradise: A Narrative of Travel with Studies of Man and Nature*, 2 vols, London: Macmillan and Co.

Watson, J. (1968). *The Double Helix: A Personal Account of the Discovery of the Structure of DNA*, London: Weidenfeld and Nicolson.

Watts, A. (1999). *The Tao of Philosophy*, Boston: Tuttle Publishing.

Whitehead, A.N. (1933). *Science and the Modern World*, New York: The Free Press (1967).

Whitehead, A.N. (1978). *Process and Reality: An Essay in Cosmology (Corrected Edition)*, D.R. Griffin and D.W. Sherburne (eds), New York: The Free Press.

Williams, C. (2011). 'Mollusc Minds: The Planet's First True Intelligence', *New Scientist*, 2816, 11 June, pp. 36-39.

Williams, H.A. (1972), *True Resurrection*, London: Mitchell Beazley.

Wilson, E.O. (1984). *Biophilia: The Creation: A Meeting of Science and Religion*. New York and London: W.W. Norton and Co.

Wilson, E.O. (1998). *Consilience: The Unity of Knowledge*, London: Little Brown.

Wilson, E.O. (2006). *The Creation: A Meeting of Science and Religion*, New York and London: W.W. Norton and Co.

Wilson, R. (1997). *Astronomy through the Ages: The Story of the Human Attempt to Understand the Universe*, London: Taylor and Francis.

Wright, S. (1964). 'Biology and the Philosophy of Science' in W.L. Reese and E. Freeman (eds), *Process and Divinity*, La Salle: Open Court, pp. 101-125.

Yong, E. (2010). 'Masters of Magnetism', *New Scientist*, 2788, 27 November, pp. 42-45.

INDEX